DOGS NEVER LIE
About LOVE

*Reflections on the Emotional World
of Dogs*

Other books by
Jeffrey Masson

FREUD: THE ASSAULT ON TRUTH

AGAINST THERAPY

FINAL ANALYSIS

MY FATHER'S GURU

WHEN ELEPHANTS WEEP
(with Susan McCarthy)

DOGS NEVER LIE About LOVE

Reflections on the Emotional World of Dogs

Jeffrey Moussaieff Masson

JONATHAN CAPE
LONDON

First published 1997

1 3 5 7 9 10 8 6 4 2

© Jeffrey Moussaieff Masson 1997

Jeffrey Moussaieff Masson has asserted his right
under the Copyright, Designs and Patents Act, 1988
to be identified as the author of this work

First published in the United Kingdom in 1997 by Jonathan Cape,
Random House, 20 Vauxhall Bridge Road, London SW1V 2SA

Random House Australia (Pty) Limited
20 Alfred Street, Milsons Point, Sydney,
New South Wales 2061, Australia

Random House New Zealand Limited
18 Poland Road, Glenfield,
Auckland 10, New Zealand

Random House South Africa (Pty) Limited
PO Box 337, Bergvlei, 2012 South Africa

Random House UK Limited Reg. No. 954009

A CIP catalogue record for this book
is available from the British Library

ISBN 0-224-04465-6

Typeset by MATS, Southend-on-Sea, Essex
Printed and bound in Great Britain by
Mackays of Chatham PLC, Chatham, Kent

For my pack:
Leila and Ilan,
and of course
Sasha, Sima and Rani

CONTENTS

Contents

ACKNOWLEDGMENTS

My first thanks go to Elizabeth Marshall Thomas for writing *The Hidden Life of Dogs*, the best book about dogs I have read. It got me thinking about that other hidden life, what they feel.

My next debt is to my two editors, Tony Colwell at my English publisher, Jonathan Cape, and my editor in America, Steve Ross who was with me on this project from day one. Tony was the primary enthusiast who helped me and Susan McCarthy to make a book of *When Elephants Weep*, and I am deeply grateful for his skill and flashes of genius in giving this new book its first scrutiny. Steve has also worked tirelessly on both books, and even came out to Berkeley to meet my dogs. He is a superb editor and a fine friend; I would feel lost without his support. As indeed I would without my agent, Elaine Markson, to whom I owe a great deal.

I owe a special debt of gratitude to Mike del Ross, a brilliant trainer at the San Rafael Guide Dogs for the Blind, who helped me find Sasha. Gary Templin, the outstanding director of the Oakland Society for the Protection of Animals provided my other two dogs and both cats.

Among those who have helped me with their deep knowledge of dogs and animal issues in general have been Professor Marc Bekoff, Dr Ian Dunbar, the Berkeley veterinarian Bruce Max Feldman, Peter Steinhart, Dr Charles Berger, Dr Robert Hack and Dr Elliot Katz, founder of 'In Defence of Animals'.

Victoria Gill and Elisa Moreno were wonderful editors in the early stages of writing this book, and I am very grateful to Joanne

9

Hill for reading the proofs and asking a few pertinent questions on the text at the final stage.

Jenny Miller has been a loving surrogate mother to the three dogs when we had to be away from home.

My thanks also go to Nina Mazur, the owner of a marvellous dog store, 'Waggers', in Berkeley.

The following friends were helpful in various ways: Marjerie Riddle, Michael Parenti, Tom and Leslie Goldstein, Laurie Goldman, Chloe Aftel, Deborah Kennoyer, my niece Justine Juson, and most important, my beloved daughter Simone who has loved all animals from the time she was born.

Without Leila, the mother of our son Ilan, nothing would be possible. She has proved my thesis about love and dogs to be true: dogs are all about love, and so is Leila. She is the light of my life.

'When a dog bites a man
that is not news, but when a man
bites a dog that is news'

Charles Anderson Dana (1819-1897)
The New York Sun, 1882

'All knowledge,
the totality of all questions and answers,
is contained in the dog.'

Franz Kafka – 'Investigations of a Dog'

In Search of Feelings in Dogs

'IT IS SCARCELY POSSIBLE to doubt that the love of man has become instinctive in the dog.'[1] These words are taken from Charles Darwin's *On the Origin of Species*, published in 1859. He continues: 'All wolves, foxes, jackals, and species of the cat genus, when kept tame, are most eager to attack poultry, sheep, and pigs; and this tendency has been found incurable in dogs which have been brought home as puppies from countries, such as Tierra del Fuego and Australia, where the savages do not keep these domestic animals. How rarely, on the other hand, do our civilised dogs, even when quite young, require to be taught not to attack poultry, sheep, and pigs.'

Darwin seems to be making an argument, only recently come into fashion, that animal emotions serve an important evolutionary function; in fact, evolution may even be grounded in emotions, since Darwin says it is 'the love of man' that brought about the change in the instincts of domestic dogs.

13

Instinctive love that crosses the species barrier is a remarkable phenomenon. We humans experience it all the time: we love dogs, cats, horses, and many other animals. Yet while many scientists will readily admit they love the animals they study, few will concede that the animals they study also return that love.

In the case of dogs, their emotional responses so resemble our own that we are tempted to assume identity; the joy of a dog appears to be identical to human joy, the sorrow of a dog the same as our sorrow. Yet we can never claim that we know precisely what a dog feels. The joy and sorrow of dogs are canine joys and sorrows and may differ from our feelings in ways too subtle to recognise or articulate. If, as I believe, we can come close to understanding the inner life of a dog, none the less we cannot enter their world and feel exactly what a dog feels. Something will always remain elusive, prohibiting us from intruding on their psyche in ways that we imagine we can enter the mind of another human being.

Long ago, the British evolutionist, Louis Robinson, had a charming and prescient way of defining the emotional ground common to humans and dogs in *Wild Traits in Tame Animals*:

> It has been said that a man stands to his dog in the position of god; but when we consider that our conceptions of deity lead us to the general idea of an enormously powerful and omniscient *man*, who loves, hates, desires, rewards, and punishes in human-like fashion, it involves no strain of imagination to conceive that from the dog's point of view his master is an elongated and abnormally cunning *dog*, – of different shape and manners certain from the common run of dogs, yet canine in his essential nature.[2]

In *When Elephants Weep*, the book I wrote with Susan McCarthy about emotions in wild animals, I avoided any prolonged discussion of domesticated animals because I thought that dogs, cats and even parrots were perhaps 'contaminated' by their proximity to humans. It seemed to me that I would discover more about emotions in their pure state if I looked only at animals who had little or no contact with people. In truth, however, my ideas about animals leading complex inner lives, filled with deep feeling, originally came from my experiences with dogs.

What I have always loved about dogs is how directly and intensely they express emotions. Every time I told my cocker spaniel, Taffy, my very first dog, that we were going for a walk, she would launch into a celebratory dance which ended with her racing around the room, always clockwise, and faster and faster, as if her joy could not possibly be contained. Even as a young boy I knew that hardly any creature could express joy so vividly as a dog. On the other hand, when I had to tell Taffy she could not come with me, and the word 'no' would come out of my mouth, she would look stricken in ways that were hard to bear. Hardly any animal can look as deeply disappointed as a dog to whom one says 'no'.

Perhaps the word 'no' should never be used with a dog, for it is simply too devastating. It is not that the concept is unknown to dogs, but somehow, when they hear that terrifying sound from their beloved friends, they enter a kind of gloom from which it can seem unlikely they will ever emerge. Of course, minutes later, they do emerge – and that is something else I love about dogs. While they experience an emotion to its full potential, once it is over, that is that, and they are ready for the next experience. Dogs do not seem to waste time brooding over the past, or anxiously awaiting the dreaded future. They are always present.

Although I have had several dogs in my life, at the time I began to think about writing this book I had no dog. I missed having a dog. Perhaps, in fact, the book was only an excuse to keep dogs once again. So I set about acquiring three dogs. Why three? One was clearly too few, four too many. Two seemed ordinary – but three, ah, with me as the leader, that was the beginning of a pack, and a pack was interesting.

I wanted at least one purebred dog, preferably an adult who had already been given some training. I had been in contact with Mike del Ross, one of the trainers at Guide Dogs for the Blind in San Rafael, a suburb some forty minutes from the centre of San Francisco. He suggested I apply for a 'career-change' dog, a guide dog that was not deemed ready to work with the blind. I began visiting the beautiful campus in San Rafael, waiting for the perfect dog to turn up.

What was the perfect dog? Choosing a dog is a little like going on a blind date, for you really don't know who you are going to meet. But while you rarely marry the person you meet for an hour over dinner, after a short visit I was expected to start a lifelong relationship with a dog. Guide Dogs for the Blind trains three breeds: golden retrievers, Labrador retrievers, and German shepherds. I was shown two labs, both male, both very large and very energetic. I liked them both. I was shown a female German shepherd, small, thin, but very sensitive. I liked her too. I asked Mike for advice. He thought I should take the shepherd, as she was so tractable. I asked about her history.

Her name was Sasha, a lean (70-pound) short-haired dog with enormous ears, a very long tail, and sad eyes. When I met her she was almost two years old. Like all guide dogs, she was given to a 4H family (people who live in rural settings, mostly on farms or ranches, and who are willing to become foster-parents to dogs) when she was about eight weeks old, and was raised by them until she was a little more than a year old. She then returned to begin her training. She was tested some six months later and given a grade of 3, which is average. She was what they called a 'poor keeper'; that is to say, she ate very little in her kennel. Moreover, according to her trainers, she was 'a bit soft' to be a guide dog. I never did establish exactly what the term meant, but I assumed they considered her too gentle, with not enough drive.[3] She was carried through (she actually finished her training) because she was such a wonderful dog. Everybody liked her.

I collected Sasha one Wednesday in late summer 1995, and so began her career change from guide dog to muse dog. She did not have to work for a living with me; all that I required of her was to feel.

A week later I went to the Oakland Society for the Prevention of Cruelty to Animals to look for a second dog. I wanted a mutt, a labrador mix, since they are such affectionate dogs, easy-going but still energetic. I decided to take Sasha with me and let her decide. Sasha was immediately attracted to a twelve-week-old golden labrador mixed with possibly pit-bull terrier and Rhodesian ridgeback. The labrador was active, loveable and very easy-going. When we walked past the cages with cats and kittens in them, she did not bark, nor lunge; she just looked at them with benevolent curiosity. I liked that trait especially, for I knew I was going to get two kittens. I wanted the puppies and the kittens to

16

grow up together; interspecies friendships have always appealed to me. She had been given the name Rajah, which is Hindi for king. I wanted to correct the gender error, but I also wanted to preserve the sound. So I called her Rat ki Rani, Queen of the Night, which is Hindi for the night-blooming jasmine. She has a sweet smell, as well as a sweetness of disposition. When I took her to my house, she seemed immediately happy and at home. She was with family. Sasha is more like us – hesitant, slower. Her emotional life seemed already more convoluted.

I returned a few weeks later to Oakland and saw a small caged puppy whose leg was in a cast. She was part golden retriever, part Shetland sheepdog. I was told that she had a bad habit of biting, in spite of her entirely innocent appearance. Evidently her previous 'owner' had kicked her and broken her leg. The SPCA was thinking of 'putting her to sleep' for that reason. I could not bear the thought and asked to take her home for a week to see how she would respond to the other dogs. She got on well with them, and I called her Sima.

While I was at the SPCA, I asked to look at some kittens. 'Oh, we have just the thing.' I was shown two small orange tabbies, brothers, just seven weeks old, who had been abandoned in a parking lot. They had been raised with dogs by a member of the volunteer staff in her foster home, and now the kittens had absolutely no fear of them. This proved to be quite true when we took all five animals – the three dogs and the two kittens – into a large room. So that was it. I call the kittens Raj (King in Hindi) and Sanjaya (or Saj for short). When I was a Professor of Sanskrit at Toronto I had read with my students the Sanskrit text of the *Bhagavadgita*, in which *Sanjaya* (meaning victory) is the King's charioteer.

At first I was apprehensive about introducing my wife Leila (at the time my fiancée) to so many animals when she had never lived with pets while she grew up in Berlin. I need not have been. Leila, a physician, is liked by everyone – her small patients, their parents, the nurses, the other doctors. She is like sunlight, bright and warm, making everything seem light. Her joy is infectious, certainly to the dogs. They adore her, and she returns the love.

The house where Leila and I and the dogs live is across the street from the Police Department in downtown Berkeley, California.

17

It is a small Victorian house on two storeys, exactly 100 years old, with a large luscious garden backing on to University Avenue. I have almost 10,000 books in the house, so space is very limited. The dogs roam wherever they want, but at night they stay in my study, in crates with no doors. They go to sleep when we do, at about 11 p.m., and wake up with me before six in the morning. I take them every morning to the Berkeley Marina, on the bay, a five-minute drive from my house.

★

My training as a psychoanalyst at the Toronto Psychoanalytic Institute prepared me for my work in the Freud Archives, but it also fostered an abiding curiosity about the emotional experiences of others, not just human beings but other creatures as well. So little was known about a person's inner life that for years analysts claimed that women who recounted episodes of abuse in their childhood were not remembering but engaging in fantasy. We know now that they were wrong. If we were so ill-informed about the experiences of our closest associates, what mysteries might still lie undiscovered in the emotional lives of animals?

In this book I attempt to get inside the mind and, more important, the heart of the dog. Besides exploring the unresolved puzzles about dogs (such as what they dream about), I wanted to pursue questions that had not yet been asked: for example, can dogs feel gratitude or compassion? Scientists often take the line that whatever cannot be proved by means of the usual scientific methods are matters that should not be raised at all. Yet only by asking such questions, even if at present we are unable to answer them, can we think about a direction in which to take our inquiries. They stretch our imaginations, and that is always a useful exercise. Some of what I write about will be from observation, but some will be pure speculation. How often has yesterday's speculation become today's fact?

I am aware that most of the 'evidence' I have presented for the reality of the emotions of dogs consists of stories – what scientists call, dismissively, anecdotal evidence. With their restricted sense of valid criteria, most scientists want to be able to test, probe, and replicate data. You cannot do that with a single story. Scientists seem to think that whereas a story can be either true or false, something that takes place more than once in a laboratory has to be true. There is no reason to believe this to be the case. Data can be faked, forged or misrepresented as easily as can a story, and what we learn from some laboratory experiments, such as those conducted by Martin Seligman and others, do not tell us anything we could not have known without the experiments. Seligman proved that a dog can become neurotic when nothing it does will prevent it from receiving a shock. Is this really an advance in scientific knowledge? Pavlov proved that a dog can be driven crazy. Did anyone ever really doubt that? Neither do I see why a laboratory scientist should be a more reliable observer than anyone else.

There is no royal road leading us directly to the inner feelings of other humans. People often do not themselves know what they are feeling, nor are they always able to express their feelings without difficulty, and so, if we are to come to an understanding, we must use reason. Since we can never know for certain what another person is feeling, anything we say about their inner world is, in a sense, pure speculation. That speculation, however, can be informed speculation. We try to imagine what we would feel in a similar situation, or we watch the expression in their eyes, and notice the movements they make in their bodies. We hear a sigh escape, or watch a cloud pass over the face. These clues to the emotions of another person are not proof in the scientific sense of the word. Why should we not be permitted to speculate similarly about dogs? We watch their eyes, their ears and their tails, we listen for sounds, we delve into ourselves and use empathy and imagination. What we come up with is no more flawed in the case of a dog than it is with another human being.

It is true that when something can be observed over and over again, and many people have seen it, reported on it, and written about it, we have a tendency to place greater faith in its veracity. Yet some things that interest me – friendship between dogs and other species, for example – have never been tested in a laboratory. We should remember, too, that laboratories have existed for only a short period of time, and it is absurd to claim that anything observed before the existence of a laboratory cannot be true. Of course I would like to have a collection of 500 stories of friendship between dogs and lions, but there are not that many on record. I have had to content myself with the one I report in this book. On the other hand, many people have told me that their dogs often become friendly with rabbits. Are these necessarily false simply because they have not been tested in the laboratory? Are we to ignore these stories? They may not be accepted in the same way as we would believe a mathematical formula, but nor should they be dismissed as mere wishful thinking on the part of naive sentimentalists.

The intelligence of dogs is not a topic I address, for it has been discussed often enough. In truth, I am not all that interested in the topic of intelligence, whether of dogs or humans. The whole idea of 'testing' somebody for intelligence is repellent to me. What does it mean? Intelligent for what? Music? Art? Research? Cooking? Fast walking? Tracking? Spanish? Doll-making? Most of us are good at *something* and much less good at a whole range of other things. It might be safe to assume that Einstein is more intelligent than most readers of this book but they could justly respond that he might be more intelligent in understanding the laws of physics, or mathematics, but might be far less intelligent in finding his way from Milan to Rome, or in building a log cabin, or in helping his daughter to make friends in a strange city.

While testing a person's intelligence has never told us much of any real value, measuring the intelligence of one species against that of another is a pointless activity. Some cats have been known to open doors. Other cats watch them, but cannot figure out how to do it themselves. These other cats, it has been claimed, are less intelligent, yet they were intelligent enough to stand around and wait for the cat with the door-opening ability to appear. If we measure intelligence by adaptability, then the lack of ability to open a door counts against a dog. On the other hand, dogs wait patiently for us to open doors, and never become angry when we fail to give in to their wishes. Some humans in a similar situation would be ready to go to war.

'Abstract thinking' is what scientists often use to measure intelligence, but that is only a special kind of skill. Some people are much better at mathematics than others who may be better at making pots, or climbing trees, or reading old German manuscripts. Every species, it seems, has certain abilities peculiar to itself. We only learn about these abilities when we are willing to observe the species on its own, without reference to human intelligence or human skills. As the naturalist J. E. R. Staddon has said: 'Bees can see ultraviolet light and bats can hear ultrasound; these abilities were not discovered by asking if bats and bees can do human-type things.'[4]

Having exceptional abilities does not necessarily entail having extraordinary emotions. Early one morning, when Sasha had been with me for only a few weeks, I went to the YWCA to exercise. While I was away, a building inspector entered my garden through a side gate and left it open when he had finished his inspection. When I came out of the gym about two hours later, there was Sasha, sitting on the gym steps, waiting for me. While I live only a few blocks away, I was none the less astonished. How did Sasha, who had never been to the gym, find me there? Was it due to a superior ability to smell? Perhaps she had followed my scent to locate me. Whatever the reason, her feelings in this situation were more mysterious than her skill – and it is feelings I want to know about, not cognitive ability.

Charles Darwin prepared the emotional ground for us 125 years ago with his book *The Expression of the Emotions in Man and Animals*. Since then scientific scholars have seen fit to close the door on this subject, and only very recently have a few field researchers begun to throw new light on the emotional lives of animals in the wild. In this book I hope to encourage a much closer scrutiny than has yet been attempted of the feelings experienced by our closest companion in the animal world – the dog.

'The dog is the only being
that loves you more than you
love yourself.'

Fritz von Unruh

CHAPTER ONE

Recognising the Emotions of a Dog

F EW WHO have lived with dogs would deny that dogs have feelings. Taking a cue from Darwin, who spoke of conscience in the dog, George Romanes, who was his great friend, wrote that 'the emotional life of the dog is highly developed – more highly, indeed, than that of any other animal'.[1] (He did not include the human animal, though perhaps he should have done so.) Of course dogs have feelings, and we have no trouble acknowledging most of them. Joy, for example. Can anything be as joyous as a dog? Bounding ahead, crashing into the bushes while out on a walk, happy, happy, happy. Conversely, can anything be as disappointed as a dog when you say 'No, we are not going for a walk'? Down it flops on to the floor, its ears fall, it looks up, showing the whites of its eyes, with a look of utter dejection. Pure joy, pure disappointment.

The question that immediately arises is whether this joy and disappointment are identical to what humans mean when we use

23

these words. What dogs do, the way they behave, even the sounds they make, seem instantaneously translatable into human emotional terms. When a dog is rolling in fresh-cut grass, the pleasure on her face is unmistakable. No one could be wrong in saying that what she is feeling is akin to what any of us (though less often, perhaps) may feel. The words used to describe the emotion may be wrong, our vocabulary imprecise, the analogy imperfect, but there is also some deep similarity that escapes nobody. My dog may *appear* to feel joy and sorrow much the way I do, and the appearance here is critical: we often have no more to go on when it comes to our fellow humans.

All dog caretakers (just another word for companion and friend) have marvelled at the exuberant greeting their dogs give them after a brief absence. Sasha twirls around in delight, squealing and making extraordinary sounds. What accounts for this display of unbounded pleasure in our return? We tend to explain it by assuming a kind of stupidity: the dog thought I was gone forever. Dogs, we say, have no sense of time. As Robert Kirk of the Cornell Veterinary School once put it to me, dogs don't watch the clock. Every minute is forever. Everything is for good. Out means gone. In other words, when dogs do not behave as we do, we assume it to be irrational behaviour. Yet a lover is entranced to see the beloved again after even a brief absence – and dogs are all about love. Of that there can be no argument, as I will show.

Another explanation for dogs' delight in our return may be found in the way in which puppies greet their mother. As soon as the mother appears the puppies crowd around her, eager to nurse or expecting her to vomit food for them. Wolves have a greeting ceremony during which they wag their tails, lick one another and bite the muzzles of other wolves. The pleasure of the puppies may be a vestige of this ceremony, as Scott and Fuller suggest.[2]

Soon after she joined the family, Sasha was sitting next to me one day as I worked on an early draft of this chapter. It was Friday evening, very quiet. I had been alone all day, working. There were just the two of us sitting in the living room. I looked over at Sasha and noticed that she was looking at me. Suddenly I was overwhelmed with the thought: there is another being in this room, another consciousness. There is somebody here, besides me.

What, though, was Sasha thinking? Why did she suddenly glance up at me? Was she just checking to make sure I was still there, that I had nothing else in mind? Or was it a more complicated thought, one that was imbued (as many thoughts are) with feelings – affection, for example, or perhaps anxiety? She looked so peaceful, lying there. Was she feeling something like tranquillity? For certain Hindu philosophers, tranquillity is the master emotion, the one that underlies all others – it has been so fascinating to me that it was the subject of my Ph.D. thesis at Harvard. Perhaps I was merely projecting my own feelings on to Sasha. It is hard to know.

As Sasha sat quietly next to me, looking contented, every so often sighing with what appeared to be contentment, I wondered what she was actually feeling. How I would love to be her for just one moment, to feel what she was feeling. I have had this desire, more than once, with people too. Does one ever know what another human being is actually feeling? It may be no harder to find out the truth about feelings in dogs than it is in people.

The question of how we know what we feel, let alone what somebody else feels, is beset with difficulties. Speaking to other people, we often use shorthand – 'I feel sad' or 'I feel happy' – but more often than not what we feel is an emotional state for which there are no precise verbal equivalents. Think of how we restrict ourselves with language. 'I'm depressed,' we say. Yet that is only the vaguest hint of a more complex set of feelings. It is probably the same for dogs; their joy is at least as complicated (in the sense that we are not always certain of its components; perhaps memory of earlier pleasure plays a role and perhaps it is entirely bound to the moment) and hard to define.

While it is clear that we can learn a great deal about dogs from observing their behaviour in terms of purely external actions, I think it is time to recognise that we could understand much more from observing how dogs feel. Moreover, we could learn something about our own feelings as well. For in the realm of feelings we can have no sense of superiority. After a lifetime of affectionate regard for dogs and many years of close observation and reflection, I have reached the conclusion that dogs feel more than I do (I am not prepared to speak for other people). They feel more, and they feel more purely and more intensely. By comparison the human emotional landscape seems murky with subterfuge and ambivalence and emotional deception, intentional or not. In searching for why we are so inhibited compared to dogs, perhaps we can learn to be as direct, as honest, as straightforward, and especially as intense in our feelings as a dog.

Freud remarked on the fact that 'dogs love their friends and bite their enemies, quite unlike people, who are incapable of pure love and always have to mix love and hate in their object relations'.[3] In other words, dogs are without the ambivalence with which humans seem cursed. We love, we hate, often the same person, on the same day, maybe even at the same time. This is unthinkable in dogs, whether because, as some people believe, they lack the complexity, or as I believe, they are less confused about what they feel.[4] It is as if once a dog loves you, it loves you always, no matter what you do, no matter what happens, no matter how much time goes by. Dogs have a prodigious memory for people they have known. Perhaps this is because they associate people with the love they felt for them, and they derive pleasure from remembering this love.

Sasha is possessed by my two small kittens, Raj and Saj. The minute she sees these two tiny fur dots she goes into hyper-alert mode. She begins to whine and to moan and to groan. She looks at me with a pleading look, as if I held the key to helping her get what she so badly wants. She sniffs them. She follows them from room to room, whining piteously. The first night they were here, Sasha never slept at all. She lay on the floor next to their cage, crossed her feet daintily, and observed them all through the night. When I let them out, she gently put her paw on them. The cats were a little dumbfounded by the whole thing, and especially at what Sasha took to doing by the second week: she would pick one up in her mighty jaws, taking great care not to harm him, carry him into another room, deposit him somewhere and then head off to find the other one to do the same. Seeing her carrying these little orange dots from room to room was as puzzling for me as it evidently was for the cats. Soon, however, they wanted to play. One of the cats rolled over and reached out with her little paw. Yet their interest in Sasha is mild compared to hers in them. There can be no mistaking the intensity of her interest in these kittens. The nature of this interest is another matter.

What does she want? Could it be that a maternal instinct has been awakened and Sasha wants to act as a mother to the kittens? Does she really think they are her puppies, and want to bring them into a den? Or is her interest predatory: she wants to eat them, and is torn between her desire to listen to me ('Do not eat the kittens!') and her instincts as a predator telling her that a kitten makes a good meal? Is she merely curious, wondering if these small beings are some odd kind of puppy? Maybe she is just herding them; she is after all a shepherd.

None of these explanations is entirely satisfactory. If it were a mothering instinct at work, she would behave similarly to rabbits, say, or geese, moaning when she sees them (instead of chasing them). Moreover, Sasha has had no pups. I doubt that she wants to eat them; I can barely persuade Sasha to eat a piece of steak. Nor is she stupid; she knows the difference between a dog and a cat. If she were herding the kittens, she would not pick them up in her mouth, nor moan and groan with some inexpressible need or feeling. The truth is that I don't know, and nobody else knows either. It would be so much simpler if only we could ask: Sasha, why are you so interested in these small fur-balls? 'Simple, just look at how adorable they are!' Or: 'They look so small and helpless, I want to protect them.' Or even, 'Beats me.' Whatever the behaviour means, it is clear that Sasha is filled with feeling for these little kittens. It is clear because she moans and groans and follows them from room to room, and cocks her head and looks puzzled and intrigued. That is why I say she is possessed. She wants something from them, she feels something for them, and she seems to want to express those feelings.

It is hard to empathise with her because humans generally do not walk behind kittens sighing and groaning. There does not seem to be an equivalent for us. Perhaps, then, Sasha is demonstrating to me one of my pet theories: as well as the emotions animals and humans have in common, animals can also access emotions that humans do not share, different from those we know, because animals are *other*; they are not the same as human beings. Their senses, their experiences, open them to a totally different (or new) set of feelings of which we know little or nothing. That a whole world of canine feelings remains closed to us is an intriguing notion. Some of these feelings could be based on the dog's sensory capacities. According to one early authority, a dog can smell one hundred million times better than we do (I will return to the topic later in the book). Even if the figure is significantly less, the face remains that when Sasha puts her nose to the ground she becomes aware of a world at which I can only make guesses. Similarly, when Sasha cocks her ears, she hears sounds of which I am altogether unaware.

In the case of Sasha's interest in the kittens, we are dealing not with a question of superior (or inferior) sensory capacities but something else, something social. We like to assume that dogs and humans are social in very similar ways, and that therefore humans are uniquely qualified to understand whatever emotions a dog may have based on belonging (like us) to a pack. We too have deep interests in one another's social lives, and the web of interrelations that creates. We assume that this is why dogs are able to understand us so well, and appear to empathise with humans from their own direct experience.

Perhaps they are so often right about human emotions because their social world is similar to ours. We are not similar to cats in the same way, and cats are not all that good at understanding us. We do not expect the same kind of sympathy from our cat as we do from our dog. A cat the size of a lion would be an animal we would approach with some hesitation. No matter what its size, however, most of us would accept a reliable dog as being reliable. The German ethologist and expert on the cat family, P. Leyhausen, makes the point that nobody chose to domesticate the cat; it chose domestication itself, while nevertheless maintaining its independent nature. He believes that the cat is domestic, but not domesticated.[5]

The German scholar, Eberhard Trumler, suggested that it was not wolves who joined the human fold but the opposite. He pointed out that wolves, phylogenetically older than us and superbly equipped for hunting, had no need of human help. Men, on the other hand, derive from plant-eating ancestors and are not nearly as well equipped for hunting as are wolves. In order to eat, wolves scarcely need us at all, but we could benefit from the help of wolves. It may well be that human groups followed wolf packs, waited until they had brought down a kill, then chased the wolves away. Indian wolves are often chased away from their kills by wild pigs, and the same could have been true of early humans and wolves.[6]

The naturalist Jared Diamond points out that the large mammals were all domesticated between 8000 and 2500 B.C. Domestication began with the dog, then moved to sheep, goats, pigs and ended with Arabian and Bactrian camels and water buffalos. He believes that since 2500 B.C. there have been no significant additions.[7] Why this is so is a question that has never been answered.

Although other animals have been domesticated – primarily the cat, the horse, certain birds, rabbits, cattle – no other animal (wild, tame or domesticated) carries such meaning for humans as the dog. We feel strongly about such non-domesticated animals as wolves, elephants and dolphins, (all of which can be tamed but over whose reproductive life we exercise little control) but our direct inter-actions with them are much more restricted. By raising all these animals over centuries, we have altered their genetic make-up to make them conform to our desires. We control their reproductive functions and breed them to suit our needs, just as we control their territory and food supply. Juliet Clutton-Brock, an expert on domestication, believes, as Darwin did, that only humans benefit from the association. She quotes Darwin to the effect that 'as the will of man thus comes into play we can understand how it is that domestic races of animals and cultivated races of plants often exhibit an abnormal character, as compared with natural species; they have been modified not for their own benefit, but for that of man.'[8]

Michael Fox, vice president of the Humane Society of the United States (in charge of bioethics and farm animal protection), points out that rapid maturation, disease resistance, high fertility and longevity, all of which we foster, would in nature produce overabundance of certain species, which would cause a shift in the ecological balance and possibly the extinction of other species.[9] Many of these domesticated animals, even when they appear to be semi-wild, are dependent on humans and require considerable attention. Hardy hill sheep still need to be dipped, wormed and given supplementary winter feed.

Even among domesticated animals the dog stands out as perhaps the only fully domesticated species. Goats are domesticated, and can be tame, but they rarely make intimate companions. Pigs probably could, if given half a chance. H. Hediger, the Director of the Zoological Gardens of Zürich, writes that the dog, basically a domesticated wolf, was the first creature with which humans formed intimate bonds that were intense on both sides. According to Hediger, no other animal stands in such intimate psychological union with us; only the dog seems capable of reading our thoughts and 'reacting to our faintest changes of expression or mood'.[10] German dog trainers use the term 'Gefühlsinn' (a feeling for feelings) to talk about the fact that a dog can sense our moods.[11]

Voltaire, who knew about the emotions of dogs, used the example of a lost dog to refute the thesis of Descartes that dogs are merely machines, incapable of any kind of suffering.

He responded to Descartes in his *Dictionnaire philosophique* with –

> Judge this dog who has lost his master, who has searched for him with mournful cries in every path, who comes home agitated, restless, who runs up and down the stairs, who goes from room to room, who at last finds his beloved master in his study, and shows him his joy by the tenderness of cries, by his leaps, by his caresses. Barbarians seize this dog who so prodigiously surpasses man in friendship. They nail him to a table and dissect him alive to show you the mesenteric veins. You discover in him all the same organs of feeling that you possess. Answer me, mechanist, has nature arranged all the springs of feeling in this animal in order that he should not feel? Does he have nerves to be impassive?[12]

It is one of the main themes of this book that the reason why humans and dogs have such an intense relationship is that there is a mutual ability to understand one another's emotional responses. The *joie de vivre* of a dog may be greater than our own, but it is immediately recognisable as a feeling that we humans enjoy as well. The closeness between dogs and people is taken for granted and, at the same time, seen as something immensely mysterious. Naturally I feel close to my dogs, but who are these dogs? They are Sima, Sasha and Rani, of course, that much is simple and obvious. Yet I will often look at them lying in my study as I work on this book and be overwhelmed with a sense of otherness. Just who are these beings lying here, so close to me, and yet also so remote? They are easily grasped, and they are unfathomable. I know them as well as I know my closest friend, and yet I have no idea who they are.

This ambiguity, which includes a certain ambivalence as well, has been memorialised in our speech, in our sayings and in our tributes to and about dogs. Sir John Davies in his epigram *In Cineam* (written in 1594) observed:

> Thou sayest thou art as weary as a dog,
> As angry, sick, and hungry as a dog,
> As dull and melancholy as a dog,
> As lazy, sleepy, idle as a dog.
> But why dost thou compare thee to a dog?
> In that for which all men despise a dog,
> I will compare thee better to a dog.
> Thou art as fair and comely as a dog,
> Thou art as true and honest as a dog,
> Thou art as kind and liberal as a dog,
> Thou art as wise and valiant as a dog.[13]

Ever since Madame Roland said in the eighteenth century: *Plus je vois les hommes, plus j'admire les chiens* (The more I see of men, the more I admire dogs), generally what has been written about dogs tends to be positive, sometimes even wonderful, as in William James's statement: 'Marvellous as may be the power of my dog to understand my moods, deathless as is his affection and fidelity, his mental state is as unsolved a mystery to me as it was to my remotest ancestor.'[14] Or it may be delicious, like Ambrose Bierce's definition in his *Devil's Dictionary*, 'Dog, n. A kind of additional or subsidiary Deity designed to catch the overflow and surplus of the world's worship.'[15] Samuel Coleridge, in *Table-Talk* (2 May, 1830), was one of the first to note that 'the best friend a man has in the world may turn against him and become his enemy. His son or daughter . . . may prove ungrateful. Those who are nearest and dearest to him . . . may become traitors to their faith. . . . The one absolutely unselfish friend that man can have in this selfish world, the one that never deserts him, the one that never proves ungrateful or treacherous, is his dog.'

When it comes to our sayings and our language, the use to which the word 'dog' has been put shows a darker side. We speak of 'going to the dogs' when we mean utter ruination. When men say of a woman that she is a dog, they mean nothing kind. Even used of a man, it suggests he is contemptible. 'To put on the dog' is to be a phoney. 'A dog's death' is the most miserable and shameful of ends.[16] As long ago as the eighteenth century, 'the black dog' on a man's back referred to depression. We criticise our own society when we speak of a 'dog-eat-dog world' though this phrase may derive from its Latin opposite: *Canis caninam non est*, a dog does not eat another dog. One of the most evocative phrases of the English language was quoted by John Lyly in 1519 as being already an old saying: 'The dogs may bark; the caravan goes on.'[17]

I take my dogs on five walks each day. People who know about us say that these dogs are living the perfect dog's life. Maybe we need to revamp our vocabulary, so that leading a dog's life is what we want, and going to the dogs is where we wish to go.

In an article on pet ideas, Joel Savishinsky notes the ambiguity in our language about dogs: 'A winning individual is top dog; a handicapped or underrated person an underdog. Pathetic individuals lead a dog's life in a dog-eat-dog world. They suffer through the dog days of August, and when they confuse their priorities or do things in an inverted way, we think of it as the tail wagging the dog. A person who hogs resources which he himself cannot use is a dog in the manger. A damaged book is dog-eared, lousy poetry is doggerel, and a pathetic look is a hang-dog expression. The best we can say about a dutiful but uninspired worker is that he is dogged.'[18]

Nobody has written about this better than James Thurber in a piece that deserves full quotation:

Dogs may be Man's best friend, but Man is often Dog's severest critic, in spite of his historic protestations of affection and admiration. . . . He observes, cloudily, that this misfortune or that shouldn't happen to a dog, as if most slings and arrows should, and he describes anybody he can't stand as a dirty dog. He notoriously takes the names of the female dog and her male offspring in vain, to denounce blackly members of his own race. In all this disdain and contempt there is a curious streak of envy, akin to what the psychiatrists know as sibling rivalry. Man is troubled by what might be called the Dog Wish, a strange and involved compulsion to be as happy and carefree as a dog.[19]

32

It is possible that we begrudge the dog its freedom to be exactly what it was meant to be: a dog. So often I will see Sasha or Rani or Sima roll over and over in thick green grass, with a look of sheer delight on their faces, and I will think they are doing exactly what a dog was meant to do. How much harder to say of ourselves that we are doing what a human was meant to do, especially as nobody knows what that is.

Setting aside what we think dogs are, what – or who – do dogs think we are? If we knew how we were represented in the dreams of dogs (for they do dream about us – see Chapter Ten), we would have an answer. But we do not, and so we must use our knowledge of dog society to extrapolate. The general observation has always been: dogs form packs; the leader of the pack is the strongest, wisest, and largest individual; a human being among dogs fits that description; ergo we are the leader of any dog pack. There are, however, a number of problems with this view. First, we really don't know all that much about hierarchy in dogs, although we think we do. We assume that dominance is a simple matter, but it is not, and we can never be certain what factors are involved, or even exactly what dominance is among dogs. Second, dogs are not stupid, and they certainly know that we are not dogs, or even superdogs. I do not believe (contrary to what some vets say) that a dog thinks a cat is a small dog. How they categorise them, I do not know, but I am confident they know they are not dogs.

Frances and Richard Lockridge find it easy to believe that a dog would like to be a man, in the same way as a man would like to cast himself in the image of God. In their book, *Cats and People*, they write that the ambition of a well-brought-up dog is to please his friend before himself: 'He is demonstrative in displays of affection as many people are, and as almost all people would like others to be toward them; the dog leaves you no doubt where you stand and when he gives his devotion, as he does readily, he is apt to give it fulsomely, so that for a little while the meanest human can see himself godlike in the dog's beaming eyes.'[20]

Do dogs think of us as gods, powerful beings who cannot entirely be read?[21] I think not, because the idea of a 'god' comes from the way humans create gods: in our own image, only more powerful. Gods grant us wishes and decide our fate. It is true that dogs are entirely dependent on us when they are with us. We decide where to go, how long to stay, when to leave, what they can and cannot do.

Some people compare dogs with slaves, but does the fact that we have created an almost complete dependency in dogs make them similar to slaves? We should remember that dogs have no choice in the matter. The Stockholm-syndrome, where the kidnapped fall in love with their jailers (sometimes well beyond the limits of their confinement) may well apply here. To a certain extent, we are the jailers of dogs, since any freedom they achieve must be acquired by wheedling it out of us. This is one good reason why they come to read us so well. Survival dictates that dogs learn about us and learn to play us to some extent. Dogs must negotiate whatever freedom they achieve within the confines we assign them. They seem to accept this control we exercise over them as the way things are. Those who rebel we call problem dogs. Perhaps they are merely independent thinkers, wondering why they should accept the status quo.

Given the fascination almost all dogs feel for small children (it is mutual), what do dogs think small children are? Do they think: 'Aha, this is more like it, they are like us'? Do they see the dependency? Is that what they see as the similarity? Is it the size? Or is it just part of neoteny; since they are like children to us, do they have a desire to be with other children?

One reason for dogs playing havoc with so many of our theories is that they do not have feelings toward *all* humans, only some. So a dog can be extremely aggressive toward some human beings and very gentle toward others. The famous protectiveness of the dog speaks for the distinctions dogs make: stranger/friend, master/enemy, and so on. We must not forget that a dog is really a wolf, and thus in much of its make-up and behaviour is a wild animal, albeit one that has allowed us to become a part of a dog's world. This is something that no other wild animals would ever do, even when they seem in some ways to respect humans.

For animals in the wild, humans are usually something dangerous and to be avoided. Though not always. Killer whales, for example, seem to have an almost superstitious interest in us: there are no documented cases of killer whales killing a human without provocation, although they could easily do so. After all, they eat just about anything that moves in the ocean, even polar bears, so why not us? They seem to recognise some affinity.

That affinity may have to do with living as social beings in well-defined groups. In this way dogs, whales and humans share much in common – although whales never show a desire to spend time with us rather than spending time with other whales. We could never become part of any killer-whale pod, which is one reason for so little being known about killer whales. In fact, no other species has ever indicated that it regularly prefers the company of a human to that of members of its own species, with the single exception of the dog. While we have domesticated many animals, only the dog has domesticated us. The dog chooses us, not because it is confused about our identity, not because dogs think we are the marvel of creation, but merely because dogs love us. It is such an amazing fact, and so counter-intuitive (so profoundly unlovable do we think we are) that almost nobody can accept it as fact. Dogs love us not only because we feed them, or walk them, or groom them, or protect them, but because we are fun. How astonishing!

Even if we are not gods, dogs make us feel as though we were. Aldous Huxley said that 'to his dog, every man is Napoleon; hence the constant popularity of dogs'. I recognise the problem here: humans confuse love and adoration with entitlement. We sometimes feel we are entitled to 'own' a dog because it treats us as so much its superior. Throughout this book I have refrained from turning dogs into objects by avoiding the word 'owner', for a dog is not a thing that we can own and dispose of at will, giving it away, abandoning it or even having it killed when we move from one city to another. What I am hoping for is greater equality. Long ago Darwin recognised that animals whom we have made our slaves we do not like to consider our equals. Nobody should be a slave, not even a dog. How much more interesting to interact with peers, friends and equals.

Since Darwin, animal behaviourists have been notoriously resistant to the notion of animal consciousness. The scientist most responsible for changing this attitude, Donald R. Griffin, pointed out that in university courses about animal behaviour students are taught that it is unscientific to ask what an animal thinks or feels. When students pose such questions they are ridiculed, and treated with hostility, which discourages open investigations.[22] Professor

Griffin told Roger Caras that 'many comparative psychologists seem almost literally petrified by the notion of animal consciousness'.[23]

Perhaps our unacknowledged envy of the dog's life has something to do with why those who are curious about animals' emotions are often accused of anthropomorphism. One scientist may reduce another to silence merely by conjuring up this dreaded spectre: 'Why are you engaging in anthropomorphism?' Anthropomorphism means ascribing human characteristics – thought, feeling, consciousness, and motivation – to a nonhuman incapable of experiencing them. Many scientists regard even the notion that animals feel pain as the grossest sort of anthropomorphic error, and referring to deep emotions in animals as a grave mistake, even a sin. It is common in some scientific discourse to speak of 'committing' anthropomorphism. The term originated in religious discourse, when human form or characteristics were assigned to God – the hierarchical error of acting as though the merely human could be divine – hence the connotation of sin. In a long article on anthropomorphism in the 1908 *Encyclopedia of Religion and Ethics*, the author writes: 'The tendency to personify objects – whether objects of sense or objects of thought – which is found in animals and children as well as in savages, is the origin of anthropomorphism.'[24]

Men, the idea goes, create gods in their own image. The best-known example of this tendency comes from the Greek writer Xenophanes (fifth century B.C.) who notes that Ethiopians represent the gods as black, Thracians depict them as blue-eyed and red-haired, and 'if oxen and horses . . . had hands and could paint', their images of gods would depict oxen and horses. The philosopher Ludwig Feuerbach concluded that God is nothing but our projection, on a celestial screen, of the essence of man. In science, the sin against hierarchy is to assign human characteristics to animals. Just as humans could not be like God, now animals cannot be like humans.[25]

To accuse a scientist of anthropomorphism is to make a severe criticism, and yet to ascribe to an animal emotions such as joy or sorrow is only anthropomorphic error if one knows for certain that animals cannot feel such emotions. Many scientists have made this decision, but not on the basis of evidence. The situation is not so much that emotion is denied as that it is regarded as too dangerous to be part of the scientific colloquy – such a minefield of subjectivity that no investigation of it should take place. As a result, any but the most prominent scientists risk their reputations and credibility in venturing into this area. Thus many scientists may actually believe that animals do have emotions but be unwilling to say so, unwilling either to study it themselves or to encourage their students to investigate it. They may also attack other scientists who try to use the language of emotions in discussing nonhuman animals. Anyone who seeks to retain scientific credibility must tread carefully.[26]

Some of the caution is valid. There is a billboard on a Los Angeles freeway that says 'maybe there are traffic jams because cars like to be together'. Although it is only meant as humour, this statement is an example of the true anthropomorphism that can easily invade our language. Cars have no wishes. If we say that the clock is tired, the bicycle is fed up, or our telephone is on strike, we are engaging in a form of anthropomorphism, because clocks and bicycles and telephones have neither thoughts nor feelings. They are inanimate objects.

Similarly, when the renowned French naturalist, Georges-Louis Leclerc, Comte de Buffon, wrote that 'of all quadrupeds, the pig seems to be the ugliest animal; its imperfections of form appear to influence its nature; all its habits are clumsy, all its tastes are filthy; all its feelings amount to no more than violent lust and brutal greed which make it devour indiscriminately anything it happens to find',[27] this is pure anthropomorphism, a catalogue of human prejudices and errors in the guise of observation.

An even more obvious example of anthropomorphism comes from the father of animal classification, Linnaeus himself. He wrote of Amphibia (a broader term in the eighteenth century than now):

These foul and loathsome animals are distinguished by a heart with a single ventricle and a single auricle, doubtful lungs and a double penis. Most Amphibia are abhorrent because of their cold body, pale colour, cartilaginous skeleton, filthy skin, fierce aspect, calculating eye, offensive smell, harsh voice, squalid habitation, and terrible venom and so their Creator has not exerted His powers to make many of them.[28]

This account is scientifically, emotionally, and psychologically wrong; these are merely venomous opinions, and say more about Linnaeus than about Amphibia, although at the time, these words may well have appeared to Linnaeus's contemporaries as based on scientific fact. How do we distinguish false anthropomorphism from a valid attempt to enter the world of another creature?

Sasha has a way of lying on the floor and crossing her front paws. She looks dainty, delicate, but this is almost certainly just an anthropomorphic projection of mine: I mean only that it looks dainty to me, that *I* find it delicate, because it resembles behaviour that would look dainty in a human being. I doubt that she thinks: 'How dainty and delicate I look with my paws crossed.' Not that such thoughts are impossible for a dog, but they are unlikely, because daintiness and delicacy are not categories that dogs use – as far as we know.

So much for anthropomorphism based on error and bias. On the other hand, if we say that our dog is bored, or our cat is sad, or the bird is lonely, this is not necessarily anthropomorphism, for although we may be mistaken, we are not engaging in flights of fancy. As anyone who has spent considerable time with these animals knows, a dog can be bored, and cats and birds can become lonely, sad or even deeply unhappy. To proclaim loudly by fiat, as it were, that a dog or a cat cannot feel emotions is to close the discussion we ought to be having before it begins. If we say that it is merely projection to speak of a dog suffering, because dogs cannot suffer, then we have lazily disposed of the question we were supposed to be asking. We have not kept an open mind, we have simply stated a prejudice. The question that needs investigation is: are dogs capable of suffering? If they are, then to state that in any given instance they are suffering is not anthropomorphic. We cannot legitimately decide this matter in advance. To invoke the term anthropomorphism as an argument is often nothing more than an attempt to forestall a discussion, a refusal to grapple with a central question: just how much like us are dogs?

Moreover, many researchers before me have pointed to a basic contradiction. You cannot have it both ways: it is unreasonable to claim that animals do not feel pain or sorrow and then test hypotheses concerning human pain and depression by conducting experiments on animals. The philosopher Mary Midgley puts it well when she criticises Harry Harlow's monkey maternal deprivation experiments in which infants were forcibly separated from their mothers and subsequently developed depression:

> The existence of the species barrier confronts experimenters like Harlow with only two clear alternatives: (1) Human beings and rhesus monkeys are indeed very closely comparable emotionally. In this case his results, though slight, may have some validity for human beings, and he is guilty of cruelty so enormous that hardly any theoretical advance could justify it. (2) Human beings and rhesus monkeys are not closely comparable emotionally. In this case he may be guilty of callousness ... but is convicted of enormous and wasteful intellectual confusion, and his results are void.[29]

The accusation of anthropomorphism has become a rhetorical device for silencing an opponent, a way of avoiding any genuine discussion. There are legitimate reasons why the phenomenon behind this word has been so mistrusted, but they are probably not the ones usually given. When we refuse to use our imagination, when we are intellectually lazy, and say: Oh, the dog is simply (this word is often the clue) in the throes of an instinct, or is merely exhibiting typical hard-wired behaviour, then we are indulging in mental nihilism, substituting the easiest explanation for the correct one. Or, as Thurber suggests, we feel unacknowledged envy for the dog, and thus may meanly wish to deny that dogs have any of the gifts or powers – such as insight or a broad range of emotions – usually ascribed only to humans.

CHAPTER TWO

Why We Cherish Dogs

IT IS IMPOSSIBLE to observe dogs for long without noticing what appears to be not only genuine emotion but distinctly canine emotions. When Sasha follows me from room to room, she seems to be expressing some emotional need that is not quite like any need we have. We are often too eager to explain away behaviour that puzzles us with behaviouristic clichés. It is not that Sasha is anxious or afraid I will disappear; to offer these as explanations is anthropomorphism. Even if we claim that what Sasha feels is instinctive, that does not negate its potency. Mothers feel instinctive love for their children, but the emotions are still powerful. In Sasha's case, I am convinced that some emotion is involved, but it is not clear which one.

Sometimes the emotions of a dog are crystal clear. I drove to Gilroy, the garlic capital of the world, to see some greyhounds who had been rescued by a woman whose ranch had been turned into a sanctuary for them. These animals were in danger of being shot, either because they had lost a race, or because they were not fast enough. Many people assume that because racing dogs make money for their owners they are treated well. In fact, they are kept confined in small cages except during the race, and are never shown any affection on the grounds that they need to be aggressive to win and affection lessens the aggression. Racing greyhounds can reach speeds of 40 mph. Although gentle, they are never socialised and spend their entire lives in cages. After brief careers, they are no longer profitable and are difficult to place as pets, so they are often simply destroyed. It is truly a gruesome sport that allows this infamy.[1]

What struck me – indeed, what struck the woman who rescued the greyhounds – was their extraordinary forgiveness. They forgave all the terrible things that had been done to them. When you step on a dog's foot by mistake, somehow it knows that it was a mistake. The dog will immediately make up with you, lick your hand and let you know that it holds no grudge. The greyhound does this at an even more profound level: 'Yes, I have been beaten and hurt and I suffered. I remember, but I forgive. I want to be friends.' I was so deeply impressed with the gentle demeanour of these animals that I wanted to take one home. As the dogs were brought out of their cages to see me, I found the way that each greyhound gazed up at me with absolute trust and sweetness to be almost unbearable. How could their friendliness have survived their traumas? Racing greyhounds are neglected and abused then simply discarded, like so much rubbish, yet the emotion they so clearly manifest is forgiveness. This almost supernatural capacity to forgive was recognised in the very earliest writings about dogs. In a strange book entitled *Animal Biography*, published in 1842, there is the following heartbreaking story from a French newspaper:

> A young man took a dog into a boat, rowed to the centre of the Seine, and threw the animal over, with intent to drown him. The poor dog often tried to climb up the side of the boat; his master as often pushed him back, till, overbalancing himself, he fell overboard. As soon as the faithful dog saw his master in the stream, he left the boat and held him above water till help arrived from the shore, and his life was saved.[2]

41

Mercifully we are spared from learning whether this cruel man found a less dangerous way to rid himself of his dog. Perhaps, though, this deed was able to touch his heart.

This drive to be friends is sometimes explained away as the need to be in a pack; to my mind it is more like an emotion incompletely developed in human beings – a yearning for friendliness. Eberhard Trumler ends his book *Understanding your Dog* by stating that the true nature of the dog is an innate requirement for friendly contact with others. One is almost justified in calling this friendliness an instinct, since it is so hard to extinguish. When my three dogs run up to people and attempt to make friends, persisting even when the people strenuously avoid the attention, it always astonishes me. The parallel would be our approaching people at a cocktail party only to be yelled at and cursed, yet continuing to seek affectionate contact. It is more than just loneliness, or the desire to play, but some combination of the two that comprises another emotion altogether. Once again, the parallel with children is striking: abused children often seek the protection of the very people who abuse them over and over again.

A dog's capacity for friendship may indeed far exceed our own. Their primary friendships are with other dogs, then with humans, and sometimes with cats. In *The Soul of a Dog*, Daniel Pinkwater once observed a dog called Arnold taking care of an eight-week-old kitten. Arnold wanted to go and sleep in his private corner, but every time the kitten cried, he would drag himself to his feet, slouch over to the kitten's cage and lie down with his nose between the wires so that the kitten could sink its tiny claws into it. When the kitten became quiet, Arnold would head for his corner and flop, exhausted. As soon as the kitten started to cry again, Arnold would haul himself back to the cage.[3] From my own childhood, I know that dogs make friends with other animals too, sometimes very odd ones: one of my childhood dogs would sit for hours in front of my hamster cage, seemingly entranced. I began asking people I knew whether they had direct experience of unusual friendships between dogs and other animals and was overwhelmed with a wealth of stories.

The most unusual friendship I have heard about was between a lion and a dog. Rick Glassey, who for twenty years has been training exotic cats for films (such as *The Jungle Book*), received a call one day from Lauri Marker who worked in the Winston Wildlife Park in Oregon. She had a favour to ask of him. She was leaving for Africa to continue her study of cheetahs and wanted Rick to take one of her animals. 'Sure, no problem,' said Rick. 'What have you got?' Just a dog. A Rhodesian ridgeback, a female, about a year and a half old. Rick liked dogs and was willing to help. Rhodesian ridgebacks originate from South Africa where once they were bred to hunt lions. They are large, brave dogs, wonderful with people, but fearsome in the field. One other thing, added Lauri: the dog comes with his best and only friend, a lion called Wazoo.

It seems that the lion was housed from the day he was born with a family of dogs: the mother, a Rhodesian ridgeback, and her four puppies. The father was probably a border collie, and the puppies were smaller than normal Rhodesian ridgebacks. They were a few months older than the lion. The dogs and the lion had grown up together as brothers and sisters. One puppy in particular seemed even closer to the lion than to her own litter-mates. This was the puppy Lauri wanted Rick to take, along with the lion. The puppy had grown into a handsome bitch, weighing about 50 pounds. The lion was also handsome, but he was enormous, weighing more than 500 pounds.

Rick agreed and accepted both animals. He took Janee, the female Rhodesian ridgeback, and Wazoo, the lion, to a preserve in Soledad Canyon, California, just north of Los Angeles. Shambala Preserve was founded and is now directed by Tippi Hedren, the actress who played in Hitchcock's *The Birds* and now has dedicated her life to helping lions, tigers, leopards and other big cats who have not been able to find homes. There the two lived in a one-acre compound with a river running through it.

The lion and the dog Janee (an African word meaning both yes and no) were inseparable friends. The lion would spend hours licking the dog's ears and face, and when he had finished, she would begin grooming him all over his enormous body. At night they would sleep in a tight ball, each holding on to the other. How could this unlikely bonding be? Rick explained to me that it wasn't only out of pure love that they stayed together and remained as bonded as they did. No doubt the lion loved the dog and the dog loved the lion, but there was something else at work

43

here, at least in his opinion, and being one of the world's foremost trainers of wild cats, he has some authority in the matter.

Rhodesian ridgebacks are famous for their ability to bluff. Lions come from tight-knit social groups, the lion pride, consisting of between four and twelve related adult females, their offspring and one to six adult males. In the pride hierarchy plays an important role. Every animal needs to know where he or she stands in rank, and it is rare that any attempt would be made to break out of that rank. Somehow Janee had convinced the lion that she was his superior, that she was dominant over him. During the early years of their time together the lion completely accepted this as inviolable fact. The dog was his boss, no question about it.

The smallish dog, on the other hand, knew that she was physically far inferior to the 500 pounds of solid muscle that was her best friend. None the less, she had a mental toughness that allowed her to insist on being deferred to by the larger animal. It meant she could maintain her edge over him. She demanded respect, and she got it. Wazoo was very good-natured and rarely did anything to offend the dog. If he did, Janee quickly brought him round: she would attack him with fierce barking, snarling, growling, and even occasional bites to the ear. The lion would slink away, apologetic for having annoyed his friend and master.

For seven years the two animals romped and played and got intense pleasure from one another's company. Is it possible that the dog believed she was a lion, and the lion believed he was a dog, or were they simply not aware of any species barrier? They would eat together, though if push came to shove, Janee got the lion's share. They would split a baby-bottle of milk, each licking from it at the same time. If the dog had to leave the large fenced area for any reason, the lion would begin to pace up and down, manifestly anxious. He found the separation unbearable. There was no doubt that Wazoo missed Janee. When his friend returned he would greet her as if she had been gone for years, running up to her and licking her from head to toe, as if to examine her and make sure nothing bad had befallen her. Janee would wag her tail in ecstasy, equally happy to be back with her close companion.

One day, after seven years of happiness, the inevitable happened. Rick noticed over the space of a single week that Wazoo was undergoing a sea-change. He could see something dawning in his eyes as he slowly came awake, like watching somebody emerge from a long sleep, as if he were saying to himself: 'Wait a minute, I'm not a dog, I'm a lion, and that inconsequential small animal over there, she's no lion, she's a mere dog.' One day, when Janee started to punish the lion for some minor infraction, the lion's eyes grew dangerous, and he turned and uttered a deep growl that was unmistakably a threat, and one to be ignored at peril. The dog was puzzled, but when she tried to force her dominance, it was clear that the lion would take it no more. Wazoo ran at the dog, and Janee, realising the game was up, turned round and went racing for the water. Fortunately Rick was there in time to take the quaking dog out of the compound. Had she been there another hour, Rick told me, the lion would undoubtedly have killed her.

What happened? How is it possible that these two lived like intimate friends for seven years, and then it all just came apart? It is impossible to say what was going on in the mind of the lion. The dog's fear was obvious, the lion's awakening more obscure.

Wazoo still lives by himself at the Shambala Preserve, sleeping peacefully as lions will most of the day. Janee is living with Rick's father-in-law in Ukiah, in Northern California, a dog who loves being a dog now and is best friends with her human companion.

I wonder if either animal is ever nostalgic. Does the dog think back with longing for the day when her closest friend was a lion? Does the lion ever wonder why he spoiled a beautiful friendship?

Memory and emotions seem linked together in the dog just as they are in human beings. Dogs clearly like seeing people they recognise. I took Sasha to the Oakland Home for Jewish Parents, to see Kucci, my ex-mother-in-law, a Polish Jew who survived the Holocaust in the Warsaw Ghetto. Kucci is 86, has suffered three strokes, and cannot speak or move. It is hard to know how much she understands – I suspect that she understands a lot more than commonly supposed. One of the activity assistants took Sasha to see each and every resident of the back ward, the people who can no longer feed themselves or communicate with others. She paid attention to each person in turn as if she knew that special kindness was required of her in this situation, but she was at her best when she saw Kucci: she tried to jump up into her wheel-chair and lick her face. Kucci was thrilled. I saw her laugh, really laugh, for the first time. Sasha did not do this with any other resident. Clearly she recognised her from the two earlier times we had visited. Beyond some early German work, I know of no contemporary research having been done into memory in dogs. Most dog caretakers I've spoken to think dogs are like people in this respect, that their memory depends on how interested they are. Sasha clearly felt pleasure at seeing Kucci, probably the pleasure of recognition. Perhaps it makes a dog feel safe to repeat an experience, especially one that brings with it good sensations.

Sima, the golden retriever Sheltie mix, squeals with delight when she recognises somebody. I have never seen her fail to do this. Clearly she is remembering. The very act of remembering seems to give her pleasure; for even when she has no particularly close relationship with a person but merely remembers seeing them earlier, she begins her little dance of delight. She invariably rushes off to get a favourite toy and brings it to the visitor in her mouth as a kind of offering, squealing and making strange little sounds of joy in her throat. Nostalgia in people provides a particular kind of pleasure. Visiting the small town in which we grew up, seeing the houses now inhabited by a completely different set of people, can evoke very strong feelings based on memories that may not even surface. When we think back on events, they often appear suffused with romance and mystery, even though at the time they seemed banal. Dogs seem to carry this ability to marvel at everything past to an even greater degree: for a dog, every memory is a delight.

Some people have questioned whether dogs, like humans, can have feelings of which they are unaware. The notion of unconscious emotions is a familiar paradox: how can we have a feeling and yet not know that we feel it? Is it not in the very nature of a feeling to be consciously felt? Freud noted the paradox but nevertheless maintained that it is in fact characteristic of humans that they are often unaware of what they are feeling. By now we are accustomed to the notion of unconscious aggression – somebody who bears us ill will but does not know it. Depression, too, can be felt but not recognised, and even denied by the person who is in the grip of it.

Certain feeling states we find difficult to imagine as unconscious: unconscious love, for example. Freud once speculated that a man could be in love with a woman for six years and not know it until many years later. This may strike us as odd, but it is not impossible. Jealousy is an emotion that is perhaps more often unconscious than conscious. We all know when somebody is jealous but will not acknowledge it, usually because he or she is unaware of it.

The idea of an unconscious emotion, like the unconscious in general, depends on a particular mechanism humans use to defend themselves against hurt: repression. When a thought, memory or feeling becomes unbearable, we put it out of consciousness, we repress it; dogs lack this luxury. I do not believe that dogs are capable of repression; that they can feel sad or happy and not know it. There is a sense in which the dog is its feelings, whether sad or happy. Much as it might wish it could, it seems incapable of denying how it feels. This provides much of the pleasure of being in the company of dogs. As Mike del Ross, of Guide Dogs for the Blind, said to me: 'Dogs never lie about love.' This is also the opinion of Anatole France who asks what could be 'the meaning of the obscure love for me that has sprung up in your little heart?' It is a mystery he accepts.[4]

Dogs do not lie to you about how they feel because they cannot lie about feelings. A dog can deceive another dog, but only about facts (pretending, for example, not to see a bone the other dog has temporarily left unattended), not about feelings. Nobody has ever seen a sad dog pretending to be happy, or a happy dog pretending to be sad. When a dog is sad or happy, that feeling occupies its whole being; the dog becomes pure happiness or pure sadness. As Roger Caras wrote in *A Dog is Listening*: 'A dog is utterly sincere. It cannot pretend. . . . People use you and pretend they don't, while dogs use you in complete honesty because they have no choice, and they have not an ounce of deceit in their soul nor self-consciousness about any of this.'[5]

An interesting facet of canine emotional life is the emotions dogs don't seem to experience, such as the self-conscious emotions. They show no sign of feeling self-pity, for example. While walking the dogs on the University of California campus in Berkeley, I saw a black labrador mix chasing a frisbee down a hill. He looked joyous and completely absorbed in what he was doing. When he ran down the hill I noticed with a shock that he was dragging his two hind legs behind him. They were in fact paralysed. His companion, a graduate student in English named Victoria Pond, told me Cinder did not seem to notice that he had a disability, much the same way as children can seem oblivious. A year earlier, when he was ten months old, he had been struck by a mysterious virus which left his whole backside paralysed. He wears special boots that protect his feet and part of his legs from the abrasions he would otherwise receive from dragging them on the ground. In spite of these disadvantages he was happy – and my dogs were delighted to play with him. They either did not notice his disability or thought nothing of it.

How different from us! Many people who experience lesser loss that this would whine and curse the heavens like regular Jobs: 'Why me? Why do I have to suffer this?' We would feel sorry for ourselves. While we would feel, above all, self-pity, for this dog it was just something that he lived with. He seemed totally unaware of being different from any other dog, and was clearly determined not to let the disability interfere with his capacity to enjoy life. His emotions were so clearly in the present that nothing could interfere with them, not any past event nor any thought of how he differed from other dogs.

An astonishing story, graphically illustrated with photographs, appeared in a German research journal concerning a German shepherd, Rolf, who lived with a railroad-crossing guard and his family in 1929. The dog constantly accompanied the children everywhere. One day, while walking across the tracks (possibly he was trying to protect the children from an oncoming train), the dog was struck by a train which took both his left legs off cleanly. The children ran back to their mother who found the dog, evidently dead. She dragged him to a wood pile, but when the guard went out to see for himself, he found that the dog had regained consciousness and had hauled himself into a cave that was lined with straw. Amazingly, the dog lost less blood than might be expected. He licked the wound steadily for days (more proof that dog's saliva has healing properties – an old wives' tale that I happen to believe is true) and seemed to get better. Yet the stump on the back leg was in very bad shape, with bits of bone splinter hanging out. The dog himself pulled them out of the suppurating wound with his teeth. Just two days later, to everybody's astonishment, he appeared 'on his feet' in front of the house. Within three weeks the stumps were totally healed, and he was like his old self: he played with the children, guarded the house, and was a spectacular rat-catcher. He began to enjoy swimming again, took to running faster and faster, and even jumping over ditches – all on two legs. When he came to the burrows of rabbits, he would try to dig them out, but would of course immediately fall on to one side. Not to be beaten, he soon learned that he could stick his whole head into the warren and bite the earth. The accident left him with no visible fear of traffic or of trains. He would still run alongside the trains, barking as he had done before the accident. So remarkable was the behaviour and plasticity of this dog that he was given to the dog-training unit of the German army for a study.

The military dog trainers decided that perhaps the animal was subject to retrograde amnesia, so severe was the shock he had suffered after the accident, and remained unaware of what had happened to him. He never walked again, but only galloped, even when he was standing still. Put to the test, to see how well he would perform on the various obstacle courses they had prepared for their own dogs that were used in war, Rolf was able to accommodate his own handicap. He learned to climb stairs, and even a ladder, to walk over a narrow gangplank across a deep ditch, and to go into pitch-dark caves.[6]

★

Charles Kingsley, the nineteenth-century Cambridge scholar and storyteller, once wrote: 'I took her, my dog, for my teacher, and obeyed her, for she was wiser than I, and she led me back, the poor dumb beast, like a God-sent, and God-obeying angel, to human nature, to mercy, to self sacrifice, to belief, to worship, to pure and wedded love.'[7]

I am not alone in my love for dogs: 35 per cent of American households owned a dog in 1994, representing a dog population exceeding 52 million.[8] It hardly seems worth asking the question of why we love them, so obvious does the answer appear to all: we love dogs because they love us, unconditionally. No matter how we treat them, what we do to them, how little attention we pay to them; they are anxious to please us, eager to be with us. I asked this question of Craig Stark, from the Los Angeles based Last

Chance for Animals, a dog expert who has done a great deal of work trying to stop pet-dog-theft, and he had a wonderful response: 'It is the only love money can buy.'[9] Dogs are ready, to the point of cosmic love, to forgive anything we do to them.

Many writers have noted that we speak to dogs much as we speak to children: our voices become high-pitched; we lean down close to them; we touch them as we talk; we play word games, give them alternative names, coo, sing, chant and lose ourselves in a more innocent world. We are surprised when a child tells us that we are boring. We do not expect to be judged – and a dog, with very few exceptions, will never judge us.[10] When asked why they love their dog, many people will bring up this point. In fact failure to judge our actions is no reason for loving anybody. In a person, such non-judgmental behaviour would strike us as either apathetic or immoral. A dog, on the other hand, somehow belongs to another realm or a different world. Dogs make certain distinctions, but in dog terms, and we may never know how our dog sees us in that language. We don't have access to it. Moreover, just as we might think one thing but feel another, loving the person but hating what he does, so might the dog disdain how we act but love us none the less.

Jerome K. Jerome wrote in *Idle Thoughts of an Idle Fellow*:

And when we bury our face in our hands and wish we had never been born, they don't sit up very straight, and observe that we have brought it all upon ourselves. They don't even hope it will be a warning to us. But they come up softly; and shove their heads against us . . . he looks up with his big, true eyes, and says with them, 'Well, you've always got me, you know. We'll go through the world together, and always stand by each other, won't we?[11]

There may be another reason why so many people love dogs with passionate intensity. Men who gradually become misanthropes explain their distaste for other people (misanthropy rarely extends to include the speaker) with a reference to selfishness, to the fact that so many human beings seem absorbed in their own affairs, self-preoccupied, obsessed with matters that refer to them exclusively. Narcissism has become the great catch-all term of opprobrium to describe man in the twentieth century. This is, I think, by and large true: some people do have a remarkable ability to remain fascinated with the minutiae of their own lives that others find puzzling, in as much as they reserve such fascination for *their* lives.

Humans have a tendency to immerse themselves in their own narcissistic concerns, losing awareness of the world around them. Not only pity for the self, but self-concerns of many varieties preoccupy us. Perhaps one central reason for loving dogs is that they take us away from this obsession with ourselves. When our thoughts start to go in circles, and we seem unable to break away, wondering what horrible event the future holds for us, the dog opens a window into the delight of the moment. Walking with a dog is to enter the world of the immediate. Our dog stares up into a tree, watching a squirrel – she is there and nowhere else.

'What are dogs interested in?' asked Elizabeth Marshall Thomas, who came up with the obviously correct answer: other dogs. But not just that. I have watched the faces of my three dogs freezing with intense interest; whatever the task at hand is, they bring such focused intensity to it. They turn to watch which way I will go at a fork in the road. They are *so* interested. It is extraordinary how much interest they can invest in the most ordinary thing. I find it entirely humbling. That concentrated, full, complete, undisturbed interest is what everybody wants from their own human companion.

Rani almost never stops wagging her tail. She seems to be pure happiness, all the time, everywhere – as long as she is outdoors. We humans are artificially confined, even though we confine ourselves. Our light is artificial, as is our food, our clothes, and much of our conversation, as well as the objects that surround us – cars, clocks, computers and washing machines. When we are out with our dogs, we are able to leave this world of artifice behind. Many people report the therapeutic effects of walking with a dog, how it is stimulating and soothing at the same time.

Later in the book I dispute the philosophical claim that dogs have no conception of time, but there is a sense in which this claim is true: dogs do not appreciate time that is set by convention; they do not divide a day up into minutes or hours, neither do they think in terms of weeks or months or years. A dog does not tremble at the thought of its own mortality; I doubt if a dog ever thinks about a time when it will no longer be alive. So when we are with a dog, we too enter a kind of timeless realm, where the future becomes irrelevant.

When I was growing up, my family habitually judged one place in comparison with another from their memory. The present, of course, could never compete with the past, especially an idealised past. I too picked up this bad habit. A close companion would often have to admonish me: 'Why do you compare one beach to another? You are here now; enjoy it for what it is.' I learn the same lesson from watching my dogs: they are never paralysed by the need to judge and to compare. They are never gloomy at the thought that this walk was not as nice as yesterday's walk, this forest not nearly as interesting as last week's forest. Each walk is new, unique, and uniquely interesting, with its own set of smells and delights. I keep looking for my dog's favourite walks, but the truth is, they have no favourite walks; only I do. They love all walks. They love walking. They love being wherever they are. The reason, and it is a great lesson, is no doubt that they are perfectly content to be who they are, without torturing themselves with alternatives: they love being dogs.

Marjorie Garber speculates that dogs allow us to fantasise about spontaneity, emotional generosity and togetherness. This is right, partly I think because dogs 'are strangers to cynicism'.[12] Dogs are not worried about how they will be perceived by other dogs. They do not have to hide their *joie de vivre* for fear of appearing naive, and they do not need to feign boredom when they are in fact interested for fear of appearing unsophisticated. Dogs never stand around at parties wondering what to say, or why they came, or how pitiful they might seem to more elegant or more amusing or more important guests. They do not struggle to be witty, getting right to the point, going straight for the source. Yet they manage to come away with a greater and more accurate fund of information than humans do at their parties. For the dog sex may or may not be present, in deed or thought, but information, knowledge is critical: what kind of dog am I dealing with? Who stands before me? Where have you been and what did you do there? But even more basic: who are you really?

Questers of the truth, that's who dogs are; seekers after the invisible scent of another being's authentic core.

CHAPTER THREE

Love: The Master Emotion of Dogs

THERE HAS BEEN so much theoretical work written about human love, almost all of it, it seems to me, far less convincing than a demonstration of the real thing. Does love resist being contained by a theory because love is best expressed through deeds rather than words? Does talking about love too much devalue it?

Dogs register no need to theorise about love (or about anything else for that matter), they just show it. And show it and show it and show it. I am continually amazed by the dog's ability to love so unconditionally and without ambivalence. Indeed many people will have heard at one time or another of a cruel or neglectful owner whose dog loves regardless of how he or she is treated. The capacity for love in the dog is so pronounced, so developed that it is almost like another sense or another organ. It might well be termed hyperlove, and it is bestowed upon all humans who live closely with a dog.

Learning to know somebody intimately is often the beginning

53

of dislike, sometimes even of contempt. Among humans love often does not survive a growing acquaintance, but in a dog love seems to grow with acquaintance, to get stronger, deeper. Even when fully acquainted with all our weaknesses, our treachery, our unkindness, the dog seems to love strongly – and this love is returned by most dog-owning humans. We too seem to love our dogs more the more we get to know them. The bond grows between us and our dogs.

It is not clear whether the love a dog feels for a human being differs from the love it feels for another dog. The bond between dogs can be a strong one, and some authors even speak in terms of falling in love. Elizabeth Marshall Thomas refers to the bond as a kind of 'marriage'. Of course that is only an analogy, but the faithfulness, the duration and the intensity are in fact very similar to these aspects of human marriage.

Where does it come from, this love? Often it is assumed that providing food to puppies and dogs lies at the heart of a dog's attachment (a similar theory has been posited for the emotional bond between an infant and its mother). A series of experiments conducted by A. J. Brodbeck in 1954[1] showed this not to be the case, and feeding not a necessary part of the development of the social bond. One group of puppies were automatically fed by a machine, the other group were fed by a person. The hand-fed puppies vocalised more at the sight of the experimenter, but this was the only important difference between the two groups of puppies. So love on the part of the dog does not seem conditioned merely by what we provide the dog, nor simply a recognition that we are a source of food. A dog does not love a robot that gives it food, but is capable of loving people who never feed it.

The signs of love in a dog are unmistakable, although each dog shows love in a slightly different manner. When Sasha greets somebody she remembers, she begins a kind of howl mixed with a whine that accompanies other gestures showing her delight: her ears go flat, her eyes take on a lustre, she smacks her lips and rubs her body against the person. Unmistakably she feels happy; it is hard to imagine a different feeling (unless it goes by a different name in dog language, which is always possible) and she is expressing it by being loving. Rani displays a totally different look on her face, and when she wags her tail, her whole body wags with it. She looks at you with what appears to be shyness, but her pleasure at seeing you cannot be mistaken. Sima cannot stop squealing and charging round in circles. She is tireless, racing between the person she remembers meeting before and that person's dog, pushing her nose into the dog's mouth, or rushing up to the caretaker while making urgent noises. All of these gestures of pleasure and happiness are a kind of love – or so we humans would call it if we felt such intense pleasure at seeing somebody. With dogs, unfortunately, we tend to speak of such gestures as a type of submission.

If a human exhibited indiscriminate affection for everybody he or she met, we would think it promiscuous. We speak of people who are friendly, outgoing, engaging, but none of these adjectives fully describes the friendliness that a dog displays. Dogs express love for just about anyone who shows friendliness toward them.[2] That is why some people (me, for example) claim that the dog *is* love, that dogs are all about love. Perhaps my favourite response to those who claim dogs cannot possibly love comes from Roger Caras, who writes about two dogs: 'I think Luke loves Chloe Sweetpea and she loves him. Since I can't define love in my own species (I do believe it is more than a glandular disturbance and an opportunity to file joint income tax returns) I won't try to define love among our dogs. But as sure as I am that I love my wife of thirty-seven years, and that she is more than just conditioned to me, so I believe those two dogs at my daughter's place love each other, too.'[3]

There are well-documented stories of intense interspecies love – of dogs who mourn their caretaker's death, grieving to the point of endangering their own lives, or even dying from refusing to eat. Consider Hachi Ko, the Akita from Tokyo, who kept a ten-year vigil at the train station, waiting for his dead owner to return; was he hopeful, or was this his own private mourning ritual? Could he have had an all-too-human fantasy that he would be reunited with his friend in some other place? What, too, were the thoughts and feelings of Greyfriars Bobby, who lived for fourteen years on his master's grave? Alas, however familiar to us a dog's emotions may appear, they still belong to a different universe. The key to the canine world of feeling will forever elude us precisely because we belong to a related but different species. At the same time, humans and dogs seem to be the only two species capable of great love that crosses the species-barrier. No other animal mourns for a lost human friend in the way that a dog does. It is possible too, that dogs – like humans – recognise this similarity between the two species, this ability both have to love a member of a different species.

Humans often confuse love and lust. A dog never lusts for us. Dogs who mount their owners are not showing desire, but rather a need for dominance. A dog loves with its body, and its heart, but probably not its mind. Dogs have minds, of course, and they use them for many things, but they do not make calculations about the advantage they might obtain from loving (temporary flattery is another matter). Nor are they inhibited in their love by thinking about its possible disadvantages. And so dogs do not make the mistakes about love that humans frequently do, though they often love a human who brings them nothing but suffering. The human brain is the primary sex organ, but this is not so for the dog. You cannot impress your dog with beauty, wealth, possessions, power, or physical prowess. We might fall in love with somebody for any of these qualities. A dog does not fall in love, the dog merely loves.

What is it that makes a dog follow us from room to room? At first I thought it was insecurity, fear that we were going to leave them. Then I decided that it was the fear of losing out on an adventure; they thought that maybe we were going somewhere interesting and they might be left behind. Nothing is worse for a dog than telling him that he cannot come with you on an outing. He cocks his head, as if in disbelief. Perhaps, though, they follow us around the house *just because they like to be near us*. What makes dogs want to be near us, and to touch their bodies to ours? There is something wonderful about my dog stretching its body along my body at night, something about the trust it shows. That is one of the most touching things about being in a deep relationship with a member of another species: the mutual trust. 'I know', the dog seems to be saying, 'that nothing bad will happen to me if I'm with you. I can relax my whole body and trust this person not to harm me while I sleep.' A dolphin would keep an eye on us, but a dog or a cat will put himself entirely at our mercy.

Is love a 'deep' feeling? I know that my capacity for deep feeling is greater when I am outdoors, when I see beauty in the physical world around me. On one May day I took the dogs to a new park, a wetlands near the Oakland Airport. There were ground squirrels everywhere, and large jack rabbits running about the fields. It was on the edge of a vast marsh, and the dogs were allowed to be there off leash. When I let the dogs out of the car they were off and running, and when they returned a minute later, there was visible excitement in their eyes. They looked at me as if grateful, as if saying to me: 'Yes, this is exactly the kind of place we love. Thank you for taking us here. Thank you, thank you, thank you.' (Of course these are my own thoughts, for dogs are unlikely to make comparisons, rooted as they are in the moment.) As we walked along the water's edge, feelings very difficult to articulate were aroused in me by the sound of the leaves rustling in the breeze, by the smells of the marsh, by the sight of the wild flowers coming up in the grass fields. Those feelings had something to do with love, in this case the love of this outdoor dog-paradise. It seemed to me that the dogs had intimations of it too: they were smiling, thrilled to be here, happy, loving. Their capacity for deep feeling, for love, may also be contingent on being in a place that makes them happy.

The feeling world of dogs is suffused with innocence, purity and lack of self-deception, something that dogs have in common with children. Both children and dogs have a certain openness, a lack of guile, and also a similar vulnerability. Dogs remind us of our children. We have the same irresistible urge to use baby talk with both. We give them nicknames; we use facial expressions that make people without children or dogs think we are demented.

There is a tendency to think of a grown dog as being psychologically similar to a small human child. This has been encouraged as a result of serious research (primarily by Michael Fox, of the Humane Society of the United States) showing that, in certain conditions, both dog and child can develop similar behavioural disorders. 'These can range from psychogenic epilepsy to asthma-like conditions, compulsive eating, sympathy lameness, hypermotility of the intestines with hemorrhagic gastroenteritis, possibly ulcerative colitis, not to mention sibling rivalry, extreme jealousy, aggression, depression, and refusal to eat food (anorexia nervosa).'[4]

Dogs in turn seem to see humans as functioning much like their own parents. Many researches have observed that dogs are only infantilised wolves stuck in an early stage of development; cubs who never mature. So we are *in loco parentis* to dogs. This is why, in 1949, E. Dechambre[5] spoke of the phenomenon of 'foetalisation', where we try to breed gentle and friendly dogs, and in 1963 (in *The History of Domesticated Animals*), F. E. Zeuner developed the idea of neoteny, the persistence of juvenile characteristics into adulthood. Immature features, such as drooping ears, smaller canine teeth, small head, are selected so that the animals are dependent on humans in the way that a small wolf puppy is dependent on its parents. In terms of behaviour, Konrad Lorenz,[6] the founder of modern ethology (the study of animal behaviour), points to the 'peculiar form' of the domestic dog's attachment: 'The ardent affection which wild canine youngsters show for their mother and which disappears completely after they have reached maturity, is preserved as a permanent mental trait of all highly domesticated dogs. What originally was love for the mother is transformed into love for the human master.'[7] We value, reward, and breed for neotenous traits in our dogs. Wolves and dogs are different in this respect. A wolf is the least neotenised of animals. Unlike the domesticated dog, a grown wolf is a fully independent being, and this contrast has been highlighted in a noteworthy passage written by Erich Klinghammer and Patricia Ann Goodmann:

> Dogs enter our world, and, to a large extent, can be trained to behave according to our rules. In working with socialized wolves, the human enters the wolves world and must behave according to wolf social rules. It is widely accepted that dogs have been neotenized during the course of domestication. Because dogs retain many infantile characteristics, it is relatively easy to impose your will on them. The wolf is a fully adult form of canine.[8]

Though the leader of a wolf-pack is nothing like a dog, subordinate wolves have rather more in common with domestic dogs. The traditional wisdom, then, that we humans act as the pack leader, and that all dogs are subordinate to us, may be correct in terms of the psychology of the dog only in so far as dogs see us as surrogate parents.

If neoteny does explain certain behavioural traits, dogs certainly know that we are not their real parents. When I watch Sima begging Sasha, who could easily be her mother, for food, she does something very specific: she sticks her snout into Sasha's mouth and licks her teeth. A wolf cub does this to get the mother to regurgitate food. Sima knows she won't get food that way, but some instinct urges her to do it, to make up to Sasha, to flatter her. The point is, however, she does not do the same to me. She must recognise an important distinction, having something to do with species. Dogs know, I am convinced, that we belong to a different species. Trainers often say that we must become the lead dog, the top dog, in any relationship we form with our dogs. Yet dogs know we are not dogs. Even when I play with my dogs, they treat me differently from the way they do each other. It is somewhat humiliating, because no matter how much pleasure I give the dogs in terms of taking them to interesting places, when it comes to real play, they would all rather play with one another than with me. They play with me in an almost condescending manner, the way that a somewhat bored adult plays with a child who is pestering him.

When I took my dogs to a dog park one day in June, the gate opened and a tiny little puppy resembling a weasel came flying in and began rushing up and down the park, stopping to greet every dog and every person by rolling over on to its back and then crawling rapidly on its belly. Every dog seemed enchanted, every human smiled. Here was the quintessential puppy, adorable, irresistible. I was mistaken. It was not a puppy, but a grown dog. Only its behaviour was that of a puppy. And it is this behaviour that so appeals to humans and that makes them want to protect and take care of puppies. When such behaviour extends into adult life, this is what scientists call neoteny. It is something we have bred into adult dogs because we prize it so.

Stephen Jay Gould, in a popular article entitled 'Mickey Mouse Meets Konrad Lorenz' (subtitled: 'Both animal behaviourists and Walt Disney have made similar discoveries about our responses') argues that the animals in the comics elicit our affection because they are given juvenile features, which, in the dry words of Konrad Lorenz, 'trigger innate releasing mechanisms' for nurturance. Gould says that when we see a creature with baby-like features, we feel an automatic surge of disarming tenderness.

Humans, explains Gould, are neotenic (the word means literally 'holding on to youth'); that is, we have evolved by retaining into adulthood the juvenile features of our ancestors.[9]

Neoteny, then, has been invoked as the prime explanation for our 'innate' love for certain animals, especially dogs. For me, however, this explanation is insufficient. There can be no doubt that infantile members of just about any species elicit a peculiar response in us; for who can resist affection for any creature newly born? When I go for walks with my dogs and meet puppies, I notice that almost nobody simply passes them by without commenting on how cute they are, how adorable, followed by a desire to touch them, stroke them, hold them close to one's body.

Part of this fascination with puppies has to do with a habit they display to which we are immensely attracted: puppies follow us. Almost no other domesticated or wild species does this to the extent that a dog does. When Lorenz discovered 'imprinting'[10] and found that his grey-lag geese followed him down the street, he received the same appreciative comments from passers-by as a puppy owner experiences on his walks. In the case of the geese, they were under the endearing but mistaken impression that Lorenz was their mother. For geese, imprinting is genetic; the animals really have no choice. Moreover, the critical period for socialisation may be only a question of hours.[11] A puppy, however, is not under the delusion that any of us is its mother. It follows us because it wants to do so. A dog retains this and other juvenile characteristics well into adulthood and, in fact, behaves much like a child for its entire life, with its human companion *in loco parentis*. Some female elephant cubs and female whale calves will also follow their mothers their entire lives. Once a certain relationship has been established, it maintains itself. This may be what happens with dogs and humans. We become intimate family for a grown dog. But whereas in the case of a wolf, any substitution is unacceptable, even traumatic, a puppy and even a grown dog generally adapt very well to a change in home, though sometimes after a period of great difficulty, as my veterinarian friends remind me.

Dogs do not seem to need the same kind of constancy that a wild animal requires. When we are walking in a park, and my dogs meet up with some especially fascinating member of their own species, their joy knows no bounds. They seem destined to be best friends. And yet when I call, or the other dog's companion calls, the dogs follow us and leave their new friends behind with barely a parting glance. We become more intimate family with our dogs than any other dog seems to be. When our dogs accidentally become separated from us, the look of panic that crosses their faces is genuine. Nothing could be worse than being separated from us. It is like a cub being separated from its parent.

Neoteny seems to decline as a dog ages. Many people note the dignity of an older dog, the almost royal bearing, the forbearance for the antics of younger dogs. The dog is no longer a puppy, no longer our child; it is more like an equal. Yet the love and affection we feel for our dog – and it feels for us – do not diminish. If, as Konrad Lorenz suggests, we were simply programmed to love juvenile characteristics in animals, we would abandon our older dogs. What ties us to them, and what ties them to us at later stages of their life-cycles, is something more profound and more complex than a biological urge. Could it be a recognition that we share with them a capacity for emotional depth and intensity? Perhaps we even recognise in them a capacity superior to our own in this respect.

What is Sasha's passion for very small children all about? At first it was hard for me to believe it was genuine; it seemed so calculated to please me. I now know that it is not. She just adores small children. She runs up to every one she sees and immediately plants a large wet kiss on the child's face. (Bruce Max Feldman, my veterinarian friend, tells me that this is most unhygienic, since dogs carry salmonella and other pathogens in their saliva – but I take refuge in denial.) Strangely, almost no child seems to mind. They all smile and quickly announce to their parent that 'this dog kissed me'. Indeed she did. It is eerily similar to the way we will grab an adorable child and kiss it over and over. It is a sheer outpouring of affection. Sasha likes all adults, but she does not reserve for them this unbridled passion. Neither does she ever do the same to another dog. I therefore ask myself what children mean for Sasha? What do they represent in her mind? Sasha likes me more than she does most other people, but she does not greet me with kisses to the face; only children receive this royal treatment. Is there some hidden similarity that I have not yet uncovered between dogs and small children? Does Sasha see a connection that remains hidden from me? Perhaps it is the recognition that children and she are somehow siblings – an acknowledgment of emotional similarity that is deeper than the recognition of specieshood.

Sasha loves to raise her face up and plant a kiss on anyone who pets her. This seems to lend credence to the neoteny theory that she is behaving towards all people as if they were her mother. Yet Sasha knows full well that such people are not her mother, nor are they dogs. She seems just to love them. The neotenist would still argue that this is no more than mother-love. Here is a circular argument: we know she responds to them as she would to her mother because she tries to kiss their faces, and wolf cubs kiss their mother's face because they want her to regurgitate food. If a wolf cub never got any results, it would soon stop. In contrast, Sasha knows that these adults are not going to bend down and vomit their food up for her to eat. What she gets from them is exactly what she gives them: love.

Is this not precisely the same as an expression of emotion between two humans?

CHAPTER FOUR

On Loyalty and Heroism

O<small>N A MONUMENT</small> outside a courthouse in Missouri there is recorded one of the most moving statements ever made about the abiding love of a dog. It was made in the nineteenth century by George Graham Vest, before he became a senator, when he was legally representing a neighbour whose dog had been killed by another man and who was suing the accused for $200 damages. By the time Vest had finished his summing up, the jury was in no mood to prevaricate: it took them two minutes to reach their verdict. The plaintiff was awarded $500, but the judge was unable to grant their wish that the dog-killer be sent to prison as the law did not permit such a punishment. These are the words that Senator Vest spoke:

> Gentlemen of the Jury: The best friend a man has in this world may turn against him and become his enemy. His son and daughter that he had reared with loving care may become

63

ungrateful. Those who are nearest and dearest to us, those whom we trust with our happiness and our good name, may become traitors to their faith. The money that a man has he may lose. It flies away from him when he may need it most. Man's reputation may be sacrificed in a moment of ill considered action. The people who are prone to fall on their knees and do us honor when success is with us may be the first to throw the stone of malice when failure settles its cloud upon our head. The only absolutely unselfish friend a man may have in this selfish world, the one that never deserts him, the one that never proves ungrateful or treacherous is his dog.

A man's dog stands by him in prosperity and poverty, in health and sickness. He will sleep on the cold ground, when the wintry winds blow and the snow drives fiercely, if only he can be near his master's side. He will kiss the hand that has no food to offer, he will lick the wounds and sores that come in encounter with the roughness of the world. He guards the sleep of a pauper as if he were a prince.

When all other friends desert, he remains. When riches take wings and reputation falls to pieces he is as constant in his love as the sun in its journey through the heavens. If fortune drives the master forth an outcast into the world, friendless and homeless, the faithful dog asks no higher privilege than that of accompanying him to guard him against danger, to fight against his enemies, and when the last scene of all comes, and death takes his master in its embrace and his body is laid away in the cold ground, no matter if all other friends pursue their way, there by his graveside will the noble dog be found, his head between his paws and his eyes sad, but open in alert watchfulness, faithful and true even to death.'[1]

The *Oxford English Dictionary* defines loyal as 'true to obligations of duty, love, etc.' Loyalty in its deeper sense seems to me more intimately linked to feelings of love than to a sense of duty. The dog is faithful or loyal (I use the terms synonymously) not because it feels an obligation but because it feels love. Dogs are loyal to other dogs; that is, to their own family, their pack. This loyalty can reach proportions that we can hardly imagine, yet we know they are real.

In *Animal Psychology*, R. H. Smythe offers an illustration of such loyalty in the story of a friend, living in Cornwall, who lost his mongrel terrier dog. As countless dogs disappear down disused mine shafts in the vicinity in pursuit of rabbits, it was assumed that this was what had become of the terrier. A search, however, revealed nothing. Smythe writes: 'The dog had a friend, a smooth fox terrier bitch, and the two had been in the habit of going off hunting together. Someone noticed that the bitch went off alone, always travelling in one direction. This led us to an old shaft from which we could distinctly hear barking. When a rescue party descended about forty feet they found the dog on a ledge, uninjured. Also on the ledge was a fresh bone which the owner recognised as that from a leg of mutton of the previous Sunday, together with several bread crusts. As no person had visited this shaft it can only be presumed the bitch carried them to the mouth of the shaft and dropped them.'[2]

One of the first books ever written about dogs, Richard Blome's *The Gentleman's Recreation*, published in 1686, already gives evidence of canine loyalty:

> *Spaniels* by Nature are very loving, surpassing all other Creatures, for in *Heat* and *Cold*, *Wet* and *Dry*, *Day* and *Night*, they will not forsake their *Master*. There are many *Prodigious Relations*, made in several Grave and Credible *Authors*, of the strange Affections which *Dogs* have had, as well to their Dead and living *Masters*.[3]

For reasons that remain hard to fathom, humans have become part of the pack world of the dog, and this inclusion is why dogs are loyal to us. People who have no direct experience of this loyalty tend to dismiss it as herd mentality or instinctual behaviour, bearing no resemblance to the loyalty that humans display among themselves.

If canine loyalty were purely mechanical, an instinct to love whoever protects the dog, it surely must follow that dogs find it easy to move from one caretaker to another. Yet think of how long it can take a dog to transfer loyalty from one human to another. Sometimes it never happens. There are reports of dogs who tried to commit suicide, so loyal were they to the family they knew.[4] In a wonderful nineteenth-century book about dogs, a story is told of a gamekeeper belonging to the castle of Holstein (in Denmark), who returned one evening from a long and tiring chase and deposited the game in his larder, unaware that his dog was locked inside at the same time. Unexpectedly called away immediately afterwards, he did not return for five days. Then, when he went to the larder to retrieve his game, he found the dog there, stretched out dead by the door. 'The gamekeeper stood extremely affected; but what were his sensations, when he saw on the table eleven brace of partridges, and five grouse untouched! This admiration increased his grief, when he found the poor dog had suffered starvation rather than transgress his duty.'[5]

The Spanish novelist Cervantes, in his *Coloquio de los Perros*, written in 1599, has Bergansa say: 'I know well enough, that there have been dogs so loving that they have thrown themselves into the same grave with the dead bodies of their masters; others have staid upon their masters' graves without stirring a moment from them, and have voluntarily starved themselves to death, refusing to touch the food that was brought them.'[6] A more recent account reads: 'Years ago in California, Ben's breeder, Allen Ransome, had a call about a Newf whose family had divorced. The husband, furious, had insisted on having the dog because the wife had the children, but afterward he gave the dog up to Newf Rescue, a group that places Newfs in need of homes. The dog had willed himself to die. He would not move, would not lift his head to eat.'[7]

The raging firestorm that devastated the hills above Berkeley and Oakland, California, on 20 October 1991, killed twenty-six people, obliterated three thousand homes and left 5,000 pets either killed or displaced. Dudley, the twelve-year-old ex-stray dog of Virginia Smith, refused to leave her body when she died of smoke inhalation. Rescuers tried to take him with them, but he 'stood like a statue, rooted to the ground. They tugged and pulled and coaxed, but Dudley would not budge.'[8] With their life in danger, they had little time to lose and finally dragged the dog off. His fur was singed and his paw pads were badly burned. He was rushed to the Berkeley Dog and Cat Hospital, and although he survived, he sank into a deep depression, so much did he miss his friend Virginia Smith.

Linda Peterson tells of rescuing a greyhound, Touch, a former

Grade A racer who was going to be destroyed because of an injury incurred while racing. He had lived for six years in a kennel. She believes that the extreme loyalty of greyhounds stems from their past suffering, that they are truly thankful to be alive.[9]

People who have been sick report that their dogs knew about the illness, and showed their concern in their eyes and the fact that they stayed close to the sick person. Elizabeth Barrett Browning (1806–61) memorialised this in her poem *To Flush, My Dog*:

> But of *thee* it shall be said,
> This dog watched beside a bed
>   Day and night unweary, –
> Watched within a curtained room,
> Where no sunbeam brake the gloom
>   Round the sick and dreary.
>
> Roses, gathered for a vase,
> In that chamber died apace,
>   Beam and breeze resigning;
> This dog only, waited on,
> Knowing that when light is gone
> Love remains for shining.

Leila and I took Sima, Sasha and Rani to the most dog-friendly town in California: Carmel-by-the-Sea. We went on a walking tour where everybody we met made a fuss over the dogs. One of the women on the tour with us, Mary Silvermann from North Carolina, shares her house with six dogs and sixteen cats! We visited the hotel owned by Doris Day, where dogs are welcome, and learned that one of the early heroes of the town was a dog celebrated by several of the local artists. Perhaps best of all was learning that the marvellous white sand beach at the end of the town was open to dogs without leashes.

It was a hot crowded Sunday and, returning to the car, we noticed that Sasha was missing. I looked back down the beach to see her tearing herself away from some game she was playing with another dog to come bounding in our direction. Suddenly she stopped. She did not know where we had gone. She thought she was lost; the look on her face is difficult to describe, but impossible to forget. It was a mixture of worry, panic, despair and 'Oh my God, what am I going to do now?' We called, but she did not hear us. Rani, however, knew where Sasha was, and went bounding off after her. When Sasha saw her, her expression turned to one of utter relief. It is clear that her anxiety had to do with her thwarted loyalty to this group, to her pack. Loyalty, in this sense, is closely connected to home, to familiarity, to love. It is one more area where a dog resembles a child: a lost child behaves very much like Sasha did, and we can imagine that the emotions for both child and dog are similar.

Extraordinary tales are told of lost dogs who find their homes from great distances, using what is called the 'homing' instinct. The most remarkable story I have heard about the ability of dogs to find their way home is quoted in *The Mind of the Dog* by R. H. Smythe, who was the examiner for the Diploma of Membership of the Royal College of Veterinary Surgeons in London:

Dinah [a Red Setter in whelp] was sent from Cookstown to Lurgan, a matter of twenty-five miles, by train. Shortly after her arrival she whelped five puppies, then promptly disappeared from her new home, puppies and all. Ten days later she was found at Cookstown asleep in her old nest with the five puppies, all alive and healthy, tucked in alongside her. Her feet were raw and bleeding and she was dreadfully emaciated. She had obviously travelled on foot and must have transported the five puppies in relays of short distance, so how many times she actually covered the mileage is unknown. On her way she swam, complete with family, the River Blackwater at Mahery Ferry, where it is over eighty yards wide and very deep, a number of times in each direction, leaving some of her puppies on the opposite shore to await her return while she fetched more. Dinah recovered, reared all her puppies and remained a resident of Cookstown for the remainder of her days.[10]

It has been observed that dogs, in finding their way home, prefer to travel on a road. Göran Bergman, a Finnish scientist, suggests that this may be because dogs often walk with their caretakers on such roads. He mentions stories about dogs who board a train or a boat to find their way home: 'My dachshunds would in fact choose the right place for getting on a bus but would not be able to choose either the correct bus-service or the right end-stop.'[11] That is what I would have thought as well, had I not had my own unusual experience in Poona.

When I was living in Poona, near Bombay, in 1968, I adopted a small stray dog who lived with me in a house in Koregaon Park, some five miles from the university where I was writing my Ph.D. thesis. I never took the dog with me to the university. As I prepared to leave India, it was necessary to find the dog a new home with friends who lived some twenty miles away along the bus route that led to the University of Poona. A few days after they took the dog, I was working with my Pundit (a learned man schooled in the traditional way) in his office at the university, very early in the morning, when we heard a knock on the door. We were surprised that anybody would be calling so early. When I opened the door, who should be there but my loyal little friend. My pundit was appalled (dogs are considered very unclean to an orthodox Brahmin) but when he heard the story of how this dog had been given away and had now found me, he created a Sanskrit verse on the spot, the gist of which was that I was bound by karmic ties to this little fellow and must never abandon him again.

How did my dog find me? I asked people at the university and was told that somebody had seen him board a bus that went by the road in front of Poona University. But how had he managed to get off at the right stop? This still puzzles me.

Michael Fox tells the story of a collie named Bobbie. He was lost in Indiana and his caretakers had to return home to Silverton, Oregon, without him. Somehow he was able to find his way back, some three thousand miles, in midwinter. Fox writes that 'this dog's feat was sufficiently well publicized that people who had given him food and shelter on his long journey home made themselves known. This way, the route taken by the dog was approximately reconstructed.'[12]

Almost everybody knows such a story, but surprisingly little research has been done on the topic.[13] Veterinarians have no clue as to what senses are involved in this homing instinct. Certainly smell and visual clues are critical, but beyond that, could there be a sense completely unknown to us that dogs are able to call into play? What enables some dogs to find their way back over vast distances while others are forever getting lost a block from their homes? Here is an area where experiments could easily be conducted, without putting the dog under great stress, by simply making the test a game.

In the 1930s in Germany Bastian Schmid (1870–1944) conducted elaborate experiments on the ability of dogs to find their way home, and concluded that neither scent nor vision are involved, and he felt forced to speak of an unknown factor, that should perhaps be called an absolute sense of orientation.[14] It is clear from this literature that dogs do possess extraordinary abilities to find their way home. What drives them – as even the popular literature (*The Incredible Journey*) recognises – is love. The German research I read even speaks of *heimweh*, literally 'homepain', i.e. homesickness.[15]

What intrigues me most about this unusual canine ability is the feelings that these lost dogs have as they attempt to make their way home. They seem to be using something deeper than mere instinct. As Smythe points out, the return of the dog is very different than the migratory instinct in birds: 'Most birds fly south-east or south-west in September and retrace the same route in April or May. The directional guide, be it what it may, is inherent in the bird, fitted somewhere into its mentality and highly dependable. The dog seeks its home purely from nostalgia.'[16] What is called 'pack loyalty' is also a sense of the place where one is supposed to be, of love for one's friends and a desire to return to scenes of earlier happiness. Nostalgia and being homesick are emotions very familiar to humans. One is more likely to understand them from descriptions in literature than from the few experimental or scientific studies.

An almost equally puzzling mystery, which argues against the existence of a homing instinct, is the fact that so many dogs do not find their way home, but simply get lost.[17] At the opposite extreme of the dog who finds his way home over a long distance is the fascinating case of a Shetland sheep dog who went feral. I first heard the story from Dr Kathy Houpt, who suggested I contact her colleague, Dr Julia Blue, on the faculty of the Department of Pathology in the College of Veterinary Medicine at Cornell University. She told me the story of her four-year-old Sheltie, Dolly.

Dolly was originally intended to become a show dog and a breeder, but when she was nine months old she was brought to

Cornell suffering from a rare heart problem. Dr Blue took her home, and she became a normal, home-loving dog. One cold night in February 1991, she was let out with the other two dogs in a large (acre-and-a-half) back yard. Soon afterwards, when Dr Blue called the dogs in, Dolly did not appear. She was gone. The Blues live on the outskirts of a small town near Ithaca, surrounded by woods, forests and a mountain with a high ridge just beyond a row of houses. They searched for Dolly all night, but did not find her.

When they advertised her loss in the local paper, somebody called to say they thought she was in their back yard. The family drove over. They saw their dog, but when they called her, much to their shock, she appeared not to recognise her owner and ran away through the fields into the woods.

During the next three weeks several people called to say they had seen Dolly but could not approach her. She would come down from the hills at night and again between nine in the morning and three in the afternoon, when children were in school and everything was quiet. But the minute she caught sight of any human being, she was off like the wind. *She had gone totally feral.* One day a call came from a house high in the woods: Dolly was there. A 'have-a-heart' trap, which does not harm the animal, was set, and the next day she was caught. When Dr Blue and her family arrived to see her, Dolly went wild, this time with happiness. She was ecstatic to see her family and could barely contain her joy. From that moment on she became a clinging house dog, not wanting to let anyone out of her sight for even a moment.

Dolly was hardly a wild dog, and yet it took but a few minutes for her to go feral. Dr Blue thinks she had been startled and scared by two stray black labradors that had been wandering in their neighbourhood. Once she had started running, she suddenly found herself in unfamiliar territory, unable to find her way home. She just ran, for weeks, living from minute to minute. In some deep sense, she was spooked into the trappings of wildness. Yet, when trapped and unable to flee, a single glimpse of her family brought her straight back to her former self.

It is an intriguing story, and a reminder that dogs are mysterious creatures, whose ways we still by no means fully understand. In

December 1996, Rupert Sheldrake, former director of cell biology and biochemistry at Cambridge University and a Royal Society Research Fellow, presented a paper to the Society of Companion Animal Studies at Cambridge University's Veterinary School in which he reported on tests that had been carried out to determine the dog's capacity for intuitive precognition. Pets in the city of Manchester were videoed in their homes as their owners, away at their places of work, prepared to return home. Up to 46 per cent of the dogs knew that their masters were coming home up to an hour before they arrived. Dr Sheldrake calls the bond between dogs and their owners a morphic field, a kind of 'invisible stretched elastic band'.[18]

For dogs, loyalty is the desire to be together with the loved one, *to be where one belongs*. Consider this story from 18 March, 1996: 'A loyal dog quietly held an overnight vigil next to the hole where his master apparently fell through thin ice Saturday in Marblehead and drowned in frigid pond water, police told a reporter from the *Boston Herald*. "The dog didn't make a peep," Marblehead police Detective Marion Keating said, describing the helpless dog's reaction yesterday. "She just sat there and stared." ' The three-year-old golden retriever, Jasmine, 'was paying very strict attention to what we were doing, just intently watching', said Lt Robert Coyne.[19]

Many people have heard the story of the Akita dog Hachi-Ko (recently the subject of a popular Japanese film, and mentioned earlier in this book), owned by a professor at Tokyo University, who became a national folk hero: Hachi-Ko used to meet his master's train every evening and fetch the absent-minded professor home from the station. One bitterly cold day in 1925, the dog waited in vain. He could not know that his master had died at work and would never catch the train again. Given a new home by the professor's friends, the faithful dog ran away every evening for ten years, returning to Shibuya Station to wait for his master who never came. Hachi-Ko had a statue erected at the station in his honour and when he died, aged 12, a day of national mourning was held and the breed declared a living monument. School-children were told his story to encourage loyalty.[20]

The protectiveness of dogs is also a form of loyalty, faithfulness, and love. Jean Kundert from Castro Valley in California wrote the following in a letter to me: 'My grandson is five months old. The other day I was holding him on my lap, playing with him, when my husband walked over to us. My husband said 'Hi, Daak,' but a little too loudly. Our shepherd/chow mix walked over to us, put her head between my husband and the baby, looked at my husband and gave him a short growl. Little Daak is the newest member of the pack.'[21]

The Ken-L Ration Dog Hero of the Year for 1995 was Bailey, a three-year-old mixture of Chesapeake Bay retriever and chocolate labrador. Chester Jenkins was pinned by an angry bull to a fence, with the bull raking its sharp hooves repeatedly over the man's back. The dog went for the bull's head, biting its nose and ears, allowing the man, by this time severely injured, to drag himself under the fence. Leaning on Bailey, he made his way back to the house. Intensive care and a long recuperation have led to his recovery, but his life was definitely saved by a courageous dog.

Among the runners-up in the annual search, co-sponsored by the American Veterinary Medical Association, was Boo, a two-year-old Newfoundland from Bakersfield, California, who pulled Link Hill from the raging waters of the North Fork of the Yuba River near Indian Valley last August. Hill can neither hear nor speak. He had lost his footing on slippery rocks and was struggling against the current when the dog dived in, grabbed the man's wrist in his mouth and towed him back to shore.[22] Boo had obviously assessed the danger simply by seeing it with his eyes.

Newfies often tow boats that have got into trouble to shore. They are capable of pulling upwards of three thousand pounds. Their caretakers report that they always look so proud afterward, as if they know precisely what they have accomplished. Is the pride connected to knowledge that a life has been saved or is it merely pride in a game well played? Nobody can know for certain, but in as much as dogs are heroic in such varied situations which require what in humans we call 'insight', we can be certain that far more than 'training' is involved. There are reports of dogs saving dogs: what we don't know is whether wolves or wild dogs do the same thing.

The capacity for loyalty is so deeply ingrained in the dog that one might think that it would feel impersonal. However, by all accounts, the loyalty of a dog feels entirely personal to the caretaker. The concentration is so intense that one never feels part of an instinctual urge. There seems to be no doubt that the dog is feeling intense love and loyalty for a specific person (you) and not for the abstract category of 'member of the pack' or 'superior human being' or 'master'. Dogs love us and are faithful and loyal to us, because they are capable of these deep emotions. Cats like us. Cats can take great pleasure in our company, but I find it difficult to imagine that my cats would risk their lives to save mine. I can easily imagine my dogs doing this without hesitation.

CHAPTER FIVE

Dogs Smell What We Cannot See

WHEN I WAS about nine and my family lived in Los Angeles, we would drive at weekends into the desert to Palm Springs. I have a visceral memory of the pleasures of that two to three hour drive, especially the last hour when we began to reach the edge of the desert. My dog Taffy, a gentle and much-loved cocker spaniel, came with us, and it was always such delight to see her stick her head out of the window, her ears flapping in the breeze, her eyes half-shut to protect them from the wind. But my greatest pleasure was to see her react to the desert: her nose would begin to twitch and she would give every indication that she was smelling smells of which the rest of us were completely unaware. We knew this to be true; right outside the window of our car was an entire world of smells to which we were denied access while Taffy and her canine friends held the key. They had but to point their noses in the right direction to be offered a powerful and never-ending bouquet.

Mazo de la Roche gives a fine portrait of a similar dog, a totally blind Scottie who 'always delighted in motoring and this delight increased with her blindness. She had been a great hunter and, in my opinion, she recaptured something of the exhilaration of the chase in the swift movement of motoring. . . . She never sat down in a car but stood, braced tense, facing the wind. Now and again she would turn her face toward me with an apologetic expression as though to say: "I have not forgotten that you are here but there are certain pleasures I cannot share with you." Her nose never ceased its sensitive quivering.'[1]

I take my dogs to the same spot every day, yet each day I am surprised to see them act as if they are in a new and magic land for the first time. Their noses go straight down to the ground and they are off, in a world of their own, completely happy, sniffing life, in the phrase of one dog-lover. Everything there is new for them, for the smells are new, or so nuanced as to seem entirely new. A dog's keen sense of smell does not become jaded. A dog running free through the countryside never looks bored, and is never bored. In this ability to seize the world anew at every moment, the dog is our superior.

The dog's nose is an exquisitely sensitive organ. Whereas humans have five million ethmoidal (olfactory) cells in the nose, the German shepherd has 200 million. The dog's experience of smelling is therefore far more powerful than we can imagine, more in the nature of an emotion than merely an experience of the senses. When we smell something, we can be reminded of an emotion, but for a dog the sensual act of smelling itself is so much more intense that I believe memory need play no role for the dog to have an immediate emotional experience. Thus for dogs, smelling and feeling are essentially the same. To smell is to feel an emotion.

Dogs do not just experience single elements of feeling (feeling sad, for example); they live in a whole world of feeling. One might even say a dog *is* feeling. If humans are defined by what they think, a dog can be defined by what it feels. Taffy, with her little head hanging out of the car window, sniffing the desert air, was pure feeling. When Sasha, Sima and Rani are running joyously, with their noses to the ground, they are the essence of pure feeling. Whether there is a cognitive element to this feeling eludes us for the moment. It is not entirely clear whether humans can think and feel at the same time. People in a rage rarely think rationally. Artists report that some of their most creative 'thinking' is done when they are lost in a feeling world and are no longer using their ordinary mind. When we feel love for the beloved, we rarely at the same time calculate the benefits of that love. And when we are making such calculations, we are probably not transported by love. Smelling is so intense for dogs that it may well preclude the kind of thinking that they are otherwise capable of demonstrating.

Exactly how well do dogs smell? This question is frequently asked, but it is in fact unanswerable. It depends on what the dog is smelling. A dog is much more interested in some smells than in others. A wine connoisseur, or a person whose job it is to create perfumes, probably smells things that a dog has neither the motivation nor the capacity (or rather the interest) to smell. When dogs enter a rose garden they do not fall into rapture.[2] What dogs need to smell, or wish to smell, they do so far better than we can.

Estimates of just how much better dogs can smell than humans vary. A French author writes: 'One of the odours released by perspiration – either human or animals – is butyric acid, one gram of which contains seven thousand million billion molecules, an ungraspable number! Imagine that this acid is spread at a precise moment throughout all the rooms in a ten-story building. A man would only smell it if he were to take a breath of air at the window, and then only at that precise moment. But if the same gram of odour were spread out over a city like Hamburg, a dog could perceive it from anywhere up to an altitude of 300 feet!'[3]

The German canine expert and scientist, Walter Neuhaus, conducted what are considered the most elaborate experiments on the sensory capacity of the dog's nose and published the results in a series of articles in the 1950s. With perhaps over-elaborate precision and ingenuity, he built an olfactometer. The conclusion in his most important article reads as follows (my translation from the German): 'The olfactory sensitivity of the dog is 1,000,000 to 100,000,000 times greater than that of a human being.'[4] This is probably the original source of the comment often heard that a dog can smell one hundred million times better than a human being, though in *Dogwatching* the ethologist Desmond Morris qualifies the comparison by restricting it to certain chemical substances that are perceived 'one million times better' by dogs than by humans.

No human-built machine has yet matched the acuity of the dog's nose. This is why dogs are used in airports, rather than a machine, to check for food products or drugs in passengers' luggage. It has been claimed that dogs can pick up some odours in concentrations of one part per trillion. Roger Caras has written of a bloodhound who followed a scent trail over a stretch of 114 miles.[5] It has even been suggested that the dog actually has a memory bank of scents that acts much like our visual memory. Our memory for smells is poor. If we concentrate and try to remember as many odours as we can, at best we come up with a limited number. A dog, however, can probably remember thousands of such smells. It is this ability to remember specific odours that no doubt aids the dog in finding its way home when lost.

The sense of smell in a dog is never dormant, even when the dog is asleep. The Israeli dog-trainer, Sapir Weiss, tells me that if you play loud music, a dog can and will sleep through it, but if you put a hamburger under a sleeping dog's nose, the dog will immediately wake up. This is true of wolves as well. Sapir believes that this accounts for the rather mysterious rituals that a dog performs as it prepares to lie down, circling in ever tighter circles. The dog, like the wolf before it, is seeking to remain downwind. A sleeping wolf can smell danger a mile and a half away, and will then immediately take appropriate fight or flight action. (As I was sceptical, Sapir suggested I might try a simple experiment on my dogs by bringing something close to my dogs' noses to see if they will awaken. He was right.) Eberhard Trumler, on the other hand, thinks that dogs are simply attempting to get their spines in the best possible position, and notes that research undertaken on jackals, wolves and foxes show this to be definitely the case.[6]

Darwin's friend George Romanes says 'the external world must be to these animals quite different from what it is to us; the whole fabric of their ideas concerning it being so largely founded on what is virtually a new sense; not simply our own sense greatly magnified.'[7]

Humans have a tendency to dismiss what we find difficult to imagine. But as Elizabeth Marshall Thomas warns us in her new book *Certain Poor Shepherds*, 'sounds too high or low for human ears are nevertheless sounds; odors too faint or pure for human nostrils are nevertheless odors'.[8] It is almost impossible for us to imagine living in a world where we could smell one hundred million or even one million times better than we can now. What would that world be like? Would we be happier or more harassed? Many people feel that they are already too burdened with smells as it is, their sense of smell embarrasses them, makes them feel too much like an animal. We are ashamed of our own body odours, and are repulsed by those of other people, whereas dogs clearly revel in theirs, and, more important, in those of other dogs. For dogs, the stronger the scent the better. Dogs always sniff the uro-genital and anal areas of other dogs with gusto and sometimes with a pleasure that resembles human enchantment. True, they pick up important information – gender, sexual readiness, and where that dog has been lately – but they also seem to enjoy the experience of smelling.[9] Everybody has seen, sometimes with horror, how a dog will find a foul-smelling object, often a rotting carcass, and proceed to roll in it with abandon. Rani does this constantly on our walks, whenever she finds bird excrement. But when she rolls from side to side, her mouth is open in the dog equivalent of a broad smile. She may be doing it to disguise herself (so that a bird will not notice her approaching downwind?), but that is merely a genetic throwback: for her, whatever its source, it is now pure pleasure.

Sigmund Freud's most protracted reference to dogs occurs in a famous passage in his *Civilization and its Discontents*, written in 1929:

> The existence of the social factor which is responsible for the further transformation of anal erotism is attested by the circumstance that, in spite of all man's developmental advances, he scarcely finds the smell of *his own* excreta repulsive, but only that of other people's. Thus a person who is not clean – who does not hide his excreta – is offending other people; he is showing no consideration for them. And this is confirmed by our strongest and commonest terms of abuse. It would be incomprehensible, too, that man should use the name of his faithful friend in the animal world – the dog – as a term of abuse

79

if that creature had not incurred his contempt through two characteristics: that it is an animal whose dominant sense is that of smell and one which has no horror of excrement, and that it is not ashamed of its sexual functions.[10]

Freud evidently thought that the dog sniffs at faeces because it enjoys the smell. In fact, since the dog is gathering information, it would be more accurate to say it is engaged in research. J. R. Ackerly, in his charming book *My Dog Tulip*, writes of how her dog reads other dogs' stains, 'and the care with which she studies them is so meticulous that she gives the impression of actually identifying her acquaintances and friends'.

All three of my dogs are spayed, and I have seen no evidence that they think about sex at all. I would like to say that they don't miss what they have never known, but of course I do not really know. Many dogs today are neutered. It is interesting that we don't think this deeply affects the personality of a dog, whereas with a person we would believe that he or she would no longer be a full person without a sexual life. It is possible that I have undervalued the importance of sexuality in the personality of the dog, but it is equally possible that we have overvalued its importance to our own emotional core. My own belief is that it is the intensity of emotional experience which gives existence its value and is an essential ingredient of leading a full life. Dogs derive a great part of their intense emotional life through their nose. This does not deprive dogs, however, of forming strong bonds with other dogs (and people) even when their nose is not involved. I don't think we smell all that interesting to dogs, but they seem to like us nonetheless. And we love dogs, often with great intensity, in spite of having no sexual relationship with them. What matters to us and to them is to be able to feel the full force of the world around us as it enters our minds, our bodies and our senses as profound emotional experience.

CHAPTER SIX

Submission, Dominance and Gratitude

WOLF RESEARCHERS WILL sometimes use the terms alpha (dominant) wolf and omega (most subordinate) wolf, even though it is not clear precisely what these words mean. Some dog caretakers refer to their animals with the same words. Do these words really mean what they seem to mean, and do they mean anything at all in relation to dogs?

Superior, inferior, submission, dominance, hierarchy – these are all highly charged terms, with political connotations (mostly in the form of gender politics). To apply them to dog behaviour is potentially hazardous, since dogs are not soldiers in the military whose ranks can be read from their uniforms.

It may be easy for us to understand the concept of rank, but to assume that dogs pay the same attention that we do to external markers (the size of a dog) is less the result of observation than projection. They recognise authority, but for different reasons and without our gradations. Because dogs are, like us, highly social and

81

sociable creatures, and because they do things that we think we recognise, we assume that there is identity, or at least similarity, when it comes to the concepts we use to explain behaviour. Dominance and ranking are two of those concepts.

If a dog caretaker tells me 'my dog is a dominant female', he will be using a term that is meaningful in the case of humans but less so for dogs. What makes for dominance in a dog? Size and strength are certainly relevant, perhaps for intimidation. Willingness to fight may be less important, in as much as it increases the chances of injury. Age, along with cunning and intelligence, contributes to dominance, because it brings a certain maturity, and perhaps even wisdom plays a role (as in the case of older elephants who know where the water holes are during a drought). Yet a puppy can often bring out the puppy in an aged dog.

Sima, as the youngest member of our little pack, displays something that we label or think we recognise to be submission. In fact, she positively adores submitting; when she meets certain dogs she begins a little dance that has all the classical features of what has been called 'active submission', licking their mouths, squealing, looking away and finally abjectly rolling on to her back. She ends her approach with passive submission, adopting a posture that Rudolf Schenkel called 'full of trust, devotion, and demonstrated helplessness', in *The American Zoologist*.[1]

Most humans call such behaviour cute, like that of a small child. Submission is a form of flagging one's childlikeness (what I have described previously as neoteny) or non-aggressiveness. Schenkel, who is an authority on wolves, speaks of a 'an overwhelming offer of friendly affection'. By begging, the submissive animal expects to be accepted or at least tolerated. These submissive gestures are peace offerings, something like our handshake. 'Symbolised and ritualised cub-behaviour' is what Schenkel calls it. Perhaps the wolf-cub or puppy is reminding the other dog of a time when he too was a small animal; or he may be appealing to maternal or paternal instincts. A more dominant dog rarely rejects such an offer of submission.

Sometimes we do not even recognise these signs of submission because we are looking for something that resembles more our own concepts than those of a dog. Rani, for example, is pure friendship. She lives for friendly relations and, of all my dogs, she is the only one who engages in a behaviour that many dog care-takers have seen, one which may be submissive because it reduces the likelihood of attack by other dogs. Whenever she encounters any foul-smelling substance, she immediately rolls in it with evident glee. Then she rushes up proudly to the other two dogs to demonstrate what she has done. They oblige by taking a good long sniff.

The experts have given me more than one explanation for this strange behaviour. Michael Fox, one of the leading authorities on dogs and related canids,[2] postulates that dogs returning with a strange odour about them will excite more social investigation from certain pack members who would otherwise begin asserting their dominance aggressively. In other words, Rani might simply be making herself interesting to her friends. While agreeing with the idea that the dog is engaging in this activity to attract the attention of fellow pack members, Desmond Morris believes that this could be a call to hunt.[3] In laboratory experiments dogs have been known to roll in substances not found in the wild – lemon rind, perfume, tobacco, rotting garbage, for instance – and this weakens the call to hunt theory, or any idea of camouflage.[4]

On any walk with dogs you will see what scientists like to call 'inguinal orientation and presentation by a subordinate to facilitate genital investigation' – the circling that adult dogs do until the subordinate allows the other to investigate its anal and genital regions. Approaching the bigger dog with its hind end lowered and back arched (to look as small and harmless as possible), the smaller dog will extrude its tongue to signify its intent to lick. In as much as staring down another dog is a prelude to a fight, dogs will look away to indicate that they have no desire to fight and have come in peace.

Of my three dogs, only Sima will suddenly become possessed to lick the corners of Sasha's mouth and, if permitted, will stick her entire small and pointed face right down Sasha's large throat and squeal and jump about with delight. Sasha is very tolerant but not about to perform what the ritual is meant to solicit: regurgitation of food. This is how wolf-cubs cajole their mother into giving them food after the hunt. She comes back to the den sated, and regurgitates the meal for her cubs. Dogs do not actually regurgitate for a pup, so when Sima does this as a greeting and a bonding gesture, it is what is called a 'phylogenetically emancipated and ritualised social gesture' – like the gesture of a handshake, an open hand concealing no weapon. To my knowledge, the Cape hunting dog is the only breed which well into adulthood still solicits and regurgitates food. With these dogs, rather than establishing hierarchy, it is a means of maintaining social cohesion by mutual aid and comfort.

Dogs have many ways of showing their intent to be friendly: they avoid eye-contact, look away, and lick their lips, indicating that they mean no threat and only wish to lick the other dog. Almost every part of the body carries a message to another dog, especially the tail and the ears. Tails, we all know, are subtle and marvellous carriers of meaning, but when I acquired my present dog family I was not prepared for the complexity of a dog's ears. The expressiveness of Sasha's ears is something to behold. She can say as much with her ears as we do with our mouths. Sasha has a way of very quietly approaching small children and then surprising them with a lick on their lips. Her ears are then put down and back in the most endearing way, indicating to all that she is the embodiment of friendly feelings and gentleness. Her eyes, at these times, take on an unmistakable shine of enormous friendliness. I still don't know how her eyes and ears can communicate such deep feelings, but they do, and everybody recognises it immediately.

More important than any physical and possibly any mental attribute is what humans do to encourage or discourage these traits. Dogs are 'contaminated' by humans; by this I mean that they take on emotional coloration from contact with humans. It is, therefore, impossible to know what dogs would be like if they did not live in human communities. Wild dogs and wild wolves are notoriously difficult to observe up close. Unlike chimpanzees, gorillas, and even elephants, wolves will not tolerate human observation, and there are virtually no detailed accounts of their behaviour, let alone their possible emotions, in the wild, a point often stressed by experts such as L. David Mech.

In attempting to understand human relationships, dominance and subordination are often invoked, but with wild dogs and wolves, the very notion of a 'fact' becomes questionable because of the difficulty of observation. An accurate picture may take years, even centuries, to develop. With humans, new biographies of historic figures are written anew every decade, often providing a very different evaluation of prominent people. The relationship of one dog to another may change over time. Moreover, what we describe as a dominant relationship may well entail disadvantages we did not consider. We may observe a large dog eating before a smaller one in the same household and conclude that the larger one dominates, and this acts to his advantage, for a more complex dynamic could be escaping us. The larger dog might suffer from stress symptoms related to his dominance. A dog could find that having to keep a constant vigil over one's status is exhausting, and may not contribute to fitness in the long run, let alone to immediate happiness.[5] It is not a question of importing prejudices that are valid for humans though not for dogs; these same prejudices limit our understanding of humans too. Our need to simplify, to categorise, to rank, to objectify, to pretend we have comprehended something, is as pernicious in our human relationships as it is destructive of our ability to understand an alien species.

In an influential article written in 1975, R. Lockwood reminds us that, despite the generalisations we can make about the social behaviour of the wolf, it is important to remember 'each wolf, like each human being, is an intelligent and flexible individual, and is, in many ways, unique'.[6]

What does it mean for a human to be superior or dominant? Shelley, in 1817, wrote eloquently about the folly of human domination:

> 'My name is Ozymandias, King of Kings:
> Look on my works, ye Mighty, and despair!'
> Nothing beside remains. Round the decay
> Of that colossal wreck, boundless and bare
> The lone and level sands stretch far away.

Upon closer inspection, or in the light of other times, certain achievements, especially those involving subjugation of a place or a person, appear very different. It is only by viewing the entire lifespan of any given dog that we can see what he has derived from the position he seems to occupy, whether in the end it was good for him or not. He might have paid a very high price (early death, for example) for dominance and have little to show for it.

Dog-trainers warn us: do not let your dog dominate you. We

all know cases in which the dog does precisely that. We hear stories of some dogs who prefer dogs to humans and dogs that prefer humans to other dogs. In France they often say: *Il ne lui manque que la parole* ('He only lacks words'). When a caretaker boasts, 'My dog thinks she is human', I am inclined not to dismiss this. A dog does not make a 'species mistake', in the way that philosophers make category mistakes. On the other hand, dogs may come to think of themselves as more like their caretaker than another dog.

Sasha, who knows she is, or could be, dominant over a one-year-old child, adores one-year-olds: she rushes up to kiss them, not subserviently, but with delight. Her behaviour manifests a complete disregard for hierarchy.

Perhaps when dogs appear to seek out a superior, canine or human, somebody to whom to be subordinate, they are merely attempting to bring some excitement into life. What we see as submission may be an activity entirely enjoyable to the dog. The English writer Elizabeth von Arnim, in *All the Dogs of My Life*, describes how she met her second husband, Francis, second Earl Russell, brother of Bertrand Russell, whom she calls Doom. Her dog, a Swiss mountain dog, wanted a man in the house with whom to play and go for long walks. The dog decided it was time for her to marry. When the Earl paid his first visit, the dog 'rushed to give him the welcome suitable to so important an arrival. He was, in fact, all over him. "Come in, come in – oh, *do* come in! This is our house, but from now on it is yours and everything in it," he seemed to be passionately conveying by leaps, licks, waggings, and loud, glad yelps.'[7]

Dominance in dogs may bear no resemblance to the hierarchies that exist in the board rooms of our corporations or even in the universities. It is rather a way of relating socially, a way of establishing a friendly atmosphere, one of peace and pleasure.[8] It is part of play, and of the dog's search for a world of good feeling, of friendship, and especially love, the very *raison d'être* for a dog.

★

The most effective antidote to the excesses of hierarchy may well be gratitude. Gratitude has a way of stressing equality and undermining dominance. When we are grateful to somebody, we acknowledge a shared humanity, we recognise limitations and strengthen social bonds.

As a student of the Sanskrit language, I was struck by so many of the ancient texts, in particular the great Indian epic, the *Mahabharata* (dating from about the second century B.C.), mentioning gratitude as one of the most valuable and highly esteemed of all human emotions. To feel gratitude was common to all, but to show gratitude was the sign of a great man, a kind of inverse hierarchy. At the time, I found this silly; now that I am older, I understand. When we do something particularly kind for someone, and the person does not acknowledge it, fails to show gratitude, we are hurt. It feels good to be acknowledged, to be shown gratitude. We expect this of people, and especially of our friends.

Can dogs feel gratitude? If they can, do we expect them to show gratitude? I think it is important to keep this central point in mind: a dog rarely feels something that he or she does not express. We might miss the sign or we may be unable to read the expression, but it is almost a contradiction in terms to say that a dog feels something but does not show it. What a dog feels, a dog shows, and, conversely, what a dog shows a dog actually does feel.

Everyone who visits me comments on how lucky my dogs are. I take them for five good walks a day, I feed them well, I talk to them, play with them and just sit with them. Leila asked me the other day: 'Do you think they are grateful?' I wondered about that, about the mechanics of this feeling. I have no doubt that my dogs are happy when I walk them, but are they capable of comparing their lot with that of other dogs and thinking how lucky they are measured against them – and then, as a consequence of this thought, feeling grateful to me? It seems highly unlikely, for dogs do not, I am convinced, have a concept of gratitude in the abstract, as opposed to feeling grateful for a specific thing. Nevertheless I think dogs are capable of both feeling and expressing the latter type of gratitude.

We took the dogs to visit my parents, who live in Southern California, just north of San Diego, in Laguna Hills. It is a long trip of about eight hours, but the dogs clearly liked being on their special futon in the back of the Toyota Camry wagon, surrounded by toys and little treats, as long as we stopped every hour or two for a short walk. On the way back, we stopped in the desert, and went outside for a walk. Sima got a thorn in her paw. She sat down and tried to remove it with her teeth. When she failed, she limped across to me, held up her paw, looked at me pleadingly and began to whine. I took the thorn out, and she looked relieved and licked my hand. It immediately occurred to me that she was grateful. A few moments later Sasha also got a thorn in her paw. She was limping but did not come over to me. I went to her, took it out, and waited for her reaction. Sasha showed neither relief nor gratitude. She did not even look at me.

It was such a different reaction from Sima's that I had to wonder: did she just accept what happened as her due? Was she being brave, putting on an act, in denial, or just plain indifferent? Maybe for her it was enough that something had hurt her and now it didn't, without giving thought to the cause. A few weeks later I discovered that I was wrong, and that Sasha could feel gratitude.

I was sitting in the garden, reading. Sima and Rani, as usual, were playing tug of war with a stick. Suddenly I heard a strange sound coming from Sasha, a sound like strangulation. The two dogs ran across and stared at her. When I arrived she had a look of terror on her face but was not making a sound. Her head was in an odd position. She looked as if she were choking. Her collar had somehow twisted into the grooves of a large oak table, and she was caught, unable to move an inch. Quickly I undid the collar and freed her. She gave me a look, the first of its kind I had seen on her face, showing profound gratitude. The two dogs started to lick her. Somehow they all sensed danger, as if they were thinking: 'Uh-oh, this is serious.' Maybe Sasha was able to feel (and show) gratitude under the impetus of an even stronger emotion, terror. It frightened me as well.

What if the hurt is not real? Rani came over to me recently, limping badly. She held up her paw for me to inspect it. I did so, and then I rubbed it, warmed it, praised her, encouraged her, told her she was now fine, and sent her off, running. She was fine. Had she just been pretending to be hurt when she came up to me? Or was she faking health when she ran off? Was this a delusion of disease, or an illusion of health? My standard poodle, Misha, used to do the same thing, approaching me with a limp, whenever he was afraid I might be angry over something he did. Parents notice something like this with their children; it is a desire for attention. In *Animal Intelligence*, Darwin's friend George Romanes noted this ability on the part of dogs and classified it under deception: 'Having hurt his foot he became lame for a time, during which he received more pity and attention than usual. For months after he had recovered, whenever he was harshly spoken to, he commenced hobbling about the room as if lame and suffering pain from his foot.'[9]

We do not feel gratitude toward somebody when we expect something from them. Often we are not grateful when a teacher teaches us something, or a mechanic fixes our car, or the dental hygienist cleans our teeth. But if my car breaks down on the highway, and the car behind me stops and the woman in it helps me repair my problem, I am grateful to her. While her foot was hurting her, Sasha did not look reproachfully at me, as if to say: 'This is not supposed to happen to me with you around. Fix it fast, buster.' It was more like: 'Well, I got into this mess by myself, so I guess I will have to get out of it the same way.'

Several times Sasha has intervened when a larger dog intimidated little Sima. Afterwards Sima would run across to Sasha and lick the side of her mouth. It resembled gratitude, a visual equivalent of 'thanks'.

We are grateful for the very existence of dogs, and I like to think that they feel the same way about us. Both species have a lot for which to be grateful. It is one of the great miracles of nature that we have come together in love and friendship in a way that no other two species ever have.

CHAPTER SEVEN

The Great Dog Fear:
Loneliness and Abandonment

VISITING A ZOO as a small child, I remember thinking that the
animals, many of whom were isolated in cages, seemed
lonely. I am sure now that I was right. Zookeepers recognise that
animals do not like to be secluded, isolated from either their
companions or those animals who live in a community in their
natural setting. Even when such animals as wolves, who live
together as a pack, are housed together in a zoo, they are not
happy. Removed from their natural environment, they appear
bored. Wolves want to do the things that wolves do. Twelve
wolves kept together in a pen, though not isolated, are still bored
because they are not permitted to behave as they would in the
wild.

Who dictates what an animal requires in order not to be lonely?
Wolves need to travel. Traversing a thousand miles and more is
not unusual for wolf packs. Perhaps they also need to hear
songbirds, and see flowers, trees, sky, rivers, mountains, valleys.

Perhaps they need the company of other inhabitants of the forest. How do we know that wolves don't miss their play with ravens? In *The Wolves of Minong*, Durward Allen notes that wolves never seem to harm ravens, though it would be easy for them to do so. He says that in eighteen years of winter watching he has only one record of violence done to a raven by a wolf.[1] David Mech, the wolf expert, would sometimes watch ravens diving at a wolf's head or tail, making the wolf duck before leaping at them:

> . . . once, a raven waddled to a resting wolf, pecked at its tail, and jumped aside as the wolf snapped at it. When the wolf retaliated by stalking the raven, the bird allowed it within a foot before arising. Then it landed a few feet beyond the wolf, and repeated the prank. . . . It appears that the wolf and the raven have reached an adjustment in their relationships such that each creature is rewarded in some way by the presence of the other and that each is fully aware of the other's capabilities. Both species are extremely social, so they must possess the psychological mechanisms necessary for forming social attachments. Perhaps in some way individuals of each species have included members of the other in their social group and have formed bonds with them much as wolves raised with humans are able to form social bonds with them.[2]

Is it enough that they have full bellies, or do they long for the hunt, the chase, the movement, the sights, sounds and smells of their natural surroundings? Even if, born in captivity, they have never seen it, they may have an innate longing for a more natural existence than the one forced upon them in even the most well meaning and progressive of zoos. They need to be in their natural environment.

Just as being in jail or in exile will produce a loneliness of spirit in a human being, so, it seems, will captivity produce the same in a wild animal. Perhaps even dogs, the most domesticated of all domestic species, long for their original lupine-like freedom. Dogs occasionally howl, as if they miss something they may know only from a genetic memory running through their blood of having once been wild. Maybe you have woken at four in the morning, visited by a strange sensation, an eerie feeling, a longing for some other kind of life. Could this also be an atavistic memory of having once lived in the hills, jungles and forests, surrounded by other free beings? Maybe we miss this just as our cousins in the zoos and entertainment parks do.

In his introduction to a book on socialisation, John Paul Scott points out that dogs are the prototype of a highly social species whose young are born in an immature state. Unlike sheep, which can be induced to form attachments to humans only by isolation from their parent species, dogs normally form social attachments to both dogs and people.[3]

If you or I were confined to a small room all day, without anything to engage our interest, we would soon feel bored and lonely, and our behaviour would certainly reflect it. Countless books about 'problems' in dogs are published,[4] and one of the best of these, written about dog-training by Carol Lea Benjamin, states that dogs get anxious because they are pack-animals, and when forced to spend much of the time alone, they become lonely, which makes them anxious.[5]

Desmond Morris, in *Dogwatching*, writes that dogs 'are social beings and they are also intensely exploratory. If they are deprived of companions – both canine and human – or if they are kept in a constrained or monotonous environment, they suffer. The worst mental punishment a dog can be given is to be kept alone in a tightly confined space where nothing varies.'[6]

In *Domestic Animal Behavior for Veterinarians and Animal Scientists*, the authors cite the case of an adult spayed German shepherd who was kept in a basement while the owner was at work: 'The dog tore up the rug on the basement stairs and then began to eat the wood of the stairs themselves ... Neither tranquilisers nor anticonvulsants attenuated the behavior ... The owner tried behavior modification for a few weeks, but there was no improvement and the dog was euthanized. There were no abnormalities on either gross or microscopic examination of the tissues, including the central nervous system.' Is it any wonder that putting a dog in the profoundly limited environment of a basement would cause the dog anguish that might well express itself in destructiveness? Even the authors write: 'It may sound anthropomorphic to speak of bored dogs, but animals appear to need environmental stimulation just as humans do. Dogs will work to see other dogs by pushing a panel with their muzzles; and other animals will work for light, to obtain access to another environment, or for brain stimulation. Dogs, therefore, may find chewing and scratching less boring than just lying around. In more scientific terms, they find such activity rewarding.'[7] Killing a dog because it is crying out for companionship is ignorant and cruel. Dogs want and need what we do: friends, sunshine, play and love.

Maybe what feels like loneliness to us feels like abandonment to a dog. Everybody has seen the characteristic worried look on the face of a lost dog searching for its caretaker. Clearly, the feelings it is experiencing at that moment are intense, similar to the feelings a child has when separated from its parents. The exuberant, often almost hysterical greetings we receive from an animal we have left only moments before suggests either that the dog has a different sense of time from that of humans (which they obviously do) or that it thought it had been abandoned. (Of course, it could simply be expressing its joy at seeing you again.) No matter how many times a dog has seen its caretaker return, it repeatedly greets the caretaker as if to say 'I thought I would never see you again!' This is one reason for many people feeling guilty about leaving their dogs all day; the cocked head and the puzzled expression seem to ask, 'Are you leaving forever?' Many dog experts dispense advice, such as, 'It is imperative that little or no attention be given to the dog prior to departure, and that greetings upon return be subdued.'[8] However, this seems counter-intuitive. Rather, we want to assure them we will return, and let them know how happy we are to see them again. Likewise, they let us know how happy they are to see us again; they greet us exuberantly, just as wolves greet members of the pack who have returned from hunting.

The loneliness a dog experiences when a beloved companion – human, canine or even feline – has died is entirely analogous to what we experience in similar situations, and little can be done (or perhaps should be done) to relieve what is a natural condition. Mourning, after all, has beneficial aspects, and perhaps we are in no position to designate arbitrarily what constitutes a respectable grieving period, for humans or for dogs.

Most problems in dogs are the result of injustices which the animals have suffered. Humans who have suffered intensely stressful situations often respond through violent or self-destructive acts. Dogs respond in a similar manner. To remove a dog from its own pack without providing a substitute pack causes great distress to the animal. In such conditions a dog will demonstrate despair by tearing up furniture or other household items, digging, running away or even self-mutilation, an act which provides at least a sort of distraction. Self-cutting in humans is often a result of early childhood abuse, where the scars are proof that something real, something that cannot be denied, did actually happen, but in cases where children have been isolated for long periods of time, the psychology of self-mutilation may be similar to that which obtains in dogs, namely a means of providing stimulation from the external world.

Of all the acts which demonstrate despair, however, it is barking, incessant barking, that, along with aggression, usually brings dogs to the attention of a specialist in abnormal dog behaviour. Nobody is quite sure why dogs bark in general, though Charles Darwin noted that 'this habit is soon lost by dogs when they become feral and is so reacquired when they are again domesticated'. Wolves make a small 'wuffing' sound, but do not normally bark, nor do any of the other wild canids, or members of the dog-family.[9] Only the dog routinely barks. It has been suggested that it is the dog's attempt to imitate human speech, to communicate with us.[10] The first impulse of a dog who is left alone is to bark furiously. Clearly it is seeking somebody's attention: 'Help me, I am here and miserable.' A dog who is getting plenty of outdoor walks and much human attention and affection is less likely to bark uncontrollably. Dogs kept chained in back yards bark incessantly. They may simply be asking to be freed.

It is easy to know when a dog is lonely, even if it does not display unusual behaviour. A dog is lonely when it is alone, and in loneliness it is bored. When a solitary dog is regularly taken out on long walks, and gets to see other dogs and spends time with them each day, he seems not to be readily bored. However, if he lives without other animals, it is more likely that he will become bored. Ideally dogs should live with other dogs or other animals in a family. They should go on several daily walks in places where they can meet plenty of other people and other dogs. Dogs need to love other dogs and people. A dog with plenty of love in its life, both giving it and receiving it, will be neither lonely nor bored.

CHAPTER EIGHT

Compassion: The Essence of a Dog's Inner Life

IN RECENT YEARS, there has been an explosion of interest in the subjects of compassion and altruism among animals.[1] Hitherto it was widely believed that no other animal besides humans can display genuine compassion even for another of its own species, let alone for a member of a different species. Yet confounding stories abound. In *A Natural History of Love*, Diane Ackerman tells of a young couple on the island of Jersey who took their infant son to the zoo. The little boy fell from a wall into the middle of the gorilla enclosure. 'A huge silverback – the dominant male – ran over to the baby and sat between him and the rest of the gorillas, and there he stayed, protecting the baby, until a keeper could be called.'[2] Recently, the world was electrified by a story, captured on video, of a three-year-old boy who fell 18 feet on to concrete in a gorilla exhibit at the Brookfield Zoo in Chicago. Binti, a seven-year-old female with a baby gorilla on her back, picked up the child, cradled him in her arms, and placed him near

95

a door where keepers could retrieve him. The child survived with no permanent injuries.

In some extraordinary wildlife footage I was privileged to watch, a small impala antelope in Africa races away from a pack of wild dogs into a river where it is immediately seized by a large crocodile. Suddenly a hippopotamus rushes to the rescue of the dazed antelope. The crocodile releases his prey and the hippo then nudges the small animal up the bank of the river and follows it for a few feet until it drops from exhaustion. Instead of leaving, the hippo then helps the little creature to its feet and opening its mouth as wide as possible, breathes warm air on to the stunned antelope. The hippo does this five times before returning to the forest. There is no possible explanation for this remarkable behaviour except compassion.

Primatologist Frans de Waal recorded an incident which occurred at the Wisconsin Primate Center. The adult males in a group of stump-tail monkeys became extremely protective of Wolf, an old, virtually blind female. Whenever the caretakers tried to move the monkeys from the indoor to the outdoor section of the enclosure, adult males would stand guard at the door between the sections, sometimes holding it open, until Wolf had gone through.[3]

In December 1995, a feral domestic cat squeezed through a hole in a fence that corrals a 560-pound bear at Wildlife Images, a wildlife rehabilitation centre in Grants Pass, Oregon. The cat approached the bear as he was eating from a five-gallon bucket. So hungry was the cat that he was seen to walk up to the bear and beg for food. Dave Siddon, founder of the centre, thought the bear would kill the cat. Instead the bear pulled a little piece of chicken out and dropped it beside his forepaw, and watched the cat walk up and eat it. Afterwards, the cat and the bear remained together – eating, sleeping and romping round the pen – the best of friends.[4]

Sceptics may be reluctant to see any of these stories as an example of compassion. Perhaps the silverback was curious, they will say; it could be that even as experienced a primatologist as Frans de Waal had fallen into the mire of anthropomorphism and was projecting his own emotions on to the stump-tail males; the bear was probably lonely and glad of companionship. When interpreting animal behaviour, some scientists seem to apply

Morgan's Law[5] as a reflex response: never explain something by resorting to a higher order of explanation when a lower one will suffice. This often results in finding a less noble interpretation than the behaviour merits.

Yet feeling compassion and committing compassionate acts make sense from an evolutionary point of view. Solitary animals – cats, for example – do not need to show compassion to survive, and examples of compassion among the big cats are scarce. On the other hand, humans and dogs are social animals, and all social animals must learn to get on with one another to survive. As Auden wrote: 'We must love one another or die.'

The animal that lives in a community learns the value of helping another individual. Rats are reluctant to press a lever to get food if doing so will also deliver an electric shock to a companion. They will invariably press the lever that will not deliver the shock, and some will even forego food rather than hurt their friends.[6] Maybe this is why rats make good companions for children, why *rattus Norvegicus* can be so affectionate with children. Scientists, however, tend to search for less noble traits.

The distinguished ethologist Irenäus Eibl-Eibesfeldt raised a wild badger, but he never succeeded in forbidding it to do anything. 'If I scolded it when it opened a cupboard and pulled out my linen, the most it did was to stare at me, and if I gave it a smack on its nose it attacked me. It would not subordinate itself. A dog, on the other hand, quickly learns to obey.'[7]

The observation is valid, but the point is not well taken. This obedience, a quality implied by so many authors to be no more than merely submission to a higher ranking individual, may in fact be more than just an instinct to obey, a fear of being punished, or respect for a superior. (Eibl-Eibesfeldt points out that in German 'respect' is *Ehr-furcht*, a combination of two words, honour and fear). It may be related to love and compassion, and wanting to be loved.

Dictionary definitions of compassion include pity, sorrow, sympathy over another's misfortune, all states which are thought to be part of the human experience. Dogs feel pity and sorrow, I am sure, but I am not so certain that they can sympathise over another dog's misfortune, or at least that they do so in ways that are recognisable to us. A short time ago I was taking the three dogs for a late-night walk when Rani disappeared, and I spent an hour searching for her. Clearly she was lost. Sasha and Sima did not seem at all concerned, but when we found her, and she came bounding up to us, the greeting they gave her was not just the usual acknowledgment of a friend who has been away for an hour. Their behaviour suggested they knew she was especially glad to be back. Somehow, I sensed, they recognised from her reaction that she had been in trouble. I would call this sympathy.

Compassion among dogs seems to me closely connected to feelings that cluster around love, such as friendship, companion-ship, nostalgic memories of having done things together, being good-natured and feeling good will towards a member of one's own species, or a different species.

Rick McIntyre tells the story of an injured and limping all-white alpha male wolf who always fell behind his pack. The wolf would rush forward on three legs and momentarily catch up. Then he would drop back several hundred yards behind, and the other pack members would halt and patiently wait for him to reach them.[8] This act seems to illustrate the complex state we refer to as compassion. I would suggest that waiting for the animal is of the same order of compassion as we witness among humans. We can dismiss it, and say that the rest of the pack needed their leader, and thus their waiting was merely for their own benefit. Such an explanation, however, ignores the feeling component in the act. Whatever the wolves were feeling or thinking as they waited, it was not likely to be a mathematical calculation of cost/benefit or a feeling of smug self-satisfaction.

Mike Tomkies lived with Moobli, a 'gentle giant' of a dog, in a remote corner of the Scottish Highlands where they roamed 300 square miles of wild mountain terrain. This Alsatian treated with tender care the many injured creatures that came to him and his master for succour. The story is beautifully told in Tomkies' book, *Moobli*, which contains pictures of the dog ministering to wounded deer.[9] There is something deeply affecting about interspecies compassion.

When one of my three dogs strays too far from the others, and I continue walking, oblivious, I will notice that the other two stop and wait for their companion to return. They look at me as if to let me know that this is the right thing to do, and that I should wait too. They do not want to continue until the pack is complete. This act is surely indicative of compassion, just as in the case of the wolves. We could explain it in other ways; there is always another explanation, whether for human or animal compassion – it is really self-interest, for instance, or disguised selfishness, with hopes of a favour in return. Even if there is some truth in these explanations, they do not cancel out the element that derives from love and compassion because they cannot explain away the feelings that accompany those actions.

In America, almost every day newspapers and television shows report stories of dogs who have saved people's lives. The *St Louis Post-Dispatch* reported on its front page in March 1996 the extraordinary story of two stray dogs, a dachshund and a brave heeler, who kept alive a mentally disabled boy when he became lost in the woods for three 'bone-chilling' days. The boy's mother called the dogs 'angels from heaven' after ten-year-old Josh Carlisle, who has Down's syndrome, was rescued from a dry creek in Montana by a searcher on horseback. In temperatures close to zero, the dogs had played with him and cuddled him to keep him warm at night. Josh hadn't eaten while he was lost, but the dogs must have led him to water for he was not fully dehydrated. The boy had mild frostbite on all ten toes, having spent his first night with a light snow dusting the ground. When Josh was carried to the ambulance, the dachshund followed and kept jumping up to see in the window. 'I'll never forget that dog's face,' said rescuer Dana Kammerlohr. Both dogs found a new home with the child's family, and his mother told reporters, 'They fell in love with my son during those days.'[10]

These dogs did not need to sleep next to the boy to keep themselves warm. The most parsimonious explanation for their behaviour is simply that they knew or sensed that the boy would die without the warmth of their fur. I see what the dogs did as protective, as an act of compassion.

A sceptic might argue that such behaviour is simply an expression of submission. This explanation supposes that dogs are always submissive in the company of humans, and that lying with the boy was simply one way of expressing submission. Barry Lopez has noted that 'wolves will submit to dogs they have grown up with, no matter how small. I've seen a tame adult wolf act submissive before an eight-pound cairn terrier.'[11] The stray dogs, however, had no cause to be submissive to the handicapped boy. They did not know him, they did not recognise him, and dogs often shy away from human behaviour they intuit to be abnormal. Even in the case that Lopez cites, the word 'submission' seems inappropriate. Perhaps it is also a form of love. Not every interaction between humans and other species is hierarchical in nature. We tend to explain behaviour in hierarchal terms because we humans think in such terms. This may be profoundly misguided, both in respect of animals and of ourselves. Submission may be just another form of love.

Rescue dogs are taught to do their work as a game. But they display such pride in what they are doing that many trainers think they know they are doing well, not merely having fun. Therefore, we could say that they act out of a sense of compassion.[12]

Dogs are also capable of showing compassion for cats. Ginny is a little mutt who has displayed an extraordinary compassion for cats, 'stray cats, starving cats, ill cats, and especially, physically handicapped cats'.[13] The first cat Ginny rescued was deaf, the second had lost an eye, yet another rescue was of a cat without any hind feet.

Roger Caras witnessed a remarkable episode of compassion and aid by a mixed breed dog named Sheba. Her caretaker, Angie, had a very high fever as a child and suffered neurological damage that made her susceptible to thirteen kinds of seizures, including epilepsy. She has as many as a dozen seizures in twenty-four hours. During some of these, Angie stops breathing and, without immediate medical attention, could die. Angie can never be left alone, even in the bathroom. Her whole family has had to learn emergency medical procedures. They applied for a dog from a programme that trains dogs to help people with special problems. In the end it was decided that no dog could be trained to give the kind of medical help Angie required but that a simple companion dog would benefit her emotionally.

However, miraculously, Sheba learned to monitor Angie's difficulties. She never leaves Angie for a moment. She can discern somehow when Angie is about to have a seizure, and she barks, grabs Angie's hand in her mouth, and drags her to a bed or couch to make sure Angie doesn't fall on the floor. Sheba not only alerts

Angie's family, she has a special bark when Angie's breathing is threatened.

How can a dog do this? Sight, sound, smell, or even infra-red heat detection may all play a part – the latter because the person about to have a seizure has a quick fever, a sudden spike in body temperature, and may give off a different odour. All this happens in seconds. Sheba has never been wrong and Angie's life has changed. She can now take walks and play outside as long as Sheba is with her.

Caras not only saw Sheba at work with Angie during a seizure but filmed one, and his presentation was shown on ABC Television's 'World News Tonight'. He says he would never have believed it if he had not witnessed it himself.[14]

CHAPTER NINE

Dignity, Humiliation and Disappointment

CERTAIN THINGS just seem to be beneath a dog's dignity. Almost all of us have observed the older dog who does not deign to participate in some childish game of his younger companions. Watching an older dog interact with puppies is an extraordinary experience. They display patience but also appear a bit embarrassed. If dogs have dignity, and anybody who works with dogs could not deny that they do, can that dignity be abused? Do they subsequently experience humiliation?

Of exactly what does dignity consist, for a dog? Is it a consciousness of being observed and meeting a certain standard of conduct? When I take my three dogs out to the bank, for example, and I am about to tie them up outside, the two puppies begin to clown and play. At that moment Sasha adopts a look that signals to any passer-by that she, at least, is not part of this pack, that she would never stoop to such childish antics. She looks in the opposite direction, staring intently at some far distant object as if

102

pretending to be unaware of the noise and romping of the other dogs. She looks – and even passers-by have called her this – dignified.

However, when Sasha does something wrong – when rushing another dog (which, alas, may be characteristic of her breed, just as Rani's mild stubbornness is characteristic of ridgebacks) in an attempt to scare it – she always casts a glance in my direction, anticipating my disapproval, for she knows I do not like this behaviour. Then, she lays back her ears, dances over to me, bends down and attempts to appease me. If I accept the apology, she is happy, but if I do not – if I am still angry with her – then she looks sheepish and humiliated. She knew I would not like it; she simply could not help herself.

Many philosophers, and even some people close to dogs, are reluctant to acknowledge that dogs can feel something as complex as humiliation. Thus even the Cambridge philosopher Ludwig Wittgenstein, despite his genius, reveals a certain insensitivity when it comes to understanding dogs in terms of their emotions: 'Why can a dog feel fear but not remorse?' he writes. 'Would it be right to say "Because he can't talk?" '[1] He seems to be suggesting that 'primitive' emotions, such as fear and anger, are not mediated by speech, whereas the 'higher' emotions of love and remorse are. Since a dog has no access to speech, it cannot, according to Wittgenstein, feel an emotion such as remorse. I think Wittgenstein is wrong. To feel humiliated often leads to remorse in humans, and I believe it is the same for dogs. While I was visiting the canine unit of the Oakland Police Department in March 1996, one of the trainers told me that his dog had mistakenly bitten him. When the dog realised it was his trainer he had bitten, he looked completely humiliated and sank down into the car, the epitome of remorse, as if muttering to himself again and again: 'I'm sorry, I'm so sorry, oh God, what did I do?'

'And did you forgive him?' I asked.

'Oh, immediately. It was my mistake for sticking my hand in the car without warning.'

'And what did he do then?'

'He immediately perked up and the whole incident was clearly forgotten.'

Dogs love to be forgiven. They bear no grudge and are happy

when they see that you don't harbour any ill will either.

Many people have told me that when their dogs have accidentally injured them the dogs looked deeply remorseful, or at least ashamed. That has not been my experience. A few months after acquiring Sasha, I took the dogs for a late night walk in a park four blocks from my house. Sasha was chasing Rani, going in circles faster and faster. Suddenly I felt as if I had been shot: Sasha had come charging from behind and slammed into me at full speed. I fell to the ground and felt a searing pain. I must have put my entire weight (155 pounds) on my right foot. I tried to stand up, but immediately fell down again. The pain was unbearable. As I started to pass out I thought bitterly what a poor guide dog Sasha would have made, why trainers said she needed a career change. Fortunately Leila was there and she ran and got the car and we made it back home. I could not walk at all. I went to bed, praying that I would wake up fine in the morning, but the pain grew worse and worse through the night as my foot began to swell. It took six weeks before I could walk again, and then only with a pronounced limp.

How hard it is to read the emotions in a situation like this, one that can arouse considerable emotion in a human but not necessarily in a dog. While I had lain on the ground, writhing, Sasha showed no concern, not a trace of remorse or guilt, playing happily with the other two dogs who were equally uninterested in this moaning grounded humanoid. I don't think she was embarrassed. Was she indifferent? Or was she just unaware of what had happened? It is hard to believe she could not know what she had done. On the other hand, this is how dogs play, and such an accident is virtually unheard of in the dog world.

Whatever guilt I might have been able to induce in Sasha by telling her what I thought of what she had done to me would have been artificial: she would have felt it only because I was demanding it. Moreover, even if genuine, it would have been short-lived. My pain, discomfort and even annoyance with Sasha would last for six weeks or more, yet I could hardly expect her on day ten to look at me and be reminded of what she had done. I did feel a certain impatience on her part, as if to say 'Don't be such a wimp, Masson, enough is enough.'

In other words, I could have caused her guilt, or humiliation, but the reason for these feelings would not have been apparent to her. On the other hand, some animals hate to be laughed at: the great apes, elephants, and house cats among them. Dogs are not usually included in this list, but people who have lived with dogs do not doubt for a moment that a dog's dignity can be injured, and that dogs experience humiliation. In *The Mind of the Dog*, R. H. Smythe has this to say:

> Every dog is extremely susceptible to ridicule. It enjoys laughter providing one is laughing with it, but it becomes extremely embarrassed and unhappy if it even suspects that it is being made fun of, in other words being laughed *at*. I once owned a very odd-looking crossbred hound which had a massive head and body and the short crooked limbs of a Basset hound. I was extremely fond of this dog and endeavored always to spare his feelings, but whenever I turned up for a day's rabbiting with Richard at my heels, a roar of laughter would go up from the men present. Richard knew perfectly well the cause of it, and would attempt to hide. Eventually he disappeared and was never found again.[?]

In this same passage, Smythe points out that certain dogs, especially heavy breeds, wag their tails in an up-and-down direction when they are ashamed, or feel guilty, or know they are about to be scolded, thumping the floor as the tail descends. A dog who does this is anticipating punishment, and will remain in a lying position, indicating humility. When I come into my bedroom and see Rani simply lying still where she is, thumping her tail on the ground and looking up at me with the whites of her eyes showing, glancing off to the side, I know that she has found a piece of my clothing and has already chewed it to pieces.

In his book *Animal Intelligence*, George Romanes tells a story he observed himself:

> The terrier used to be very fond of catching flies upon the window-panes, and if ridiculed when unsuccessful was evidently much annoyed. On one occasion, in order to see what he would do, I purposely laughed immoderately every time he failed. It so happened that he did so several times in succession – partly, I believe, in consequence of my laughing – and eventually he became so distressed that he positively *pretended* to catch the fly,

105

going through all the appropriate actions with his lips and tongue, and afterwards rubbing the ground with his neck as if to kill the victim: he then looked up at me with a triumphant air of success. So well was the whole process simulated that I should have been quite deceived, had I not seen that the fly was still upon the window. Accordingly I drew his attention to this fact, as well as to the absence of anything upon the floor; and when he saw that his hypocrisy had been detected he slunk away under some furniture, evidently very much ashamed of himself.[3]

It is hard not to be somewhat sceptical of the 'triumphant air of success'. Romanes may be transferring some of his own deviousness on to the dog. It may also have been meant in jest, though Romanes does not think so. Whatever the significance, the dog's behaviour, if the report is accurate, displays a remarkably sophisticated awareness of human thought-processes and emotions. Romanes was humiliating the dog and the dog did not wish to be humiliated.

Laughing *with* a dog, of course, is a very different proposition, and many dogs have a good sense of humour. Henri Bergson declared that laughter is the unique prerogative of humans.[4] He was wrong, as many dog people can tell him. Konrad Lorenz, in *Man Meets Dog*, speaks of dogs who laugh when they play with an adored human companion.

Do dogs recognise our smile? Yes, says Barbara Woodhouse: 'When I speak of "expression", I really do mean that animals watch to see whether one's face is smiling or dull. If I don't smile at my dog, whilst she is working in the obedience tests, she fails hopelessly, just as when training her I used to look sad when she did wrong, and that hurt her.'[5]

Once, when I was asked to deliver a lecture to the Oakland Zoological Society, I sought permission to bring my dogs, assuming it would be a small gathering in a small room. As it turned out, there were more than 200 people present, and I was to speak from a raised platform. I decided to let the dogs loose anyway. They proceeded to attack one another playfully, to roll around and behave like puppies, to the great amusement of the audience. They were not acting; they were oblivious of the people, and totally unconcerned with what anyone thought. I was surprised at their apparent lack of self-consciousness and their total disregard for any possible humiliation or disapprobation. It seemed to them a matter of indifference whether the people were laughing at them or with them. They could just as well have been on a solitary meadow for all the attention they paid to me or to the audience. Perhaps I am not immune from anthropomorphism, and categories such as disapprobation are human concerns rather than canine ones.

★

While dogs feel humiliation, it appears that they do not blame a specific person (or other animal) for having created this distressing feeling. It is as if, once again, dogs feel the pure emotion itself, almost detached from its source. I believe the same is true of disappointment. Dogs are particularly sensitive to disappointment, but rarely connect the feeling to the people and friends they love. Dogs, it seems, are free from a need to blame somebody for their misfortune.

To return for a moment to the philosophers. Ludwig Wittgenstein claimed: 'One can imagine an animal angry, frightened, unhappy, happy, startled. But hopeful? . . . A dog believes his master is at the door. But can he also believe his master will come the day-after-tomorrow?'[6] Wittgenstein makes a valid point, but once again he wishes to confine the emotions of dogs to the most simple, physiologically-based feelings. If a dog cannot be hopeful, I think Wittgenstein would have claimed that a dog cannot be disappointed either. For him it would belong to the same category of emotion, one that involves some sense of time – even if only an imagined imminent walk suddenly denied.

While it is almost certainly true that a dog cannot have the idea that his 'master' will come at a specific time, such as in five hours, he nonetheless certainly believes his master will come at some point in the future, and the sooner the better. When this turns out not to be the case, the dog is prone to disappointment. The fact that dogs feel disappointment seems to me proof that they anticipate some kind of future, even if one confined to the present and the following second. The dashing of hope or an expectation unfulfilled is a common experience for dogs. Many people, myself

107

among them, believe that no animal can be quite as disappointed as a dog. We observe disappointment in dogs daily. Just this morning, for example, Sima, Sasha and Rani heard me get my keys and head for the door. They were in another part of the house, but immediately I heard thundering paws as they raced towards the door, tails wagging wildly, moaning with excitement: 'A walk, a walk' was written all over their faces.

'No,' I said, sadly, 'no walk now. I have to go out for a little while. But soon, soon we will go for a walk.'

The second half of the sentence was in vain. All they needed to hear was 'no' and 'walk' together. The three froze and looked as if I had struck them in the face. Their ears were cocked as if they could not believe what they had just heard. Then in a great crash they threw themselves to the floor, ears flopped down, the whites of their eyes showing, looking the way only a dog can look who is *totally disappointed*. Indeed, they were the very picture of disappointment. The emotion would have been unmistakable to anybody.

There are those who claim that disappointment is a uniquely human emotion, one that a dog cannot feel. In their mind, to claim that a dog is disappointed is pure projection. How can one answer this objection?

Take the case of a human being. If I promise my daughter (who is 22) that I will walk with her in an hour and then tell her later that something has come up and I cannot go, she may display some of the same features as did the dogs, allowing me to read disappointment in her face and in her body language. The only difference between her response and that of the dogs is possibly the degree of expression. She can hide her feelings, the dogs cannot. But I can do something with her that I cannot do with the dogs: I can say to her. 'Simone, sweetheart, are you disappointed?' And she can tell me that, yes, she is. But what if Simone were secretly dreading the walk, since she knew I wanted to ask her intrusive personal questions which she did not want to answer? Then she might be relieved, even though she answered me by saying that she was disappointed. Or she might not know that she was disappointed; she might think what a relief, while feeling deep down that I had given her false hope. Language, in other words, is no guarantee of veracity, nor is the absence of language a reason to declare the impossibility of emotion.

If this is true for humans, why should it be any different for dogs? 'Disappointment' is a word we use to indicate a feeling we all experience and exhibit in various ways to others. The same emotion we see in other humans is written in the face of dogs, in their eyes, ears, deportment. It is not anthropomorphism to observe the same signs in them as we see in other people. The degree of disappointment dogs feel, and the exact tone, the feeling-quality of that disappointment may be different from what humans experience. It may be more or less subtle, more or less intense. It may even have shades of feeling we do not recognise in it, but it is still in the same world of feeling, not wholly unlike our disappointment.

People who train dogs to do rescue work, such as finding people buried under an avalanche, or under rubble when a building collapses, say that the dogs need to find a certain number of people alive or they become so disappointed that they refuse to work any longer. After the bombing in Oklahoma city, a rescue woman found that her rescue dog was becoming depressed at having no success. So she decided to plant a live person in the ruins for her dog to find. This cheered the dog up considerably, and she was happy to go back to work, her mind relieved.

Every dog has certain expectations of consistency without which its life would be miserable.[7] If the dog lived in a world of total confusion, never knowing whether it could count on going for a walk with me, it would soon become depressed and possibly traumatised. Dogs love consistency and stability precisely because they can adjust their own expectations to reality. Of course, there is no time when a dog is not ready for a walk, but if I walk my dog every day at 4 p.m., it would surprise nobody to see him bring a leash to me at precisely that time. He is surely hoping to go for a walk. His hopes may have little to do with time in the sense we understand the word, but it is clearly connected with his feelings, anticipation of happiness for himself, pleasure in being with his friend, and joy at soon being outdoors and enjoying the external world. Anticipated time is not important to the dog, but anticipation in the pleasures of his own emotions is.

In her book *Operating Instructions*, Anne Lamott talks about her infant who at six months became shy with everyone but her.

'When I come home to him, he just goes ape-shit, like he'd given me up for dead. It's like George Carlin's impersonation of a dog – frantic and breathless with relief that his human has come back, going, "Oh, Jesus God, I'm so glad you're back, I was going out of my mind, I was beside myself, I didn't think I could last another fifteen minutes," and his human says, "I just came back to get my *hat*, for Chrissakes." '[8]

Some argue that what the dog feels is not only disappointment but something more akin to despair, because when I say 'Not now, but soon' to a dog, it cannot understand the second half of my sentence. The dog does not have a notion of soon, the reasoning goes, only of now. This is Wittgenstein's point, that the dog cannot project an imagined event on to the future, since it has no sense of measured time apart from natural cycles or rhythms. It is true that everything for the dog is in the moment, immediate. That was partially what Wittgenstein means: dogs have no sense of time. They understand 'now', but not 'in an hour', or 'next week', or 'next month', or 'next year'. There is something to this argument; yet it is not completely convincing. For me the problem is that Wittgenstein and other philosophers who compare humans and other animals to the detriment of the latter insist on using human standards. While dogs cannot understand our arbitrary (or subtle, depending on your point of view) time distinctions, they have their own sense of time which suits them fine.

After all, dogs have a circadian rhythm and are crepuscular beings – that is, they are most active at dawn and at dusk. They too have internal clocks, even if they are set differently from ours. Moreover, even if the dog cannot understand 'soon', it knows from the tone of voice I am using, a friendly one filled with hope, that it can expect something more than a flat rejection. Expectation is essential to a dog's existence. There is a difference in the demeanour of a dog that is watching me eat and expecting to be fed too, and one who knows that I will not feed him. A dog is exquisitely sensitive to these shades of meaning. If dogs did not expect anything from the future, why would a dog sit in front of a door, waiting for someone to return? While it is true that dogs seem to live in the here and now far more than we do, they have their own sense of time, which allows them to hunt and to know when to pounce, whether now or later, this moment or the next.

In a poem by Harold Monro (1879–1932) called simply *Dog*, he describes the moment when the word '*out*' reaches 'by devious means (half-smelt, half-heard), the four-legged brain of a walk-ecstatic dog'.

The words 'not now, but soon' often elicit a strange reaction from Sasha. She cocks her ears in that wonderful way dogs have of listening with complete concentration, and a puzzled expression appears on her face. The listening is intense. What is she listening for? Some idea, clearly, of just what it is that I mean by these words. She is attempting to read the message, and I believe that to some extent she succeeds. Whether this is from the tone of my voice, from my whole demeanour, from something I emit that I am unaware of, or whether she uses some other more mysterious sense than hearing, somehow she picks up what I mean. She is assuaged. Her disappointment, while still real, is not climactic, not final, not annihilating. Sasha will often sigh at such moments, as if to say, 'Oh well, maybe not now, but soon.'

CHAPTER TEN

Dog Dreams

For many years I have had a recurrent dream, a dream whose geography is familiar to me, like a place one has known as a child and visits years later as an adult. The dream takes place in a tropical forest, or on an island, or in the mountains. I am always with someone I love, and a beloved dog, as I encounter a series of baby animals – wild goats, panthers, elephants, chimpanzees – all of whom are friendly and follow me along a hillside as I walk among them. I always hope that they will follow us back home, so that I can show friends and strangers alike how unthreatening 'wild' animals really are, but I never get that far. Before I reach home the animals have all dispersed.

Freud once said that a recurrent dream always points to a repressed memory of a real event. I wonder if this dream could represent my attempt to tap into an atavistic memory of some kind of lost Galapago concord that mankind once knew? When I am sceptical, I think it is probably pure wish-fulfilment on my part,

112

the desire to live such a life of harmony. When I am speculative, I wonder if my dogs have recurrent dreams of this kind, dreams that link them to their own past or even to a larger canid past. If we are so circumspect about our own dreams, who would dare to pronounce on those of a dog? The newborn child sleeps for about two-thirds of the time, and about half of this sleeping period is taken up by REM (rapid eye movement, indicative of the dream state) sleep. We will probably never know what a newborn baby dreams about any more than we will ever know what makes up dog dreams.

The latest research reveals that dreams contain extreme emotions. In fact, that appears to be one of their functions: people who have trouble expressing emotions in everyday life can do so (*must* do so, to be psychologically healthy) in the safety of a dream. In this way, nobody else sees what we are feeling, and we need not act on what we are feeling. Anxiety is the most common emotion felt in a dream, followed by joy and elation. More than half of all dream emotions are extreme ones, either of a highly unpleasant or highly pleasant nature. In a dream emotion experiment carried out by the director of the Laboratory of Neurophysiology at the Massachusetts Mental Health Center in the Harvard Medical School, subjects were asked to quantify the emotions in their dreams and came up with a figure far higher than anything previously reported. This was due simply to the fact that, in the earlier studies, the subjects were not specifically asked about emotions in sufficient detail.[1] Few dreams, it would seem, are devoid of any emotion whatever.

For some time now, scientists have been aware, as a result of electrophysiological studies, that almost all mammals dream.[2] The sleep of more than 150 species has been studied, and only the dolphin would seem never to dream. Young animals dream more than older ones. During the first ten days of life kittens spend 90 per cent of their time in what scientists call paradoxical sleep (parallel to REM sleep in humans), almost as a carry-over from foetal life, a form of foetal sleep.[3]

Dogs dream, of that there can be no doubt. Even without sophisticated machines, one can see dogs move their legs, ears, whiskers, wag their tails, bark, whine, moan, groan and even growl (though I have never heard one do so during sleep).

Hooked up to recording instruments, they show all the evidence of the REM activity indicative of the dream state in humans.[4] REM sleep in dogs occupies approximately 36 per cent of total sleep, as measured by electrographic studies.[5] According to Frederick Snyder, humans spend less time in REM sleep than either cats or opossums. The sleep researcher William Dement and his co-authors point out that babies born prematurely (thirty weeks) spend 100 per cent of their sleep time dreaming. A full term baby spends about 50 per cent. In the teens, we spend 20 per cent of sleep time dreaming, and only 13 per cent in old age.[6] In a recent book, James L. Gould, Professor of Evolutionary Biology at Princeton University, and Carol Grant Gould, a science writer, noted that 'if natural selection has led to dreaming, it seems reasonable to think that an animal might benefit more from exploring in imagination the consequences of alternatives, rather than passively replaying the day's mental videos. Again this suggests some degree of imagination and planning, but as yet there is no way to ask an animal what it is dreaming.'[7]

Recently I visited the Stanford University School of Medicine and met the research director of the Sleep Disorders Center, Dr E. J. M. Mignot, and his colleague, Dr Seiji Nishino, to learn more about their work with narcoleptic dogs. In humans, the neurological disorder known as narcolepsy occurs in about one in every 1,000 people and is characterised by extreme sleepiness ('sleep attacks' they are appropriately called in the scientific literature), or cataplexy (sudden temporary paralysis due to a strong emotional stimulus), or even hypnagogic hallucinations, and sleep paralysis. In 1974 the same condition was diagnosed in a dog (a poodle) by Dement and his colleagues.[8]

After touring the facilities and being introduced to a dog who had had the disease for several years, I asked about dog dreams. Dr Mignot told me that his dog constantly wags her tail in her dreams. While both scientists had no doubt that dogs have elaborate dreams during REM sleep, just as humans do, they thought it would be a long time before we could say precisely what it is they dream.

When we say something like, 'I know my dog was dreaming of chasing squirrels the other night because his legs were twitching,' we are only hazarding a guess. Maybe he was dreaming of his own early life or of a long lost friend. No doubt the past activities of the dog can provide an entry point for a dream, just as they do in humans. Such dream instigators are called the 'day-residue', and they may trigger other memories which lead far beyond the day to memories of events years ago. If memories influence human dreams, why would it not be true of dogs as well? If memories are the building blocks of dreams, why would dogs not have complex dreams? Their cognitive skills may be different from ours, but they are nevertheless complex, and no doubt give rise to internal activity at night.

Virginia Woolf wrote about the dreams of the dog Flush:

Even his sleep was full of dreams. He dreamt as he had not dreamt since the old days at Three Mile Cross – of hares starting from the long grass; of pheasants rocketing up with long tails streaming, of partridge rising with a whirr from the stubble. He dreamt that he was hunting, that he was chasing some spotted spaniel, who fled, who escaped him. He was in Spain; he was in Wales; he was in Berkshire; he was flying before park-keepers' truncheons in Regent's Park. Then he opened his eyes. There were no hares, and no partridges; no whips cracking and no black men crying 'Span! Span!' There was only Mr Browning in the armchair talking to Miss Barrett on the sofa.[9]

My dog Sima greets certain people with squeals and runs about in circles in a state of extreme excitement. It is charming, because she is so happy to see the person, but it is also disconcertingly intense, as if she had never expected to see that person again, as if the visitor had just narrowly escaped death. Sima does not do this to strangers, only to people she has met before. In other words, her excitement is a product of her memory. She remembers them and is overwhelmed at seeing them again. Thus her memory is very closely linked to her emotions.[10]

Dogs have good memories. A dog will often remember a place or a person not seen for years. The excitement is evidence that the dog is remembering, and these memories are clearly linked to certain feelings or feeling-states. If we experience a long-term separation from a loved one, we begin to dream more and more frequently about that person. I am convinced that dogs do the same. It would be an interesting experiment to watch the dog's sleep (dream) pattern in the absence of a loved person or fellow dog. Would the dog dream more? If so, would it not be some indication that the dog is dreaming about the absent person or dog? Since we know that emotions are closely linked to dreams, we can assume that a dog with good memories also has complex dreams laden with emotions. The veterinary surgeon R. H. Smythe claims that dogs dream 'when they are young and inexperienced but not so apparently after they reach years of discretion. . . . Later in life I expect he [a greyhound] will still enjoy his dreams, but it is unlikely he will exhibit the same outward signs.'[11]

If dogs do dream about us, how are we represented in their dreams? This is a question my 22-year-old daughter asked me the other day, and we began to think about how dogs cognise us in their dreams. She suggested that since scent plays such an important role in the life of a dog, maybe we are present in canine dreams as a smell. By taking an informal survey among my friends, I found that it is the rare person who is aware of smells in a dream, (just as we rarely eat and drink in dreams). We see and we hear, but we rarely smell or taste. It seems likely that dogs see us in their dreams, for they too are highly visual (though not as visual as we are), and smell us, but primarily they smell us.

When I was interviewed recently in London for a BBC radio programme on animal dreams, two of the questions left me wondering. Can a dog remember its dreams during the day? If so, there is no reason to believe that they do not think about the dream; in fact, their sniffing may be related to smells from their own dreams, and there might be some dreams so powerful that they leave traces for months or even years. Indeed, it is not impossible for the dog to remember a particularly intense dream from puppyhood. A dog could be haunted by a dream from long ago, just as we can be haunted by a childhood dream. The other question was whether dogs, with their exquisite awareness of other animals with different senses and abilities, ever dream of having those capacities. Do dogs dream, as we do, of soaring through the air, or swimming rapidly in the waves? Strangely, though, people never seem to dream (at least, I have never heard of it) about possessing a dog's ability to smell.

Will we ever know for certain what dogs dream about? I find it hard to conceive of how we might. Far into the future, no doubt, electrical brain impulses will be translated directly into images and stored on tape. Then maybe we will have whole libraries of the dreams of our canine companions.

Humans have a vexing habit of wanting to tell their dreams to another person, especially if that person appears as a character in the dream. Even if a dog had this impulse, we would not know it. Though vocalisation in a dreaming dog is inhibited, it is clearly present: we hear moans, whimpers and barks, and some people have heard a dog growl. Since dogs undoubtedly dream about each other, and therefore must relive situations they have been in, such as a tense stand-off with another dog, the only reason for the rarity of growling would be similar to the inhibition of movement in human dreaming. We do not start running at great speed during a dream. The growl may represent an equally great effort of the inhibited physiological system that is at rest in sleep.

It would seem, however, that a dog is aware that another dog dreams, and can show a certain degree of sympathy for another dog caught up in a bad dream. Not long ago, when Sima was crying in her sleep, Rani went over and licked her. I think that Rani knew, from her own direct experience, that Sima was having a bad dream, and was attempting to relieve Rani's anxiety. More than just empathy, it is not only that Rani knew, cognitively, what Sima was experiencing, she actually wished to do something about it. This is the mark of sympathy, a higher order of emotion than mere empathy, which itself is already higher than most other feelings.

CHAPTER ELEVEN

Nature versus Nurture: Dogs at Work and Play

I AM FASCINATED by the phrase 'a dog's nature' as it is used in so many different contexts: 'It is the nature of a dog to hunt'; 'You are going against the very nature of a dog'; 'He can't help it, it's in a dog's nature'. I wonder how carefully we have thought about such phrases. How do we really know just what a dog's nature is? Is it merely the product of genes, a simple example of biological hard-wiring in a living creature? The people who think so act as if a dog were iike a computer. I am reminded of Descartes's idea of the robot-dog, a *machina animata*. He justified his gruesome vivisections on the grounds that the dog felt nothing.

On the other hand, one cannot totally deny a genetic component in canine behaviour. Sasha seemed to me so gentle that I often wondered why I needed a leash for her. She would never run after anything if I told her not to do so – or so I thought.

One day I went for a run with my three dogs and a friend, and all was fine until a deer appeared. The reaction was instantaneous

118

and powerful. Sasha was trembling, moaning, and every muscle in her body was quivering and straining. 'No!' I told her. She looked at me as if to say: 'What? You're not serious? *Daaaad*! This is my very first deer!' As indeed it was. As far as I know, Sasha had never seen a deer before. I did not relent: 'Stay with me,' I told her sternly.

Her excitement was unendurable. Suddenly, like a branch snapping, she veered left into a garden, took off at warp speed, and was gone. No amount of calling or whistling made the slightest difference. All was still. Not a sound could be heard. Then, from far off in the distance, I heard dogs barking. Could she be the cause of that, so far away? I was in despair. I stood there for ten minutes, trying to decide what to do. My friend's wife, who has superior hearing, urged me to be still when she met us. 'Listen,' she said. 'The jingle of dog tags.' Suddenly, crashing through the underbrush, Sasha was back.

What did I learn from this incident? Mike, of Guide Dogs for the Blind, told me firmly: 'Never let her off leash until you're certain she's trained to return on command.' But how could I bear that? And how could I correct her after she returned? She would not have understood what I was saying, and she would associate coming back with being punished. How does one justify – indeed go about – correcting a dog's nature?

We think we know the nature of dogs; we believe we can predict their behaviour. I certainly thought so, until I went to visit a friend and her companion who live in the country north of Berkeley with their four baby Alpine and Lamancha goats. They looked a little concerned when we arrived with Sasha, Sima and Rani.

'Most young goats that die are killed by dogs,' I was told darkly.

I reassured them: 'These three are gentle and perfectly safe. But just to make sure, I will put them on leashes.'

It was a good thing I did too, for the minute they saw and smelled the goats, all three began pulling on their leashes. It seemed as if they just wanted to lick the goats, but the noises they made (the same whining that Sasha had displayed with the kittens and with the rabbit) were so intense, their excitement so visible and their straining on the leash so strong that it took all my strength to hold them back. The goats were curious and charmingly unafraid, but we could not risk allowing the dogs their freedom. What would I do if one of them suddenly bit the young goat and hurt him? No matter how much I attempted to discipline them and make them remain still, they were clearly out of control, as if in the grip of some force beyond them. I don't know if it was a hunting instinct that had arisen, or a genetic memory of predator/prey relations, but the dogs were uncontrollable. I felt that in one second they could go from creatures I knew as well as I knew myself to mysterious others, a totally different order of being about whom I was and would remain profoundly ignorant.

If we are the parents of a dog, what are our teaching responsibilities? How much should we attempt to make a dog fit into the human world, and how much can we allow a dog to be a dog? For some people who own dogs ('own' is the operative word here), training is the *raison d'être* of having a dog. There are others (those who would shudder at the implications of 'own') who feel just as strongly on the other side: it is a distortion of the nature of a dog to train a dog. I can see, and have felt the justice of, both of these positions. Neither, though, strikes me as completely correct. A dog is not a wolf. Dogs are not wild animals, and they must fit into our society to some extent or their lives will end in tragedy. Just think of dogs who run loose and kill livestock or chickens. Even if they have no predatory instincts, a totally untrained dog may run into the street, and you cannot call it back to save it from being hit by passing traffic. Dogs that roam free generally have a short life; the vast majority are victims of automobile accidents. On the other hand, a dog that is never allowed to express its own nature, but must always obey and show off to other humans how compliant it is to its master's wishes, leads an impoverished life. It was hard for me to find the perfect balance, the amount of training that was necessary to make my dogs good or tolerable citizens and the amount of freedom they needed to be happy dogs.

Working dogs are often very happy indeed. Anyone who has watched them in obedience trials must gain a sense (hard to prove, of course) that the dogs are keenly competitive and hugely enjoying themselves. Left to their own devices, dogs will engage in playful rivalry. Whenever Sima sees Rani pick up a stick, she charges over and attempts to grab it out of Rani's mouth. Rani does the same when Sima finds a stick. They race around the park together with one stick between them, much to the delight of passers-by. Yet Sasha was not content as a guide dog. This is surely part of what was meant when I was told she was 'too soft' for the guide dog programme. Her true personality has only slowly come to the surface, almost as if she needed to shed the lessons she had learned as a guide dog. I say 'true' because, as Sasha becomes more confident, she seems more playful, happier, more carefree; in short, she behaves more as I would imagine a dog behaves when it has nobody to please but itself or a good canine companion. Dogs are as individual as humans, and what is good for one may be altogether wrong for another. The fact that Sasha is happier not being a guide dog does not mean that some other dog would not be thrilled to be so useful. I was a pretty useless psychotherapist, but friends of mine seem predestined for it.

I am eager not to allow my own agenda, my own ego, to get in the way of understanding what is actually going on. The other day I became angry with Rani. After a long walk, we found ourselves at the Marina on our way home when suddenly Rani ran towards a family having a picnic. I called, she ignored the call. I saw her sit down and start begging for food. I went back to the car, sure she would eventually follow me. She did not. Finally I headed back to where I had left her. She saw me coming and paid no heed even when I was standing in front of her. She looked at me as if she had never seen me before in her life. The family stared at me as if I were trying to take a dog that was not mine, hinting that I should prove she belonged to me. I was indignant. Of course she was mine. 'Rani, come on, we're going.' The look on her face unmistakably conveyed: 'Does anyone know this guy,' or 'Why is he calling me that strange name?' I was angry. After we had got away on our own, I emphatically let her know that I disapproved of what she had just done. But how did she see it in her mind? Is she just too greedy to resist a meal? And why was I so humiliated?

Why do I think that Rani is thwarting my will instead of simply being a dog? Why do I think of it as stubbornness when she wants to do what she wants to do? A day later, Rani ran under a car because she found something there to eat. She then refused to come out. I was angry again, and when eventually she emerged, I

121

grabbed her by the snout, held it tight, and told her what I thought of her behaviour. She was scared, not contrite, and immediately began trying to appease me. I had lost my temper. I have not felt that kind of anger for a long time. It surprised me. I still do not know the source. Is it only that my will was being thwarted, and I didn't like that? Most trainers would say that I was to blame for not having trained her properly. Something like that should not happen, and when it does, the fault does not lie with the dog.

In any large bookshop, there will usually be a section on how to train your dog. After reading some of these books, I am convinced that they are all right, that they all work. The dog who is trained with any of these methods learns to do what is expected of him or her. There does not seem to be such a great gulf between 'correction' (*The Koehler Method of Dog Training*[1]) and pure reward, whether verbal or with food. Guide Dogs for the Blind, which uses the correction method, also gives plenty of praise, and dogs trained with either method learn at about the same speed. People are very sensitive to the complexities of this issue. Many caretakers find it unpleasant, and some unbearable, to correct their dog, claiming that this is punishment, even though those who use the method insist that it is not. Others, however, feel that if their dog is doing something purely for the reward, then training is reduced to bribery, and they don't wish to be party to it. Of course, we all want the dog to do the work because he loves us and wants to please us. This is something we read about all the time, and most trainers (except Koehler) talk about it as if it were self-evident. But is it? What motivates the dog to do as we tell it? Partly fear, in the broadest sense of the word – fear that we will be displeased, for example – we are, after all, part of its pack, and the dog likes to be on good terms with other members of the pack. Often I don't feel as if I am the alpha of the pack, though that is the received wisdom, but I am sure we are part of it, even if in some more mysterious way than we know about.

Among the best books I have found on training are *How to be Your Dog's Best Friend* by the Monks of New Skete and Carol Lea Benjamin's *Mother Knows Best* (where Mother refers to a mother dog as the personification of the best possible trainer for a young puppy). Both books stress the natural emotions of a dog (pride, for instance) and how important it is – indeed, what a miracle it is – that we share so many of our emotions with dogs. Taking advantage of this fact in training makes sense.

★

So much for nurture: what then is natural for what we call a 'domesticated' dog?

Dogs are particularly prone to play with just about anything. The astonishing thing is that sometimes a large predator, such as a polar bear (as seen in a 1994 *National Geographic* cover photo), will play with a dog,[2] and sometimes the dog is its prey (a polar bear is only prey to killer whales, who scoop them off ice-floats as if they were a ball of ice-cream). When I walk my three dogs in the Berkeley Marina, especially early in the morning, it is very common to have a swallow come swooping by Sima's head, daring her to chase it. Sima invariably takes up the challenge, and the bird easily stays ahead, but never far ahead, so that the game can continue. If Sima tires and turns away, the bird swoops even more closely, to renew Sima's interest, which usually happens. It is clearly play for them both. What would happen if Sima should perchance catch the bird? I would think that each would be disappointed, though one certainly more than the other. As Woody Allen once noted: 'And it will come to pass that the lion will lie down with the lamb; but the lamb won't get much sleep.'

Kaspar Hauser, Germany's most famous 'wild child', was born in 1812 and kept in a dungeon for the first sixteen years of his life. When he was released, he could not speak or walk. He eventually learned to speak, and even wrote his autobiography, but the brief life he led, both in the dungeon and later, was filled with tragedy, and ended with his murder in 1833 when he was barely 21 years old. The only activity he could remember from his years in the 'black hole' was playing with a wooden horse and a toy dog. In the years following his release (as mysterious as his captivity), he learned to speak, eat, play the piano, draw, and engage in social discourse in all matters that Germans considered essential to the civilised person. He had played enough while in prison, it was thought. It never occurred to anyone that what Kaspar Hauser lost in his sixteen years in prison was the delight of playing with other human beings; consequently he was neither taught nor encouraged to play with other children.[3]

123

In the most elaborate and authoritative book so far written on play in animals, *Animal Play Behavior*, Robert Fagen writes that 'In the past, scientists who studied play sometimes encountered deep hostility from their colleagues and from the public.'[4] This despite Konrad Lorenz encouraging the ethologist to cultivate 'a playful interest in animals'. Play is natural in the healthy young of all mammals, whether they be human or other mammalian young. Even non-mammals, such as baby birds, exhibit playful behaviour. (Insects do not seem to play, although I would not be too sure about it.) Yet adult humans, most of whom enjoyed playing when they were young, seem to have little appreciation of the value of play. The play of young nonhuman animals is even more frequent and more hearty than that of human children. Although *Homo sapiens* is the only species known to fashion objects for use in play by its offspring,[5] when it comes to sheer delight in play, the human might take lessons from the dog. Erik Zimen once watched five young wild wolves play almost without interruption for five hours at a lake in British Columbia. The wolves chased each other back and forth across the beach, jaw-wrestled, played 'king of the castle' on a large stone in the water, and occasionally broke to play-bite each other or play with objects.[6]

Sometimes it is not easy for me to distinguish between a game or something more sinister that my dogs are playing. When I go running in the morning at the Berkeley Marina, Leila often comes along and we walk together for a few minutes before I announce that I am going to run. As soon as I take off, the dogs come with me, but after a few steps they stop and look back at Leila, then at me. They seem perplexed. They run another few feet, then, as if they have made up their minds, they return to Leila and walk with her while I continue my run. Leila tells me that they remain constantly alert, watching every runner who resembles me (blue running shorts, cut-off T shirt) and running after him, only to return to her in disappointment. At the end of my thirty-minute run Leila and I meet at a designated spot. Once the dogs see me, or hear me (I call to them softly), they begin running toward me with complete abandon and joy. I have returned, I am back as part of the pack. Are they teasing me and themselves, or are they genuinely worried that I have left for good? I simply cannot tell. It could be a game, or it could be the depths of anxiety for them.

Their emotions seem so genuine: complete puzzlement when I leave; pure joy when I return. I would give a great deal to enter the world of their emotions and know for certain what it is they feel.

Where we have toys, dogs have the entire natural world at their disposal. It is interesting that children are fine when left on their own, unconstrained by adult notions of what is sanitary and proper play. They gravitate to the outdoors and find, just as dogs do, an infinite number of natural toys. Dogs chase twigs and leaves and their own tails and drops of water and butterflies; they leap into the air and burrow in the sand, dig holes and throw themselves into waves. Which child does not engage in such behaviour as well? Perhaps this is why children and puppies can play together for hours on end in a garden or on the beach. They play in almost exactly the same way.

Animal behaviourists have found play to be a sign of physical and mental well-being in an animal. The kind of play engaged in is indicative of the state of the animal in general. Ethologists have noted 'defective, fragmentary, regressive or infrequent play in orphaned, handicapped, injured, or seriously ill primate infants'.[7] When the play is robust, complete, age-appropriate and frequent, it indicates that the youngster is thriving. Such play is also an indication that the young animal is capable of love, because play is a forum for friendship. Through play, bonds are forged; and continued interaction serves to deepen the bonds.

Moreover, play that is not stereotypical (by stereotypical I mean that it displays no deviation from a fixed pattern),[8] play that encourages use of the imagination, promotes psychological and physical health. For both humans and other animals, much that happens in play is 'pretend'. Play allows us to engage in behaviour that extends beyond the scope of our ordinary life experience. Normally deceptive behaviour is considered objectionable, but deception is often an element in play. Dogs engage in what has been described as cunning or imaginative behaviour in play: they feint; they pretend to go one way and then quickly change direction; they play dead, then leap up. This kind of deception is entirely acceptable to dogs. Usually when a dog looks directly into the eyes of another dog, it is a sign of aggression, a challenge. If the other dog stares back, a fight will ensue. In play, however, dogs stare at each other constantly. This is part of the fun, a reversal of the normal order of things. In play, when a dog stares, it signifies the opposite of what it means in the real world. By this simple manoeuvre, dogs are able to reverse their world. John Paul Scott discovered that playful and serious aggressiveness are not necessarily correlated.[9] A dog that is playfully aggressive is more often than not completely peaceful and friendly in 'real-world' encounters, whereas an aggressive dog is not always willing to play, even when play is rough.

This kind of reversal may be the dog's idea of a sense of humour. Play is undoubtedly connected to humour, and dogs display it in abundance. R. D. Lawrence begins his book *In Praise of Wolves* with an encounter with a wolf who teased and played with him. He notes: '. . . he stopped to inspect me again, his eyes still reflecting that gleam of puckish humour which is so characteristic of wolves who love to tease and do so frequently.'[10] Thomas Mann, in *A Man and his Dog* (1918), wrote:

> Or we amuse each other in that I flick him upon the nose, whilst he snaps at my hand as at a fly. This forces both of us to laugh, yes, even Bashan must laugh. This laugh of his – to which I must instinctively respond, is for me the most wonderful and touching thing in the world. It is unutterably moving to see how his haggard canine cheek and the corners of his mouth quiver and jerk to the excitement of the teasing, how the dusky mien of the dumb creature takes on the physiognomic expression of human laughter . . .[11]

Roger Caras tells the story of Biddie, a black poodle with whom he had worked out a vaudeville routine: she would sit on his lap with her forepaws on his chest and he would say: 'Brigitte, Petite Noire, look into my eyes. You are getting sleepy, you are falling asleep.' She would close her eyes and flop her head against his chest as if in a trance. People never failed to laugh, and even she seemed to see the joke. In fact she would demand to do it again and again until she was banished from the room. Caras comments: 'Anyone who saw that little poodle and didn't think she had a sense of humor didn't have one themselves. It existed in her every posture, her every move, very nearly.'[12]

All dogs tease one another and enjoy being teased by humans.

They tease back. The facial expression during teasing is slightly different from that during play; it seems a little less relaxed, as if the dog were getting away with something. It is another example of role reversal, a way of showing play-dominance, where the dominance lasts for only so long as the play itself.[13] When dogs deceive, they tease, which is different from cheating. Dogs do not take advantage of play to hurt one another deliberately. The same cannot be said of all human play.

Sasha weighs 80 pounds and is by far the most powerful of our three dogs. When the three play together, Sasha often reverses roles, to make it more fun, and allows herself to be chased even though she is much faster. She deliberately handicaps herself, even slowing down to allow the other two dogs to get closer or to catch her. When I first saw her do this, I thought I was observing something unique. Then I discovered that it is very common behaviour among many mammals. Apes do it all the time. The primatologist S. A. Altmann notes that a set of conventions exists through which play in monkeys is made reciprocal and fair.[14] Marc Bekoff analyses these conventions for dogs. I wonder if, in fact, all animals who play have similar signals or conventions?

The play-fighting my dogs engage in can become somewhat alarming to watch. They grab each other by the skin of the neck and move their heads back and forth with what seems enough vigour to break the other dog's neck.[15] When I first observed this, I intervened, afraid that the play would get out of hand and lead to real aggression. It never did, and after a while I saw that the bites and the shaking were not dangerous and were in fact self-inhibited. The dogs knew what they were doing. I did not understand that these actions, which in other circumstances would be taken as hostile, were play here. To stare directly at another dog is the prelude to a fight, or at least the threat of one, but in play the direct stare functions more as a joke. Dogs have even been observed to cover their teeth with their lips when playing, to ensure that no harm is done. It also appears that dogs know how vulnerable the body is, and how easy it is to hurt, even in play. I notice that in a tug of war with a neutral object, both dogs are more aggressive than they would be with one another's bodies.

In *A Dog is Listening*, Roger Caras tells the story of Sirius, a greyhound who owed his rescue to his ability to smile. 'He rolls his lips back and shows his teeth in a big wide smile. He does it to greet you, he does it when he is about to get a cookie, he does it when you ask him to.' The veterinarian, who was forced to put to sleep 21 healthy greyhounds, balked at putting down Sirius: 'How do you kill a dog that smiles at you every time you come near him with a syringe?'[16] The English naturalist, Brian Vesey-Fitzgerald, describes one of his dogs as coming up 'wagging, wriggling, and grinning, smiling, so to speak, all over his body'.[17] In play, subordination, submission, hierarchy, and all the other distinctions normally operative in dog society perform a different role. Play confers a freedom that is not available in any other realm of a dog's life. No wonder they enjoy it and want to engage in it so often.

How do dogs communicate that what they are doing is play and not to be interpreted by conventional rules of behaviour? Marc Bekoff has discovered certain acts that function like punctuation marks in grammar. They signal that everything to follow is part of a special discourse, play. That is what the dog's 'play-bow' is: a means of letting the other dog know that what he is about to see is governed by a different set of rules, the rules of play. To announce this, a dog puts that happy look on its face – with mouth open, tongue relaxed, eyes shining (this is known technically as the 'open-mouth play face'[18]) – and then lifts up its hind quarters, puts the front paws slightly apart, and begins to wag its tail furiously. How could the meaning possibly be misunderstood? The dog is saying, 'Let's play!'

I have seen dogs refuse to respond to a play-bow, but I have never seen a dog mistake the intention. Why is it that humans have far greater trouble reading one another's signals? Is it because we engage too often in irony and sarcasm, both of which seem absent from a dog's emotional vocabulary?

An interesting feature of dogs' play is the pause that takes place between play bouts. The sign is unmistakable, the pauses are kept so short that mistakes are not made. Dogs tend to look away during the pauses so that a direct stare, now part of normal life, is not mistaken for real aggression.

Many animals play and we do not recognise it as such. When dogs play, however, there can be no doubt. Even so, some people believe that their dogs are *always* playing, even when they draw blood; others will not permit their dogs to romp on the grounds that such behaviour is only disguised aggression. Bruno Bettelheim's theory about aggression in children is considered the ultimate criterion for this latter type of behaviour. He believed that the excuse 'I was only playing' was not acceptable. He decided when the aggression was unconscious, hidden, or covert. Analysts do this all the time. But dogs do not seem to engage in playful fighting that is really a disguise or a cover for real fighting. They do not deceive one another in this manner. Whether in the real world or in the imaginary world that dogs create when they play, dogs are honest and straightforward.

Erasmus Darwin, the grandfather of Charles Darwin, wanted to counter the old notion that animals had no rights because they could not make contracts:

> Does not daily observation convince us that they form contracts of friendship with each other, [and] with mankind? When puppies and kittens play together, is there not a tacit contract that they will not hurt each other? And does not your favourite dog expect you should give him his daily food, for his services and attention to you?[19]

CHAPTER TWELVE

Cats and Dogs

IN 1845, Charles Darwin was miles from any human habitation, riding in the Argentine Pampas, when he noticed flocks of sheep guarded by a single dog. This special guard dog had been raised with sheep, sucking from a ewe and sleeping in the sheep pen on a bed of wool. The dog was castrated and became 'senior ram' in the flock, with the sheep trailing after him. In the evening, he would return to the house to be fed, the sheep following. Other than the evening feeding, he had no contact whatever with humans. The other dogs of the house would turn on him and pursue him until he reached his flock of sheep, at which point he would turn and the dogs would flee. They would not attack the sheep while the dog was with them. Why? Darwin wrote:

> The shepherd-dog ranks the sheep as its fellow-brethren, and
> thus gains confidence; and the wild dogs, though knowing that
> the individual sheep are not dogs, but are good to eat, yet partly

consent to this view when seeing them in a flock with a shepherd-dog at their head.[1]

What unspoken code of moral behaviour governs this remarkable observation of the wild dogs restraining themselves from attacking sheep because a shepherd-dog is amongst the herd? A sceptic might argue that it is merely territorial, but it seems more complicated than that, as Darwin's use of the word 'consent' implies.

As I was growing up, our dogs and cats were raised together. The first time I heard the phrase 'fighting like cats and dogs' (which goes back to the fifteenth century) I did not know what it meant, as my cats and dogs never fought. In Toronto, where I first acquired Misha, a standard poodle, we already had a wise alley cat called Megals. Misha would grab Megals by the neck and bounce her down the stairs. When they got to the bottom, Misha would lie down and begin gnawing on Megal's neck. The first time I witnessed this I ran up to them, terrified that Megals was being murdered, but as I drew closer I heard what sounded like an idling Porsche engine: Megals was purring in ecstasy. Even when they were adults, Misha would grab Megals by the neck and shake her. Megals would let herself go limp and clearly enjoyed the sensation. Both animals knew it was a game. To my surprise, Sima does this to my tabby Saj, who responds in the same way as Megals did.

What does it mean, this interspecies play that so resembles predator-prey behaviour? Received wisdom tells us that dogs and cats are descended from entirely different wild progenitors. Dogs belong to a social species and therefore form friendships, while cats belong to a solitary species and do not. Traditionally, it was believed that tigers were entirely solitary creatures, but recent evidence indicates that we simply may not have been around to observe their frequent encounters. Who knows what friends tigers make in the jungle when nobody is present to record it?

Billy Arjan Singh has lived in intimate contact with tigers and leopards for the last thirty-five years on a remote farm at the edge of the jungle in Uttar Pradesh, close to the Indian border with Nepal. He brought into his house a remarkable little mongrel dog, Eelie, who became a close companion to three of Arjan Singh's leopards, as well as the fast growing tigress he called Tara. As adults the large cats not only tolerated the small dog, but played with her and never hurt her. The pictures in his book, *Eelie and the Big Cats*, show the kind of astonishing trust that can develop between species one would ordinarily expect to be only enemies with one another.[2]

It is clear that dogs and cats enjoy pretending – that they are eating their prey and that they are being devoured by a predator. Both know this is play, and both know the boundaries. Sometimes, Sima will play too rough, and Raj will yowl in protest and end the game. I have also observed that Saj prefers playing with Sima to playing with me. True, Sima may be too rough, but she must also be more fun, for I cannot engage Saj in the same way.

I have asked other dog caretakers who have cats whether they have noticed anything similar. Most of them have. Dogs like chewing on cat necks, and cats enjoy being chewed.

This mock predator/prey game is not something that, to my knowledge, anyone has observed in the wild – which does not mean it does not happen. What enables a cat and dog, two completely different species, to engage in such complex interaction as pretend slaughter, and why do they enjoy it? To answer the second question first: I have not seen cats play this game with one another, nor have I seen dogs play it with other dogs. It is precisely that they are different species, a fact of which they are somehow aware, that allows them to engage in this play. I think they enjoy it because they know it is fantasy; it is unreal. They are taking pleasure in their powers of imagination, in the ability to recognise how very odd it is for two separate species to play with one another. That may seem far-fetched, but I know that I love watching dogs and cats play because it thrills me to see this complex interaction across the species barrier. I can imagine that cats and dogs enjoy engaging in this action for much the same reason.

The mystery writers Frances and Richard Lockridge, in their book *Cats and People*, note that 'Man's conscience is uneasy; if cats and dogs think, they may think about man and, since they have many opportunities to observe him, this possibility is disquieting.'[3] Just as we can ask, 'Who do dogs think we are?', I think we can ask the same question of dogs with respect to cats. What does a cat represent to a dog? Into what category does a cat fit? Koko, a captive Lowland gorilla who was taught sign language, was able to sign 'cat' and even had a pet kitten.[4] Yet nobody asked her what a cat was. The category of 'pet' is reserved for humans. Other animals form friendships. Dogs and cats are often friends, but dogs do not think of cats as their pets. While we might be tempted to say that cats don't think about dogs at all, in fact they must. Cats distinguish carefully and precisely between those dogs who are friendly and those who are dangerous. I believe that many animals categorise other animals or other species, but just how refined and how many gradations there are in these categories, nobody knows.

As for what enables cats and dogs to engage in this kind of behaviour, it must have something to do with early socialisation. I have not heard of an older dog and an older cat, introduced into the same household, enacting this kind of intimate play. They must be raised together to develop the kind of mutual trust presupposed in the game.[5]

When Sima was very small and was first introduced to the cats, I discovered she was secretly doing a terrible thing: she was biting off Saj's whiskers, as neatly as if it were done with a razor. It felt as if the cat had a rough beard. This could be life-threatening for a cat, for cats use their whiskers to determine whether a space is large enough for their body, and without whiskers they could find themselves wedged and immobilised in a tight space. This was no game; Sima was just chewing everything she could get her teeth on, and for some odd reason, the kitten allowed it to happen. But while it was not play, neither was it dangerous aggression. It was a curious diversion that had evolved out of mutual trust.

This mutual trust that develops between cats and dogs when they live together is strangely satisfying to observe. Often my three dogs will sleep in a great tangle with the two cats. Yesterday, for instance, Sasha had placed her long nose lovingly over Raj's belly, and with Saj snuggled up to them, all three were sound asleep. This night-time co-habiting goes against expectations: after all, natural enemies do not sleep together. On the other hand, the dogs seem to feel a kind of deference for the cats. When Sasha goes into her den to sleep and finds the cat curled up in the middle of it, she backs out, rather than bump the cat out of the way as she does to the other dogs. She then goes to sleep at the entrance to the den, allowing the cat to sleep undisturbed.

She also seems to have infinite patience when it comes to being bothered by the cats. If Sasha is eating, she does not allow the other dogs near her bowl, but Raj can walk right up to her and begin munching on Sasha's food, while Sasha looks on with a quizzical but tolerant air. Or Saj will swat Sasha's nose, trying to get her to play when she is not in the mood. Sasha never loses her temper, though it is clear that she wishes Saj would stop. I wonder if she would be embarrassed to behave in this way in front of her dog friends, as if she knows that she might be found ridiculous by them. The cat is treated more like a child than like another dog.

Cats are the other great domesticated species besides dogs, but their form of domestication is quite different. Cats live in close proximity with humans, but they are by no means subservient, leading their own lives without being dominated. They can, as the classic *The Tiger in the House* says, 'revert to the wild state with less readjustment of values than any other domestic animal'.[6] Studies of feral cats living in the wild, as discussed in *The Wildlife of the Domestic Cat* by Roger Tabor,[7] reveal that the household cat differs little in its behaviour from cats living wild. Maurice Maeterlinck believed that to the cat 'we are nothing more than a too large and uneatable prey: the ferocious cat, whose sidelong contempt tolerates us only as encumbering parasites in our own homes'.[8]

This judgment may sound harsh, but there is little doubt that cats do not give their love to us as freely and completely as dogs do. Yet I have never believed that the world has to be divided into the two distinct classifications of dog-lovers and cat-lovers; I am both. Carl van Vechten refutes the usual banality by beginning his classic book, *The Tiger in the House*, with the following words: 'As James Branch Cabell has conveniently pointed out for all time, "to the philosophical mind it would seem equally sensible to decline to participate in a game of billiards on the ground that one was fond of herring".'[9]

It can scarcely be denied that cats tolerate us, whereas dogs adore us. To me the question to ask is whether dogs and cats love each other. Judging by the number of trustworthy stories of dogs and cats who not only form intimate friendships but who mourn one another's deaths, I would venture to say it is probable. It has been suggested that kittens and puppies play together for hours because of their immaturity; they are not yet aware that they belong to different species. On the other hand, many people report lasting and intense friendships between mature cats and dogs, for whom there can be no question of confusion of identity. However, these friendships seem to be very particular and individual. It does not appear as if dogs make the abstract connection between their household cat and other cats. They neither consider other cats the enemy, nor are they friendly merely because they belong to the same category of animal as their friend at home.

Most dogs chase cats. I do not think it is serious predatory behaviour. Dogs will chase just about anything that runs, especially smaller animals, such as rabbits or squirrels. Whenever I take my dogs for a walk around the block, the cats wait in the driveway for our return, when the dogs will chase them back into the house. It is all a game, as it is when they chase other cats in the neighbourhood. On the rare occasion when my dogs actually corner a strange cat, they look about, bewildered. They clearly do not know what to do with it.

When I first acquired my standard poodle, Misha, she greatly enjoyed chasing cats, and I decided to use some aversion therapy. So one day I took her to the entrance to a pet shop and told her that there was a cat inside and she should chase it. She became very excited, and I released her, having previously arranged with the owner to keep his large black panther in a cage in the store. Misha reached the cage and saw the 'cat', who did a panther's version of hissing. The poodle went racing out of the store at quite extraordinary speed. She never again chased another cat! According to Laurens van der Post, in his book *A Story Like the Wind*, dogs are generally not afraid of leopards: 'The trouble was that no self-respecting dog ever could see any reason why it should be afraid of a leopard. A leopard was hardly any bigger than itself and, in any case, was a species of cat which no dog could be expected to respect. When they found themselves faced with a leopard, the dogs had no hesitation in rushing to the attack.'

While I was observing rescued greyhounds, I was told that about half of them were inveterate cat-chasers, no doubt because they were trained to race with live rabbits as bait, and that some of them will even kill the cats when they catch them. Is it possible for a dog to love a cat at home and to kill one in the street? I doubt it. I would be deeply shocked if Sasha were suddenly to turn against either of my cats and bite with the intention of causing harm. I cannot believe it could ever happen. Chimps may go to war, and adolescent dolphins may force their sexual attention on females eager to get away from them, but no animals slaughter each other the way that people do. Can we not learn, as dogs evidently have, that it is possible to live with members of another species without destroying them, eating them, exploiting them or disdaining them?

CHAPTER THIRTEEN

Dogs and Wolves

'THE WHOLE CONTINENT was one continuing dismal wilderness, the haunt of wolves and bears and more savage men
. . . Now the forests are removed, the land covered with fields of corn, orchards bending with fruit and the magnificent habitations of rational civilized people,' wrote John Adams in 1756, revealing some of the common prejudices of the time. He should have added 'dogs', for where once wolves roamed, we now live with our dogs. Many dog caretakers have wondered – perhaps after watching dogs fight if the dog is really a wolf. Actually, it is the reverse: a wolf is a large wild dog, the original dog, as L. David Mech, the foremost authority on wolves, puts it.[1]

Somewhere between ten and twenty thousand years ago, humans domesticated dogs from wolves.[2] Every dog – from the tiniest miniature dachshund to the gentle giant Newfoundland and St Bernard – are descended from a wolf-like ancestor. There are more than 400 breeds of dogs in the world today and all belong

137

to one species, named *Canis familiaris* by Linnaeus in 1758. The dog is closely related to the wolf, the coyote, *Canis latrans*, and the jackal, *Canus aureus*, especially the golden jackal. Other members of the canid family, such as the fox, *Vulpes Vulpes*, the African hunting dog, *Lycaon pictus*, and the Indian red dog, *Cuon alpinus*, are more distantly related.[3]

How different are dogs from wolves? John Paul Scott claims 'there is strong evidence that every basic behaviour pattern found in dogs is also found in wolves. This means that, in spite of the centuries of selection practiced on dogs, nothing really new in the way of behaviour has been developed.'[4] Peter Steinhart, the author of *In the Company of Wolves*,[5] told me in an interview that although wolves behave like dogs, the opposite is not true. There are many things a wolf does that a dog does not do. Asked what they were, Peter told me that a wolf is more serious than a dog. They give you the feeling that they have a sense of purpose. They walk unwavering down a path where a dog will flit off to the side or become easily distracted. A wolf, to survive, needs to know many things. Dogs just need to know us. The wolf has a relationship to the landscape that is far more profound than anything seen in a dog. For a dog, *we* are their landscape. What they need, they get from us. The wolf must be studious and stay focused. Where the dog learns, obeys and copies, a wolf has insight. A wolf is attuned to all kinds of signals – to the song of birds and the subtle scents of plant and animal drifting on the wind – and these signals tell it where to look for prey or competing predators.

He quotes a conversation with Dr Harry Frank, Professor of Psychology at Michigan State University, who had a female wolf pup from a Chicago zoo: 'It's much more advantageous [for the dog] to develop a very keen understanding of human behaviour and to communicate wishes to a human, because the human is the most important feature of the environment, and we give a lot of visual and auditory cues.' Steinhart comments: 'Evolution hasn't honed the dog's problem-solving skills, just its people-reading skills.'

There are other differences between dogs and wolves. For instance, male wolves mature sexually much later. L. David Mech, the wolf scholar, says that 'in terms of its hormones, a wolf is not fully mature – comparable to a human of about 25 years of age –

until about five years of age'. Most dogs reach maturity by seven months. Female wolves go into a heat cycle only once a year; dogs do so every seven months on average. The St Bernard, often twice the size of a large wolf, has smaller teeth and jaws than the wolf. Dogs lack the tail gland of the wolf.

While monogamy among wolves has been somewhat exaggerated, they do not display the sexual promiscuity of most dogs. Could this have anything to do with the fact that their brains are 30 per cent larger than those of dogs? Harry Frank raised both wolves and dogs as companion animals. By watching humans open a door, wolves quickly learned how to turn the knob. His dogs never did.[6] I have been told that the brains of dogs weigh about the same in all breeds, whether it be a Chihuahua or a Newfoundland, despite the enormous body size differential. In the wolf, it is only those parts of the brain that deal with sensory perception which are larger; the more primitive brain, the centre of the emotions, remains the same in dogs and wolves.

By domesticating the wolf into a dog, we have not improved upon the wolf's physique: hip dysplasia and probably most canine genetic defects are non-existent in pure wolves. Neither have we improved canid conversation. While wolves sometimes give short sharp barks in warning, only dogs bark all day (or all night) long. Wolves will take care of sick, injured or old wolves. As far as I know, dogs, when they form feral packs, do so only rarely.

Wolves form a hierarchy that governs a great deal of their everyday behaviour. The alpha wolf, head of the pack, displays physiological characteristics that separate him from lower ranking wolves. For instance, he has a higher heart rate, presumably because of the responsibility which accompanies his role as leader and the concomitant stress. We often see remnants of this in dogs, but it is much attenuated and subject to great variation. In part this is due to the humans who replace the alpha animal being so inconsistent that dogs are perpetually confused about rank. The positive effect is that dogs become very forgiving. A mistake with a wolf is neither forgotten nor forgiven, and to hit a wolf even once means to forfeit any relationship with that animal. Free-roaming dogs follow a leader, usually the largest male, but his role is temporary, just as is the life of the pack as a whole.[7]

139

As has often been observed in this book, the dog is perpetually juvenile, for which it is selected and bred. A wolf behaves like a cub for only as long as it is one, which is why a wolf cannot be truly tamed. As a wolf cub behaves towards its parents for a short period of its life, so a dog behaves towards us for the whole of his or her life.

Apart from these differences, which within the full context of personality are rather slight, the behaviour of dogs and wolves is almost identical. Erik Zimen, a wolf specialist who studies wolves in Germany, and who has raised many wolves and wolf-hybrids, has said that there is no single element of dog behaviour known to him that is not also present in the wolf.[8] Indeed, as I was reading about wolves, the similarity seemed so striking at times that I believed I was reading about my own dogs. Sima, for example, greets people she has not seen for some time in a very distinctive manner: she squeals, licks, rolls over, her tail wagging rapidly the entire time. John Fentress found that his hand-reared wolf behaves in much the same way: 'Persons he had met before were greeted enthusiastically, even if they had not seen him for several weeks. The typical pattern consisted of many high squeaks, much tail-wagging, slightly lowered haunches accompanying approach, pawing, licking, and rolling on his back.'[9] We should remember that tail-wagging in dogs begins at a very early age and continues for as long as the dog lives. 'It has no function other than a social one, and in all these respects is much like the human smile.'[10]

Many of the qualities we love in dogs are found in wolves: Michael Fox writes that 'acceptance, forgiveness, loyalty, truthfulness and openness, devotion, and unquestioning, unconditional love are traits found in a family of wolves, the dog's pure cousin, uncontaminated by human interference'.[11] This is how a wolf behaves toward members of its family. We love dogs because they behave in this way toward us. In spite of the stories of wolves raising abandoned small children (probably a fantasy that is characteristic of our species), a human could never really become a member of a wolf pack. With dogs, however, we are the pack; that is, the pack is complete as soon as a human being joins it.[12] Just as the alpha wolf in a wild pack is deferred to and makes all the major decisions, such as where and when to hunt and rest, so dogs defer to us. As the persistent myth of the wild child raised by wolves shows, people can become mystical at the thought of being part of a wild pack. There are even reports of wolf cults. Part of the pleasure of being around dogs is a sense that we are participating in rituals that go back to atavistic pack behaviour. Living with a dog is much like living with a very tame wolf, without the dangers. There is a kind of honour in walking down the street with a dog. I feel it when I run with Sima, Sasha and Rani. We are like a small pack in which I am the alpha male. It is quite an odd sensation.

This is perhaps less surprising when one considers in how many ways wolves and humans are alike. We are social animals, even pack animals; we reflexively seek out hierarchal order; we are both at the top of the food chain. Wolves have no natural enemies other than man, and humans once hunted in much the same way as wolves do. We use sounds and postures to communicate with one another; we care for our young; we are physically symmetrical, and at times we are aggressive toward our own kind. But then, which mammal is not like this? We are probably more like prairie dogs than we care to admit.

Even a wolf's facial expressions are similar to ours and not difficult to read: the alert and happy face, the friendly grin, the closed eyes as a sign of pure pleasure. The friendly submissive face, and the submissive grin (with the ears back), first identified by Rudolf Shenckel,[13] an early expert on wolves, do not require much learning, unlike the facial expressions, say, of the grey-lag goose, which Konrad Lorenz learned to read accurately over the years.

Like us, wolves have lived just about everywhere on the planet, from Saudi Arabia and Central India to the Arctic Ocean, from Japan to Greenland, Europe to North America and Mexico. They are, just as we are, habitat generalists; that is, they can be found wherever there is food and water.

Peter Steinhart writes: 'Wolves are an essential likeness to ourselves, a mirror in which we can examine ourselves as we can with no other creature. We see in them reflections of our good or evil, our own selfless love and our own perplexing violence. We see ourselves as we are and as we might be.'[14]

Such similarities should not be exaggerated, however, because in truth we still know very little about the behaviour of wild wolves. They are elusive, and observing them up close has proved difficult. Just to see a wolf in the wild is a rare event. As a result, it is not entirely clear how a wolf pack is formed in the wild; usually it consists of litter mates, but sometimes a stranger is accepted, and to date nobody knows the basis for such acceptance into the pack. Is it merely that certain wolves are liked and not others, or are there obscure entrance requirements about which we know nothing? The same cloud hovers over our understanding of how dogs distinguish among their peers. I am constantly puzzled to see Sima, Sasha and Rani take to some dogs immediately and become definitely hostile or indifferent to others. I have never succeeded in understanding the reasons for these seemingly arbitrary decision – yet another indication that animals have hidden complexities, just as we do.

We have spent more than 10,000 years taking the wolf out of the dog, and now we sometimes wonder if this was not misguided. People who own wolf-hybrids do so because they admire the wolf in the dog, the original behaviour of a wild animal. Some of this wild behaviour, absent in dogs,[15] is indeed praiseworthy. Researchers who have attempted to socialise wolves to human beings have noticed that, when they were successful, the wolves did not revert to wild behaviour, even after a year of no direct human handling. The hypothesis is that wolves are able to utilise their innate friendliness and generalise it to all humans who act appropriately toward them. Their extreme gregariousness allows them to behave in a friendly manner to all people, not just humans they know. Dogs cannot always do this, and we find some dogs who always remain 'one person' dogs. Unlike a dog, however, a wolf cannot generalise 'my family' to another wolf family, which dogs on the other hand seem to do easily. Witness the friendliness dogs exhibit to other dogs in the park. The point is that while wolves can be friendly towards all humans but not other wolves, dogs can be friendly to all dogs but not all humans.

In her book *Adam's Task*, Vicki Hearne points out that a wolf 'will not have the courage of a good dog, the courage that springs from the dog's commitments to the forms and significance of our domestic virtues. The wolf's xenophobia remains his own. With other wolves he may, of course, be respectful, noble, courageous and courteous. The wolf has wolfish social skills, but he has no human social skills, which is why we say that a wolf is a wild animal. And since human beings have for all practical purposes no wolfish social skills, the wolf regards the human being as a wild animal, and the wolf is correct. He doesn't trust us, with perfectly good reason.'[16]

Dogs have been with us for so long now that many of their behavioural traits are practically human ones. We have selected them. If we ignore this fact, then we err, as Konrad Lorenz did when he distinguished between 'aureus-dogs' and 'wolf-dogs'. He suggested that breeds which tended to be friendly towards everyone were descended from the jackal (*Canis aureus*), while those that accepted only one master were descended from the wolf (*Canis lupus*). For Lorenz, the 'jackal-dog' was childish and submissive, regarding his 'master' as a cross between a father and a god, whereas the 'wolf-dog' is neither submissive nor obedient, and treats his master more as a colleague. The bond is stronger and far less transferable to another person. Clearly this is the kind of dog Lorenz preferred.[17]

Lorenz later recognised he was wrong. For whereas wolves and dogs are highly social animals, 'jackals, like coyotes, ordinarily form groups no larger than a mated pair'. Moreover, the vocalisations of dogs and wolves are very similar, whereas those of the jackal contain far more complex patterns. The information about vocalisation convinced Lorenz, who evidently withdrew his hypothesis of jackal ancestry.[18] None the less, as Dr Ian Dunbar points out, 'It is impossible to say for certain that jackals, coyotes and other wild *Canidae* play no part [in the domestication of the dog], especially since it is known that the jackal still breeds freely with pariah, shenzi and dingo-like dogs, in much the same way that some northern breeds, such as Huskies and Malamutes, may be backcrossed with wolves.'[19]

I have never heard Sima, Sasha or Rani howl, but my standard poodle, Misha, did so frequently. Many people have heard their dogs howl, and it is somewhat eerie, as well as simultaneously thrilling and unnerving. To the best of my knowledge, dog howls have not been the subject of any study. Wolf howls, on the other hand, have been investigated in some depth, and we continue to learn about their complexity. The wolf's howl advertises and maintains its territorial boundaries and even acts as a spacing mechanism to keep wolf packs from intruding on each other. Wolves need a lot of space to survive. It is amazing how far the howl carries. I am assured that, on quiet nights, a single howl can announce a pack's presence over an area of from 50 to 140 square miles.[20] Only a highly social species howls. It is common to the dingo, the African hunting dog, the dhole and the timber wolf. The howl, which often serves as a signature tune, also conveys the precise mood of the howler, as Desmond Morris points out. He notes that the only time a domestic dog howls is when it is forcibly shut away on its own. This 'howl of loneliness' is a way of saying 'join me'.[21] Lone wolves also howl for company; they howl to call other wolves, to let the den pups know they are returning from a hunt, and for the sheer joy of being together.

Just as a 'dog is not a four-legged and childish human being dressed up in a fur coat',[22] so also should we avoid the error of thinking that a wolf is simply a dog with a rougher coat. Although the dog has evolved from the wolf, there is an enormous difference between a domesticated and a wild animal. Even a wild animal that has been tamed, and still retains its instincts, can revert to its wild state without warning. Many people seem unaware of this. I remember my daughter coming home from school one day some fifteen years ago and telling me that her teacher was offering wolf-puppies to good homes. She wanted to know if we could we take one. I was very tempted, until I called Charles Berger, a veterinarian in Berkeley who is an expert on wolves. He warned me in most emphatic terms against the idea. Since then, I have read of terrible tragedies which have befallen people who took in wolves.

No matter how much time is spent with a wolf pup, their socialisation to humans will always be tenuous. A tame wolf is not a dog: 'Tame wolves remain handleable by the person who bottle-fed them as infants, but they may become quite timid and sometimes aggressive towards strangers once the age of six months is reached . . . a few generations of breeding within human confines will not erase the wolf's wild instincts. To domesticate the wolf would take about 10,000 years.'[23]

There appears to be no documented case of a healthy, non-rabid North American wolf in the wild seriously attacking a human being. For some reason, the wolf respects (or perhaps has learned to fear) humans. It has been claimed that the European wolf (especially in Russia) has attacked people, but this has been questioned. Perhaps the attacking wolves were wolf/dog hybrids. The Scandinavian countries have very few real wolves but tell many tales of the danger of wolves. Erkki Pulliainen writes: 'No evidence showing that wolves are dangerous to human beings has been obtained in Finland during this century. In spite of this, man's hostility towards the wolf has remained almost unchanged in the Finnish countryside.'[24] Nevertheless there is immense variety within every species, and that must include the temperamental variety. If this is so with humans, why shouldn't it be true of wolves? One is tempted to imagine a mother wolf trying to inculcate a fear of all men in her young after she had been shot at once and the cub objecting on the grounds of a friendship he has established with the son of the hunter.

Some people believe that by owning a wolf-hybrid, they will somehow contribute to the rehabilitation of the wolf, or they themselves will come closer to living with a wild animal. The former is untrue, and the latter true, which is precisely the problem. Most people who have hybrids experience serious problems with them by the time the animals are three, notes Randall Lockwood, vice president of the Humane Society of the United States. Richard Polsky has also warned potential owners of wolf-hybrids not to 'be lulled into a false sense of security because of the hybrid's friendly demeanor to family members. . . . Strong predatory tendencies are part of a hybrid's nature, thereby making it a potentially dangerous animal to keep as a pet in an urban environment.'[25]

Even sophisticated owners experience sudden and unexpected attacks from their pets. A biologist and champion of wolves, Beth Duman, used to take her female pure wolf to schools to teach children just how lovely wolves really were. She and her husband had the wolf for four years. One spring afternoon they were in the backyard pen, petting and scratching her, when without any warning she pushed Beth's husband against the fence and sank her canines deep into his forearm. The husband had hurt his lower back, and was limping on the day he went into the pen. Probably the wolf had seen this and that was all it needed to provoke the challenge, just as it would challenge another wolf. She notes that most of her friends who keep wolves have told her of similar experiences.[26]

Since wolves do not attack humans in the wild, it is odd to think that the aggression in wolf-hybrids comes from the dog element, not the wolf element. Captivity, on the other hand, alters behaviour profoundly. Almost anyone who has ever kept a wolf agrees that wolves are not the best animal to have in captivity. Many people were tempted to keep them, I think, by the extraordinary book by Lois Crisler, *Arctic Wild,* which is probably the most eloquent account of wolves living with humans. It is a very romantic book, and it should be read in conjunction with her second book, cited far less often: *Captive Wild.* Crisler took her wolves and wolf-hybrids to Colorado, with tragic results. All the wolves and hybrids died untimely deaths – some were run over, others were shot, and some had to be put to sleep. One has an almost palpable sense of the chaos they brought to Crisler's life and the destruction she brought to theirs, even though she was trying to keep them from the certain death they would have suffered if she had simply released them in the Arctic. They were no longer purely wild animals, and would not have survived. Terry Jenkins, curator at the Folsom City Zoo in California, had a wolf-hybrid that was affectionate and appeared to love babies and women, but had attempted none the less to kill her. She tried to establish herself as his superior and failed: the hybrid lunged at her and bit her repeatedly in the chest, going for her throat.[27]

Peter Steinhart ends his book *In The Company of Wolves* by noting: 'The wolf was once widely seen as a symbol of the depravity of wildness; it is now to many a symbol of the nobility of nature. Largely by the use of symbols, we nearly eradicated the wolf. Largely by manipulating symbols, we may yet save it.'[28]

Another possible source for our new-found love of the wolf comes from a continuing deeper appreciation which occurs when we observe the wolf-like behaviour of our dogs. Wolves may not love us, but dogs clearly do. For once, humanity seems to have hurdled the species-barrier. It has never happened before with any other species. It is one of the great mysteries of nature: we have become a part of the intimate world of dogs.

CHAPTER FOURTEEN

Canine Aggression: Real or Feigned?

LINDA GRAY SEXTON, the novelist, breeds, owns and shows Dalmatians. She told me a story that makes a good entry point into a discussion of aggression in dogs.[1] Rhiannon, her first Dalmatian, came to her when the dog was a year old. Rhiannon had lived with a breeder as a show prospect and, like the other dogs in the household, was crated for up to twenty-two hours each day. As the bottom dog in the pack she enjoyed few privileges. When she moved to Linda's home, her life was transformed, she was the centre of attention, loved, petted and stroked all day long. Nevertheless she remained very shy and submissive. Although there were two cats in the house, she was the only dog. She did obedience training and was shown for conformation. Her attachment to Linda grew strong, and she would follow Linda everywhere, lying at her feet, staring at her for hours, loving, devoted and barely able to tolerate the slightest separation.

147

Linda, however, wanted a puppy. When Rhiannon was nearly three years old, Tia, a seven-week-old Dalmatian, was brought into the house, and at first Rhiannon was very accepting of this bumptious little creature, making every allowance for her, permitting her to nip and jump all over her and playing with the puppy as if she were her own.

When Tia was about eighteen months old, Linda noticed that Rhiannon was starting to become protective of certain territories and objects. One day, when Linda's young son Nick was teasing the dogs with a bagel, they both tried to grab it. Rhiannon growled, indicating that she wanted Tia to back off, that she was dominant and the bagel was hers. Tia was no longer a puppy, however, and would not yield. Suddenly the two dogs began fighting savagely. They locked jaws and would only release to grab on somewhere else. They rose in the air on their hind legs, biting and slashing. There was blood everywhere. When they were finally separated, there were huge gouges in their faces and down their legs. They were rushed to a vet, put under anaesthetic, and major surgery was performed.

Afterwards, being at home with the two dogs was like living in a war zone. Dogs who previously had eaten out of the same bowl and slept in the same bed could not now be let out of their crates at the same time. Linda consulted a behavioural trainer and was taught to read their body language in a new way. For a time things seemed to be back under control, until one day Nick slipped and stepped on Tia's tail; Tia yelped and Rhiannon lunged at her. The fight was bloody and ended again at the vet with hundreds of dollars' worth of surgery. Four more times this happened, until Linda and the behaviourist sat down and tried to analyse the behaviour. It became clear that Rhiannon initiated the fights when she was on heat, no longer regarding Tia as a puppy to be tolerated, but an interloper who occupied a great deal of Linda's time. The jealousy sprang out of her intense love and devotion, the kind of love she had not experienced while living in a crate, and Tia was now a direct threat to that love.

Even though Linda wanted to breed these champion dogs, she knew that she had to spay them, which meant that she could no longer show them, for neutered dogs cannot be shown. For three months she kept them both muzzled and separated from one another while in the same room by tying them to door knobs so that they could learn to co-exist in the same space without becoming aggressive. Linda also learned to be a stronger Alpha, making it clear she would not tolerate fighting of any kind, and the dogs began to look only to her for direction. Linda now has two rehabilitated dogs, but she never takes for granted the new peace and friendship between them. She learned that where love is strong, aggression can also be strong.

Many lessons can be culled from this story, but what most impresses me has to do with my search for the origins of aggression. Whatever the stress factors were that helped to spark the fighting between Rhiannon and Tia, it is also worth asking what earlier experiences predetermined that the response would be one of aggression. I would agree with Linda that it was the fear of losing love, and the privileges that go with it, that pushed Rhiannon over the edge. It seems likely that Rhiannon acted in this way because she was so deprived of love in the first year of her life.

According to John Paul Scott's concept of the critical developmental stages in the lives of dogs, if the dog does not receive the correct stimuli during these 'windows', certain social skills or other learned traits cannot be acquired properly later. Scott's definition of a critical period is a 'special time in life when a small amount of experience will produce a great effect on later behavior'.[2] The idea of critical periods in the life of the puppy has proved enormously influential both theoretically and practically. It is the reason, for example, why we adopt puppies about eight weeks of age. In his classic book, *Genetics and the Social Behavior of the Dog*, Scott points to a profound change in behaviour at three weeks of age when a puppy becomes able to move and eat like an adult. By that time all the sense organs are functioning and easy associations are made between outside events such as being fed and an internal sensation of pleasure, linking emotions and social interaction. The puppy then quickly learns how to relate to other animals, people and places and a pattern forms that will affect almost everything in later life. 'There will be other periods of rapid organisation of behaviour in later life, at the time of sexual maturity and birth of the young, but their effects will be more limited.'[3]

Scott recognised that this key idea had also to do with the origins of aggression. In his autobiography, he wrote of 'maladaptive' behaviour in dogs that had been raised in kennels, with little interaction with people. They were frightened of anything new and had difficulty learning. If later they were placed in homes in an attempt to 'rehabilitate' them, some would run from human contact, others would bite people. According to Scott, whether a particular dog became pathologically shy or, on the other hand, became aggressive, was genetic, having to do primarily with its breed, but both kinds of behaviour were due to having been kept in a kennel for five months or more.[4]

In my view the symptoms can be broadened beyond shyness and untrainability (Rhiannon was anything but untrainable) to include heightened aggression toward another dog. If the human defence mechanism of displacement is taken as a parallel, doubtless Rhiannon was angry with Linda for bringing this dog into the home in the first place, but could not express her displeasure directly to her mistress. The ferocity of her attack on Tia may have had to do with this inability to direct her anger at its legitimate target. If a dog cannot be as deductive as this, one can conclude that one dog simply detests the other dog's presence as a direct experience rather than as an abstract grievance.

Many studies claim that a dog raised in isolation will be more aggressive than one raised with other dogs. On the other hand, extreme shyness is also characteristic of isolation during rearing, but it is not known exactly how much confinement constitutes isolation, nor have the effects of confinement been studied to the extent that isolation has. Is it a question of the breed of the dog? Scott claims that aggressiveness is inherited in certain breeds of dogs.[5] Among the experts I have consulted, a different consensus seems to be growing: no breed is aggressive by nature without some reinforcement from the external world in the form of upbringing or training. A Doberman pinscher, for instance, raised from puppyhood in a gentle and friendly atmosphere, where aggression is frowned upon, or discouraged, and not rewarded, would not grow up to be aggressive, even if it showed early signs in the litter of being prone to aggression. On the other hand, the fact that the behaviour of wolf cubs raised in human households is almost identical to that of dogs until they are sexually mature, at which point they often can no longer be kept in a domestic environment, suggests that there is an important genetic factor at work here.[6]

Mongooses raised in isolation from the day of birth onwards show threatening behaviour towards another member of their own species the first time they encounter one. The same is true of Siamese fighting fish. They seem to need no experience to trigger these reactions. Male sticklebacks reared from the egg in complete isolation from other animals will, when adult, show full fighting vigour to other males and courtship behaviour to females when faced with them for the first time in their lives.[7]

Moreover, the fact that aggression is the most significant behaviour problem that dog caretakers encounter, and is also the main reason for a guide dog to be eliminated from training, suggests a genetic component. Yet there remains a tendency among dog owners, just as among psychologists, to seek out an explanation for hyperaggressiveness that is connected to earlier experiences or to various defence mechanisms. One can speculate about a dog's fear – indeed trainers speak of fear-biting[8] – or that a miserable life is the cause. It does not matter to the victim what the psychological explanation for the brutality is. It would be small comfort to a five-year-old victim of an attack by a pit-bull terrier to learn that the dog was viciously teased and beaten by its owner. Dog bites, especially of small children, are still common and pose a significant health threat in the United States. In 1994, an estimated 1.8 per cent of the U.S. population were bitten by dogs. This amounts to approximately 585,000 injuries requiring medical attention or restricted activity as a result of dog bites. Given these figures, it is perhaps surprising that on average in the States only eighteen deaths per year result from dog bites. The main victims of fatal dog bites are children, and most of these result from fatal attacks on sleeping infants.[9]

I recently had my own experience with dog-aggression when I took my three dogs to visit some friends who keep a yellow labrador mix called Alice. While I was being shown round their new house, suddenly, with no visible provocation, Alice turned on Sasha and began biting her viciously. Sasha was screaming – at least, what she was doing sounded very much like screams. She was not fighting back; she was crying out. I managed to separate the two dogs, but not before Sasha had defecated and released a very strong odour that I had never smelt before. I thought of it as the scent of terror.[10] She was trembling and shaking. Since Sasha is normally independent and stoical, it was surprising that she came to me for protection, demonstrating once again the importance of the neoteny thesis that dogs remain permanent juveniles, with us *in loco parentis*. Sima and Rani looked on with astonishment. They clearly could not make any sense of the attack. Neither could we. Yet, although Sasha was as upset as we were, while I wanted to leave, Sasha was happy to take a walk in the park with the offending dog. Dogs never seem to hold grudges against humans, and here was an example of the same tolerance extended to another dog. In the park Alice again attacked Sasha, and this time so visibly upset was she that we took her home. I do not think that this kind of experience will permanently affect Sasha. What enables a dog to get over these traumas with no ill effect? Forgiveness, something humans could learn from dogs.

What took place between Rhiannon and Tia, Sasha and Alice, was truly aggression because we reserve this term for fighting between members of the same species. Predatory behaviour is not generally seen as involving aggression. When a dog chases a rabbit, or a cat catches a mouse, they are not said to be behaving aggressively (a subtlety no doubt lost on the rabbit and the mouse). Rivalry usually takes place within the species, though sometimes within the family, and most aggression is directed towards a rival, whether for food or territory or a mate.

Psychologists have always been fascinated by aggression. There are more than 250 different definitions of aggression in the psychological literature alone. Human aggression is a popular field for academic study, perhaps due to the hope of eliminating it. Is this why we are so fascinated by aggression in dogs, because we can feel superior when faced with what many imagine to be the dog's innate aggressiveness?[11] For indeed, aggression may well be the first thing that many people think about when they think of dogs. Dogs and other carnivores seem to make good models, not just for understanding human aggression but for learning to become more like other creatures who appear better able to curb their aggression.

Ever since Konrad Lorenz wrote his book, *On Aggression,* we have become accustomed to the idea that aggression in dogs is ritualised.[12] In what are called 'agonistic' (the complex of threat, aggression, appeasement and avoidance) encounters, a kind of formal dance takes place in which gestures that normally harm are employed as symbols of what could take place but does not. In such ritualised encounters, nobody is actually hurt. The stronger animal, the one who would win were the combat real, demonstrates superiority by ritual displays. It is more a ceremony, a theatrical performance, than a real fight. Ritualised fighting appears to be common among all social species – even, sometimes, among men, as in boxing or football. The dog, being profoundly social, could not possibly fight to the death on a continual basis, or the species would cease to exist.[13] Juveniles, who by definition are less strong, need to survive, and could not do so if fighting to death were constant. Dogs learn this early from their mothers and from play-fighting with litter mates, especially during the first seven weeks. Deprived of this opportunity, as Scott points out, dogs no longer seem to know the distinction between play aggression and the real thing.

Lorenz claimed that the loser demonstrates vulnerability by exposing its neck to the stronger dog. More recent research suggests that this is merely a generalised means of submitting and has nothing to do with any recognition that the neck is the most vulnerable part of the dog's body. In fact, it is not. When I first saw Rani grab Sima by the neck and shake her as if she were a rabbit whose neck Rani wanted to break, I was worried. Eventually I realised that the neck is chosen precisely because it is so strong, and is not in fact vulnerable to attack. Dogs play with each other by grabbing the neck because it is safe to do so.

Similarly, revealing the belly in a ritualised fight is not exposing the most vulnerable part of the body (as Lorenz and others seemed to believe), but is a ritual submission – one more connected with affection. We see this constantly in our dogs when they are feeling particularly affectionate and roll over on their backs. In three ways the posture expresses their submission: preventing us from continuing on our way; focusing all our attention on them; and encouraging us to stroke and pet them, giving them the desired physical contact. In 1872, Charles Darwin noted this in the chapter on dogs in his great book, *The Expression of the Emotions in Man and Animals*:

153

The feeling of affection of a dog towards his master is combined with a strong sense of submission, which is akin to fear. Hence dogs not only lower their bodies and crouch a little as they approach their masters, but sometimes throw themselves on the ground with their bellies upwards. This is a movement as completely opposite as is possible to any show of resistance. I formerly possessed a large dog who was not at all afraid to fight with other dogs; but a wolf-like shepherd-dog in the neighbourhood, though not ferocious and not so powerful as my dog, had a strange influence over him. When they met on the road, my dog used to run to meet him, with his tail partly tucked in between his legs and hair not erected; and then he would throw himself on the ground, belly upwards. By this action he seemed to say more plainly than by words, 'Behold, I am your slave.'[14]

This exaggeration of the ritualised aspect of fighting is what links aggression in dogs to both play and love. Rani approaches everybody by rolling over immediately, asking for, in fact demanding, affection, which she invariably gets. Sasha expresses a similar sentiment with her ears (it is amazing how expressive a dog's ears can be) and Sima with her hind quarters.

It is obvious that the dog is aware of the ritualised aspect of the aggression, and rarely makes a mistake or misleads another dog. In real aggression it is important to intimidate another dog. The dog tries to look as big as possible: the hairs on the body stand erect (piloerection), the head is held high, and the tail is up, with the dog more or less on tiptoes, to appear tall. When two dogs play-fight, the same thing happens: the hackles go up, they stare at one another and indulge in all other activities that are normally part of aggression. They each know, of course, that they are playing (humans quickly learn to read the differences as well). If, as often happens, the two dogs do not begin their encounter with a play-bow, what subsequently signals to the other dog that all this is play? The entire atmosphere in a play-fight is different from the charged one that prevails in a real fight. Dogs can see the difference, they can smell and feel the difference.

Many animals who have antlers use them only in ritualised fashion, which is why we see so many animals lock horns. They cannot hurt one another when they do this, but if they were to use their horns against the side of another animal, the opponent could be killed. This is clearly against the rules, and very rarely seen.[15] Rattlesnakes only use their poison against members of another species, not in fights with other rattlesnakes, and skunks do not use their secretions to blind rival skunks, only other animals. Although scientists claim that these 'rules' are hard-wired into the genes of animals – and I am prepared to believe it in rattlesnakes – I am not so certain with all mammals. Both my cats like to rake their paws down the sides of my legs when I am sitting in a chair with shorts on. The first time it happened I was sure that I would be scratched, but each time the cats pulled in their claws and I felt only their soft paws caressing my legs. Once, after scratching the specially designed post, Saj came up to me and began to use me as a scratch post. I winced, she noticed, and rushed off in what looked like humiliation. She certainly knew she had made a mistake and broken one of her own rules.

As everybody knows, the most dangerous wild animal is a mother protecting her young, where the love for her children makes her aggressive. Defending what one cares for is universal among all animals. Dogs care for us, and so, in dogs, love is so clearly the master emotion that aggression is intimately connected to it. A dog will risk its life to save its human family, and will become aggressive in its defence. There are many such stories from the Second World War, none more famous than Chips who took out a Sicilian machine-gun bunker in 1943. Pinned down by heavy gunfire from the Italian bunker which commanded a large area of the beach, Chips's handler, Rowell, wondered if he would survive the invasion:

. . . Chips growled and rose. Outrunning Rowell's protests, Chips charged up the beach toward the bunker. The Italian gunners aimed at the running dog, their bullets kicking up sprays of sand in his path. One bullet nipped Chips's scalp. Another tore into his hip, staggering him for a second, but Chips ran on toward the bunker. Rowell watched Chips charge over a barricade and disappear into the bunker. The gun went silent. For seconds, Rowell could only guess what was happening inside the gun placement. Then an Italian soldier emerged from the bunker, screaming. Chips held a death grip on the soldier's neck as the man clawed at him, trying to escape the furor of the canine attack. Behind the first man, three others marched out of the bunker indicating their willingness to surrender.[16]

Chips was awarded the Silver Star for bravery. The U.S. War Department later rescinded the award on the grounds that a dog could not have one of the army's highest awards. Chips did not seem to mind the affront.

During his final years in exile, Napoleon Bonaparte wrote how, at the end of the Italian campaign, a dog sat beside the body of his fallen master, licking his hand. Napoleon could not get this out of his mind, and at the end of his days wrote this:

Perhaps it was the spirit of the time and the place that affected me. But I assure you no occurrence on any of my other battlefields impressed me so keenly. I halted on my tour to gaze on the spectacle, and to reflect on its meaning.

This soldier, I realised, must have had friends at home and in his regiment; yet he lay there deserted by all except his dog. . . . I had looked on, unmoved, at battles which decided the future of nations. Tearless, I had given orders which brought death to thousands. Yet, here I was stirred, profoundly stirred, stirred to tears. And by what? By the grief of one dog.[17]

When the Nazis marched into Austria during the Anschluss, they killed all the dogs they found in the homes of Jews on the grounds that these were 'Jewish' dogs.

The Yiddish writer Isaiah Spiegel (born in 1906) spent the war years in Poland, part of the time in concentration camps and part of the time in the Warsaw Ghetto. He wrote a disturbing short story, called 'A Ghetto Dog', which portrays the destruction from an oblique angle, that of an old, frail and lonely widow and her equally old, infirm and weary dog. When the Germans began shooting all the dogs in the ghetto, she could not bear to leave her dog, so she followed him into the pound and then the field behind the pound where the dogs were massacred, winding his leash about her arm the way the phylacteries are wound in the orthodox Jewish religious ritual.[18]

Many Jews who lived through the Holocaust are still frightened of German shepherds. They remind them of the camps, where these dogs were often urged to attack and kill Jews. Pictures from Auschwitz reveal groups of Jews surrounded by menacing German shepherds. It occurred to me that no one, not even a German, has ever written about those dogs. On film, we see the Nazi guards with the dogs, and we blame and hate the guards but not the dogs. Not even the victims blamed the dogs. Why not? Surely it is because everyone recognises that the dogs were trained to behave in the way they did. They did not harbour a natural dislike of Jews. While the guards were also trained to behave in a vicious manner, it was personal. I was never persuaded by Hannah Arendt's argument that Adolf Eichmann was just a cog in the machine, that he was ordinary, and his evil was banal. We instinctively feel that any individual could have refused, could have asked to be re-assigned,[19] something a dog could not do, but if those guards were disgusted by what they did, there is little record of it.

I wonder if the dogs were ever reluctant to do what they were told to do, if they ever hesitated when given their orders. Did they ever feel compassion for their victims or wonder why these people were being murdered? Did some dogs just refuse to perform? I am sure there must have been a failure rate, dogs that were simply not suitable for this kind of work, or performed badly, or who could not learn to do what was expected of them.

I spoke of these things to Sergeant Mestas, a tough and experienced instructor (he is now assigned to the 'gang' unit) for the K-9 Unit in the Oakland Police Department, whose dogs are trained to sniff out drugs and track down suspects, primarily by scent. When the 'perp' is found, he is given a warning: 'I am armed with a police dog. Surrender, or I will release, and he will bite you.' More often than not, the suspect immediately surrenders, especially if he has had any experience with K-9 dogs. (Although some police departments train their dogs to stand and bark, rather than bite, this does leave the dog or the handler exposed to shooting.) If the suspect does not, the dog is sent in, and moving with extraordinary speed, bites the leg, thigh, buttocks or arm. He immobilises the suspect and does not tear the flesh unless there is a struggle. The person is warned to stay perfectly still and thus avoid even greater physical harm. I wanted to know how the K-9 unit trained dogs for this kind of work.

It was somewhat unnerving to discover that all six dogs used in the unit came from Germany, where they were initially trained. They are all unneuttered male German shepherds. Females are not employed because they are considered too protective of their handlers and are reluctant to leave their side to assess a situation. Not every dog is suited to this kind of work. There is a failure rate of about 50 per cent.

I asked Sergeant Mestas what the dogs felt when they did this kind of work. 'It depends', he said, 'on which part of the work.' They enjoy the training – in fact, the whole point of the training is to make it fun for the dog, like a game. For the dogs it is a game; that's why they do it. No hostility, hatred or aggression should be involved. In training them for narcotics work, for example, the important thing is to keep it light and free from tension. 'The trainer', said Sergeant Mestas, 'has to get down with the dog.' The drug (or chemical substitute) is wrapped in a sock that becomes a toy; the trainer holds the sock under the dog's nose before hiding it. The dog then races off, searching for its toy and finding drugs. As a reward, it is allowed free play time with the toy.

For attack work, the dog, at a command (in German!) from its trainer, runs at a man wearing a heavily padded sleeve and grabs hold with its teeth. The bite of a German shepherd exerts between 700 and 1,500 pounds of pressure per square inch. Very persuasive! It's a game, and the minute it is over, the dog is happy to be stroked by the man playing the role of the perpetrator. However, the handlers told me, when a criminal foolishly fights back and hurts a dog, the dog becomes angry and thus dangerous. The dogs rarely get killed.

It is different, Sergeant Mestas went on to tell me, once they are actually in the field. Dogs are reluctant to make a 'live' bite, one from which the flesh is broken.[20] It is as if they know this is more serious, so they sometimes give an inquiring look, as if to say: 'Are you sure?' They know the difference between biting a sleeve in a game and biting real human flesh.

'Are they angry?' I asked.

'Absolutely not,' the Sergeant told me. 'What is essential is control. The handler must always be in control, so that the minute we tell the dog "*aus*" [German for 'out'] the dog obeys. But of course the dogs pick up fear scent, on the side of both parties, and therefore know this is for real.'

All the officers agreed that the dogs were uncanny at picking up the emotions of their handlers. Anticipation, nervousness, excitement and fear are all quickly communicated to the dog.

When their work is over, these dogs go back to being social animals, retiring as pets kept by their handlers.

I was playing with one of the dogs in the back of Sergeant Mestas' pick-up truck. 'Watch', he said, 'how different the dog is when it is working' – and he put the dog in the back of his patrol car. As I approached, the dog growled menacingly, hurling itself against the window, the same dog who moments before had been rolling over and playing with me. When Sergeant Mestas goes home to his wife and seven children, the smaller kids dress the dog in costumes, and the 120-pound German shepherd patiently permits it all, happy to play with the kids, completely reliable and harmless.

A few days later I went out with one of the dog-handlers. Officer Barry Hoffmann, on his daily rounds with his dog Jasco, told me that Jasco was the most mellow dog in the whole unit who never became excited by what he was doing; it was clearly work for him, something he did for a living, no more, no less. He did exactly as he was told. Barry said that the dog was happy to be patted by somebody he had just bitten, and that some dogs did have an inhibition which was not easy to overcome.

'Let's experiment,' he said brightly. 'I'll tell my dog to bite you while you and I are having a perfectly quiet conversation. This is not the situation I usually give this command in, so let's see if he hesitates.'

I was less than enthusiastic, but Officer Hoffmann assured me he could stop the dog before he dog complied, and so gave the instruction. Jasco looked at Barry, then at me, then at the ground, then he lay down, gave a sigh and seemed to fall asleep! My pulse returned to normal, while Barry seemed a shade disappointed. Well, that was proof enough for me. The dog knew a just order from an unjust one. Or he knew that Barry was not serious. For me, this raised the question of whether dogs have a sense of justice. I asked Barry whether Jasco would ever enforce the law without him. If he saw a theft in progress, would he attack the thief? We both laughed at the question, and the answer was obviously no. Our laws are arbitrary from the point of view of Jasco or any other dog, but canine rules are something else. Stealing cars, dealing in dope, beating up wives – none of these are a dog's concern. On its own, the dog would definitely pass all these activities by without the slightest regard, but when Barry is there, and orders are given, Jasco is ready to comply, to be a ferociously loyal partner. That seemed, according to Barry, to be the dog's primary motivation.

'We are buddies. We look out for each other. He knows that I have fought for him, as he fights for me. We are best friends.' As I got out of the car, he said, 'Imagine being outdoors all day with your best friend and being paid for it. That is how I feel about my work.'

Vicki Hearne tells a story that implies dogs have a sense of moral order not so different from our own. It is about a 'bad-assed cop' whom she calls Philip Beem and his wonderful Doberman, Fritz:

> One night, Officer Beem stopped a young black woman for jaywalking and started clubbing her with his nightstick, for the sheer fun of it as near as anyone could make out. (There were witnesses.) Fritz attacked – not the woman, but his policeman partner, and took his club away from him emphatically.
>
> Now Fritz was not only by nature a good dog, he was well trained and had a keenly developed sense of what his job entailed, what did and did not belong in this particular little dog-human culture. Sitting by while people got beat up for no good reason was not part of his job, it simply didn't belong. While it would not be exactly wrong to interpret this story by saying that Fritz was moved by compassion or a sense of rescue or protectiveness, it wouldn't be quite right, either. He simply knew his job, had his own command of the law in a wide sense of 'law' and was putting his world back in order.[21]

CHAPTER FIFTEEN

Being Alone: The Sadness of Dogs

I AM SURE I AM NOT ALONE in a spooky, recurring experience:[1] I am walking with the three dogs along the road. I am in the middle; Sima and Rani are in front, Sasha behind. I turn around to look for Sasha. She is not there. To my left I see a path leading to a back yard, precisely the kind of path upon which a cat would sit. I call. I call again. No Sasha. I begin to be anxious, since she usually returns when I call her. How far off could she have run by now? Terrible images force their way into my mind: she has been run over; she is disoriented and cannot find her way back. I become more and more worried. I call frantically, Sasha! SASHA! *SASHA!* Suddenly I notice there are six pairs of eyes looking at me in great puzzlement. Sima, Rani *and* Sasha are staring at me with consternation, as if to say: 'Who on earth are you calling? We're all *here*.' And indeed they are.

The question is whether Sasha was there all along and I merely suffered the illusion of her absence, or whether she actually disappeared and reappeared silently without my taking notice? It felt as if she had appeared by magic; as if she had materialised out of thin air. If this had happened only once it would be easier to dismiss, but it happens at least once a week. I call and call and then see whichever dog I am calling staring intently up at my face. All three dogs look a little concerned, as if they fear I might be losing my grip on reality. It is an uncanny experience, not to say embarrassing. I have learned now not to call until I have looked around me thoroughly and have perhaps even consulted a second witness.

'No Rani in sight, right? You agree? OK, so now I will call.'

Then, *voilà*, she appears, the stealth dog. I have only ever experienced this with the larger dog, Sasha, and the smaller dog Sima. I can understand how Sima might be overlooked as she is small, and her colouring allows her to blend into the earth easily, but one can hardly overlook a full-grown German shepherd.

One day a recollection from my childhood helped shed light on this experience. When I was a little boy, my cocker spaniel, Taffy, slept every night on my bed. Like many small children, I was frightened by strange noises, especially those I thought I heard breaking the silence of a still night. I soon learned to look over at Taffy, because if she were still and unmoved by the noise, then I knew it was imaginary, or not significant. When Taffy suddenly lifted her head and became alert, I was permitted to become alarmed because I knew I wasn't hearing things. Taffy had heard it too.

The solution to my present puzzle was now evident. I only needed to look at the other two dogs when one was missing. I had noticed that when our little pack was incomplete and one member was missing, the other two would look worried (dogs' facial expressions include worry in a most poignant fashion – on some dogs it seems etched on their features). Last week, for instance, I thought that Sasha had jumped into the back of my Toyota Camry wagon along with the other two dogs before I began driving away. The dogs let out a simultaneous yelp. I turned around, and both Sima and Rani were staring intently out of the window in the direction of the hapless Sasha, who was staring back at the retreating car. She had not jumped in after all, and the others were not about to allow me to drive off without their friend.

It is the dogs who can alert me to what is happening. If I think one of them is missing, I look at the other two dogs. If they seem unconcerned, then I can look around again. They are always right. So now I know how to tell whether I am paranoid or perceptive, whether I have a problem or something is happening in the real world. All I need to do is to watch my dogs. Their reactions are much more closely tied to the real world and free from fantasy.

Dogs can be anxious, or irritable, can develop phobias and be subject to panic attacks, but it does not seem likely that they would be excessively concerned with their physical health, or have persecution delusions because of personal inadequacies. Probably no dog has ever experienced a nihilistic delusion of world destruction. Whether dogs ever experience hallucinations is not known for certain. Dr Charles Berger, a veterinarian for the Iditarod race in Alaska, told me of the vivid hallucinations that the human mushers have after days without sleeping. Sled dogs need their sleep and get it, so they probably do not experience the same level of exhaustion. However, if they did, I asked Dr Berger, could they hallucinate? 'If only we could ask them,' he replied. Short of asking, it is hard to know. Dogs will sometimes chase imaginary enemies (or friends), but it is not clear whether this is deliberate play or an actual hallucination.

Are all these emotional or perceptive disturbances symptoms of a more serious emotional crisis – depression? Entire libraries have been filled with volumes on human depression, and there are almost as many theories about its origin and treatment as there are books. A distinction is generally made between sadness (a common condition) and depression (a disease). Psychiatrists attempt to distinguish between a 'reactive' depression in which the sadness is a reaction to something that has happened and a more ominous (because seemingly biological in origin) melancholia. If you are sad because your lover left you a week ago, that is not susceptible to treatment, but if you are sad because your lover left you five years ago, that constitutes an illness. The official manual of psychiatric nomenclature, issued by the American Psychiatric Association, gives the following symptoms associated with a major depressive episode: 'Appetite disturbance, change in weight, sleep disturbance, psychomotor agitation or retardation, decreased energy, feelings of worthlessness or excessive or inappropriate guilt, difficulty thinking or concentrating, and recurrent thoughts of death, or suicidal ideation or attempts.'[2] The associated features include: tearfulness, anxiety, irritability, brooding or obsessive rumination, excessive concern with physical health, panic attacks, and phobias. There are delusions (that one is being persecuted because of a moral transgression or some personal inadequacy) and hallucinations. There may be nihilistic delusions of world destruction or of poverty.[3]

While it is generally accepted that human beings experience depression, it is not so widely accepted that a dog can be depressed by nature, or may even be genetically predisposed to depression. Some of the primary symptoms or associated features of human depression do occur in dogs. Sad dogs do not eat, they lose weight, they sleep poorly, walk slowly, have less energy. While it would take a brave anthropomorphist to suggest that the dog has feelings of worthlessness (the physiology of certain dogs – bloodhounds, for example – makes them appear forlorn, melancholy animals) many dog caretakers report that they believe their dogs experience excessive guilt. As for recurrent thoughts of death, this is almost impossible to know. I am sure that dogs do recognise death: a recent photograph in *The Animal's Voice*[4] (USA) showed a large number of dogs watching another dog being euthanised. Each was awaiting its own death. It is hard to suppose that the animals were unaware of their fate, and if they were aware of it, it is impossible to believe they were not feeling something about it. Caretakers who have their dogs euthanised swear that the dogs know what is coming, and that the dogs seem to be forgiving them, an almost unbearable experience. Fortunately, dogs live so intensely that they crowd a full lifetime into their ten to fifteen allotted years.

Depression in the dog is simply sadness at the loss of love which is not easy to replace. I think it is possible that a dog can die from grief, and even if the dog does not succumb to the sorrow, it can give evidence that it experiences it for many years. Many people have heard the remarkable example of devotion involving a Skye terrier dog who worked for a Scottish shepherd named Old Jock. In 1858, the day after Jock was buried (with almost nobody present to mourn him except his shaggy dog) in the churchyard at Greyfriars Abbey in Edinburgh, Bobby was found sleeping on his master's grave where he continued to sleep every night for fourteen years. At a street corner near Greyfriars churchyard is a granite fountain with an effigy of a dog on guard. It has the following inscription: 'A tribute to the affectionate fidelity of Greyfriarys Bobby. In 1858 this faithful dog followed the remains of his master to the Greyfriars churchyard, and lingered near this spot until his death in 1872.'[5] In *A Dog is Listening*, Roger Caras adds to Bobby's story: 'Friends whose names are recorded and who were obviously real people, not fictional ones, brought him food and water, but winter and summer Bobby stayed there, perhaps waiting, perhaps guarding his master's grave.'[6]

There are recorded cases of a dog appearing to commit suicide out of despair, and some of them are heartbreaking: 'After 6-year-old Lee Scott Campbell was taken to a hospital with severe burns suffered when his cowboy suit was set ablaze by a bonfire, Lee's dog Woodsie refused to eat. Lee died after receiving eleven blood and plasma transfusions. Woodsie died two hours later at the Campbell home.'[7]

Not long ago someone wrote to me from New York about his Samoyed who had become crippled due to a slipped disc. 'Even though he was getting better, he died suddenly of "psychological pneumonia" – he just slowed his breathing rate until his lungs filled up. The doctor told us a lot of wounded dogs in the country go off in the woods and die so as not to be a burden on their owners.'[8] Dr Robert Kirk disagrees with this interpretation. He thinks the dog is hardly reasoning, but merely wishes to be alone. It is true that most dogs, when they are going to die, seek out a place by themselves. James Thurber writes of it in these moving terms: 'Death, to a dog, is the final unavoidable compulsion, the last ineluctable scent on a fearsome trail, but they like to face it alone, going out into the woods, among the leaves . . . enduring without sentimental human distraction the Last Loneliness, which they are wise enough to know cannot be shared by anyone.'[9]

Al Graber, who is 91 years old, told me that when he and his wife Helen had to move from Escondido to the California Veterans' Home in the Napa valley in Northern California in 1980 they were told they could not bring their eight-year-old miniature poodle. 'We had to get rid of him,' Al told me, 'and somehow he sensed it. He started acting funny. We took him to the vet, but the vet said he was perfectly healthy. Just before we were due to leave, he began racing around the perimeter of the house, faster and faster. Then he lay down next to me, and died. I know he committed suicide.'[10]

Veronique Richard told me about her five-year-old Brittany spaniel called Lady. The whole family was on the beach in Calvia, Corsica, in 1978, and Lady was her usual healthy self, swimming, fetching, running about the beach. Her father was swimming, watched by both his daughter and his dog, when he suddenly disappeared. The dog and daughter both ran to the water. He was taken out of the water and flown by helicopter to the nearest hospital, where he lay in a coma for the next four days. Lady would not touch her food or water, and seemed to go into a coma herself. When the hospital called to say that the father had died, the family drove – with the dog – down to retrieve the body. On the way the dog died as well, on the very same day.[11]

I have also been told the story of a terrier who was so unhappy at being given to a new family that she lay down in the middle of traffic and was run over. The observers all felt that the dog knew what she was doing and did it deliberately.[12] Of course there is a subjective layer of interpretation in these accounts. Affection and grief are felt not only by the dog with respect to its caretaker, but also by the caretaker for his or her dog. Yi-Fu Tuan tells the story of the tender romance between the lonely writer T. H. White and his red setter, Brownie, which began coolly on White's part. He recalled how at first he thought of his pet as simply 'the dog', rather as one thinks of 'the chair' or 'the umbrella'.

'Setters', he said, 'are beautiful to look at. I had a beautiful motor car and sometimes I wore a beautiful top hat. I felt that "the dog" would suit me nearly as nicely as the hat did.'

This casual appreciation later deepened into love. Brownie's near fatal sickness and White's nursing of the setter back to health triggered the change. When, after eleven years of companionship, the dog finally died, White wrote to David Garnett: 'I stayed with the grave for a week, so that I could go out twice a day and say, "Good girl: sleepy girl: go to sleep, Brownie." It was a saying she understood. . . . Then I went to Dublin, against my will, and kept myself as drunk as possible for nine days, and came back feeling more alive than dead.'[13]

When a dog's affection is repeatedly rebuffed by either a human or a canine companion, the dog seems to suffer from the rejection and gives some evidence of a broken heart. Examples of this, however, are more rare than of those losing a close companion, probably the primary cause of canine sadness.

What else makes dogs sad? Dogs grow sad when they are alone. In extreme cases of abandonment, it is possible that the dog could cross the line from sadness into depression, but abandonment is something that only a human does to a dog, sometimes with great cruelty. In the 1960s John L. Fuller, the senior staff scientist at the Jackson Laboratory in Bar Harbor, Maine, reported on experiments he conducted on deprivation, in all of which the same basic isolation procedure was used.[14] 'Puppies are removed from their mother at the age of 21 days, when they can for the first time survive independently without special handling. They are placed in cages about 60 centimeters square which permit feeding, watering, and removal of wastes without physical or visual contact with a human being. The cages are furnished with a one-way observation window, are kept constantly lighted at a low level of illumination, and are ventilated by a blower, which provides some masking of external sounds.'[15] The aim was to prove that dogs do not thrive without other dogs.

If a dog is raised in such horrendous conditions, perhaps it is legitimate to speak of depression as opposed to sadness, but we must bear in mind how this situation has been artificially created. These puppies evinced behaviour that would look bizarre to any observer, behaviour that one would not expect to see in the wild. Any creature, man or animal, raised in these circumstances, is likely to exhibit classic psychiatric symptoms of depression as outlined in the *Diagnostic and Statistical Manual*, the bible of psychiatrists, mentioned above. As John Paul Scott noted in an article on the emotional response to separation in dogs: 'There is nothing in human experience comparable to the degree of change experienced by the isolated dog, with the possible exception of the culture shock that is described by anthropologists who go to live in a completely foreign culture apart from their own kind.'[16]

These experiments were conducted partly to determine the exact period beyond which, if it were not socialised, a dog could never be counted as normal. This is the theme of one of the most famous of all books on dog behaviour, Scott and Fuller's *Genetics and the Social Behavior of the Dog.* They determined the critical period to be between three and a half and twelve weeks of age. That is, 'all puppies are capable of forming firm attachments to people and places beginning at about three weeks of age',[17] and after twelve weeks of no contact with a human being, a puppy can no longer be completely socialised, avoids human contact and remains virtually untrainable. As Michael Fox, the canid expert, puts it: 'Thus even in a domesticated species, lack of exposure to man during this formative period (when brain centres are integrating and emotional reactions developing) will greatly limit the social potentials of the species.'[18]

Another classic experiment in bringing about an artificial depression in a dog was performed by the University of Pennsylvania's Dr Martin E. P. Seligman, famous for his 'learned helplessness' model. In 1967, Seligman delivered electric shocks to dogs through a steel-grid floor with such intensity and persistence that the dogs stopped trying to get away and 'gave up'. In 1978 an entire issue of the *Journal of Abnormal Psychology* was devoted to the topic of 'learned helplessness' as a model for depression. According to this notion, feeling helpless is not an innate state, but must be learned through experiences which convince one that no amount of effort will alleviate suffering. Since Seligman's original experiments on dogs with inescapable electric shock, many investigators have developed their own learned helplessness models, including forcing animals to swim until they give up, or, in the language of behaviourists, 'learn to be helpless'.[19] Seligman was much impressed with the 'striking findings' of C. P. Richter, who observed that after he had squeezed wild rats in his hand until they stopped struggling, they drowned within 30 minutes of being placed in a water tank from which there was no escape. Rats who had not been squeezed, swam for 60 hours before drowning.[20] Seligman hypothesised that dogs who do not become helpless, even after inescapable shock, must have had a history of controllable trauma before arriving at the laboratory. He tested the hypothesis by raising dogs singly in laboratory cages, allowing them almost no contact with other dogs or humans; these dogs became helpless after only two sessions of inescapable shock. He noted that dogs reared in isolation find it difficult to escape shock.[21] That the normal nature of a dog can be permanently modified in this manner hardly seems to require scientific proof; neither does it teach us much about human beings who experience learned helplessness (such as battered women) that could not have been learnt by merely speaking to the victims.[22]

Psychiatrist Dallas Pratt wrote, 'Surely these experimenters are contributing little or nothing to an understanding of the complexities of human anxiety or depressive states. If anything, these tortured and terrified dogs appear to be suffering from a traumatic reaction similar to the soldier's "shell-shock". . .'[23]

Where does one find depressed dogs? At dog races, where chasing the rabbit for fun is ominously shrouded in an atmosphere of tension and even death (greyhounds who consistently lose are killed); on breeding farms known as puppy mills, where the physical conditions are abominable;[24] in an area where dogs form free-roaming packs, and loners cannot join or are not accepted into the group; and, of course, in an experimental laboratory. Nobody who knows anything about the use of dogs as experimental animals in laboratories can doubt that these animals become depressed. The depression might be artificially induced, but the condition is real.

Indeed the problem is extensive. Dr Robert Sharpe points out that, according to the Department of Agriculture, which compiles statistics of animals used for 'research, experiments, testing and teaching', more than 100,000 dogs are consumed every year in the United States alone. A 1994 survey conducted by the National Association for Biomedical Research indicates that the total number of dogs and cats used in research is more than three times greater than the official USDA figure.

I wished to see dogs used in experiments, and to ask the scientists if they had dogs at home, and how they could bring themselves to do these experiments on such sensitive animals. I called the Research Animal Facility at the University of California (Berkeley) and was told that the Lawrence Laboratory was using beagles[25] in an experiment. Though I left five messages with four different people who worked in the laboratory, none of my calls were returned. I am not surprised that people who engage in this kind of work keep it hidden from public view.

One only has to look at experiments conducted within the tobacco industry, in which dogs are forced to inhale poisonous smoke for hours on end, to understand why researchers in animal laboratories are reluctant to inform the public of their work.[26]

Ivan Pavlov received the Nobel Prize for torturing dogs and creating an artificial insanity in them. He did not understand what he was doing to the dogs and blamed them for the pain they felt, as we see in this passage where he describes a dog intelligent enough to understand what was happening to her:

> She slinks behind the experimenter on the way to the ex-perimental rooms, always with her tail between her legs. On meeting members of the staff, some of whom constantly try to make friends with her and pet her she invariably and quickly dodges them, draws back and squats down on the floor. She reacts in the same manner to every slightly quicker movement or slightly louder word of her master, and behaves toward all of us as if we were her most dangerous enemies from whom she constantly and most severely suffered.[27]

His successor in Leningrad, I. T. Kourtsine, wrote the following sentence: '*Parmi les 350 chiens soumis aux expériences dans nos laboratoires au cours de ces 10 dernières années, sur 5 seulement nous n'avons pu réussir à provoquer expérimentalement une névrose.*'[28] (Among the 350 dogs subjected to experiments in our laboratories over the last 10 years, only in five of them were we unable to produce an experimental neurosis.) His colleague, V. K. Fedorov, also from Leningrad, tells the horrifying story of the most friendly dog they had in the laboratory, who was always shown to visitors as the model 'experimental model'. One day this kindly dog was subjected to an agonising experiment in which she was intravenously injected with high doses of camphor, and as a result suffered severe convulsions. From that day on the dog exhibited what Fedorov calls 'une grande pusillanimité' (a great cowardice): she would place her legs in the door jamb to avoid entering the room: 'We could only get her into the room with the greatest of efforts.' To Fedorov's puzzlement, the dog was totally transformed and 'behaved very strangely', shaking and sniffing objects with great suspicion and refusing to eat. She had become a paranoid schizophrenic![29] Do humans respond any differently to torture?

A contemporary of Claude Bernard (1813-78), the father of the use of biochemistry on the bodies of large dogs, described him in the narrow, damp corridor that was his laboratory, where he stood 'before his animal table, his tall hat on, his long grey hair dangling down, a muffler about his neck, his fingers in the abdomen of a large dog which was howling mournfully'.[30] Bernard's wife was so horrified by the cruelty of his experiments that she tried to stop him, in the end separating from him and giving large sums of money to humane societies to help counteract the effect of his work.

I do not believe that a dog becomes depressed for no reason. While some scientists have a tendency to think of it as having a biological basis – something in the dog's genes – I feel certain that there is always a reason and one that is not difficult to understand. Such reasons include being left alone; being without a playmate; having suffered a similar deprivation in puppyhood; having too little interaction; suffering loss of a beloved. There is nothing sadder for a dog than being alone. Loneliness was never programmed into the dog. When forced to be alone, a dog becomes sad. This sadness need not remain incurable. The cure is companionship, love and attention. The easiest and most effective therapy is not prozac or other awful psychiatric drugs, but simply frequent long walks in the country.

In a reversal of domestication, dogs are now being used in nursing homes, in homes for the elderly, in psychiatric hospitals and in individual therapy as a means to draw patients, the elderly and children, out of isolation or depression by interacting with dogs. Whenever I visit the Home for Jewish Parents in Oakland, California, to see my ex-mother-in-law, I take my three dogs. I go to the back ward, where the most severely disabled people live, men and women who can no longer eat by themselves or forego the use of a wheel-chair. On one visit, there was a very old woman suffering from dementia who kept repeating over and over again: 'I lost my key. I vant my key.' Then she saw Rani and mumbled something. I came closer and heard distinctly: *'Ay, vos far a sheyn meydl'* (Yiddish for 'what a pretty little female'). The dog seemed to pierce her dementia, drawing out of her some old recognition that here was a female dog and she was cute. An old man, also demented, could only clap his hands over and over again. He saw Sasha and immediately reached out and patted her, totally appropriately, as if he had been doing it every day. Dogs used in this way for therapy often have surprising results, and lead one to wonder if the very notion of dementia might not need to be rethought.

Dogs often seem to be empathic with suffering human beings. Flapper is a therapy dog who walks the halls of a hospice in Dayton, Ohio, visiting people in the last stages of a terminal illness. 'I remember a man who had cancer but who was also diagnosed with Alzheimer's,' Deborah Jay, his caretaker, told a reporter on the *Dayton Daily News*. 'He would sit in his room in silence. Flapper would climb up in the chair next to his bed, and a transformation would take place. The man began talking, saying over and over again, "what a pretty dog – is a pretty dog." The whole time he was talking to Flapper, he would stroke his face, pull his ears, and Flapper just let him.'[31]

Such people have every reason to be depressed, but seeing these healthy happy animals lifts them, momentarily at least, from their sadness. I think it may have made the dogs feel good too, as if they knew that they were bringing some pleasure to otherwise dreary lives.

CHAPTER SIXTEEN

Thinking Like a Dog

IT IS NOT EASY to experience the world as another person does, even when that person is very much like oneself, much less if the person is from a different country and speaks another language. That is one reason why we read novels; they draw us into the inner experiences of others without our having to become too personally involved. To imagine yourself inside the inner world of another species seems impossible.[1] Yet if it were at all possible with any animal, it would surely be so with the dog, partly because the dog is a social creature, like us, and partly because so much of our time is spent with dogs that we are able to observe them closely as they experience their environment. Sometimes the dog's 'language' seems almost indistinguishable from our own.

A human smile and a dog's tail-wagging are similar forms of communication. Yet until I read Stanley Coren's *The Intelligence of Dogs*, I did not realise that a dog only wags its tail for something that has life.[2] Dr Coren claims that a dog lying alone, with something lifeless that it enjoys before it, will not wag its tail. The dog may be delighted to eat a bowl of food, but it will not wag its tail while doing so unless a living creature is present. The same point was made by Jean Craighead George in her book *How to Talk to Your Animals*: "The dog wags its tail only at living things. A tail wag, the equivalent of a human smile, is bestowed upon people, dogs, cats, squirrels, even mice and butterflies – but no lifeless things. A dog won't wag its tail to its dinner or to a bed, car, stick, or even a bone.'[3] There is some controversy over this matter, however. Marc Bekoff, one of the foremost scientific experts on dogs and the dog family, tells me that this is simply wrong: he has observed his dog wag its tail over dinner when he was watching from another room. Did the dog think he was being observed? Very unlikely. (This would be a non-invasive experiment that readers could carry out on their own.) Dr Feldman, my Berkeley veterinarian friend, agrees with Dr Bekoff. Whether or not Dr Coren's claim is true, the dog's tail is a powerful communicator. Even if dogs wag their tails at things either living or inert, it remains true that dogs revel in close emotional contact. That is why they wag their tails when they see us. Nor is this meaning lost on any human. Just witness dogs walking up to strangers and wagging their tails: many if not most people will immediately begin an almost embarrassingly affectionate conversation with the dog: 'Well, you sweetheart you, you darling, adorable dog, look at how beautiful you are, how wonderful. Come, give me a kiss.' And the dog obliges.

Some people begrudge dogs this quality, which they sometimes call dogs' 'promiscuous behaviour'. It is true that dogs generally like most people, even if they prefer some they know better. They are rarely stingy with their love; indeed, I am often left in awe at how much Sasha loves to love. She approaches just about every person we meet who shows the slightest interest in her (and even many who don't) with the same beseeching demeanour, the same licks on the face, the same look of pure adoration in her expressive eyes.

The love of a dog is so often freely given, that some people refuse to accept it; others have trouble even believing it. So they say they are 'cat' people, because they think the cat is more discriminating, or they call the love something else, like slavish dependency. Yet small infants are like this for some time; they also look upon everyone as a protector, a friend, somebody who deserves their love. Experience may teach them better, just as it may affect the life of an individual dog. A child can easily be traumatised for life; it takes more to turn a dog against all humans, though it has happened. It just seems in their nature to go on loving through all their experiences, even the worst.

If our search for their inner life moves from the dog's tail-wagging to its bark, we immediately notice an important difference: everybody thinks they know why a dog wags its tail, but nobody knows for certain why a dog barks. There are many hypotheses: it is an alarm function, signifying that friend or foe is approaching; it serves to define space, much like other kinds of territorial marking behaviour (urination, for example); it is purely social – 'Here I am!' In a fascinating article in the *Smithsonian* entitled 'Hark! Hark! The dogs do bark . . .', biologist Raymond Coppinger and linguist Mark Feinstein claim that barking is not an adaptive trait, and that it has no purpose. In effect, they conclude, dogs bark for the hell of it. Most wild dogs (the Australian dingo, the New Guinea singing dog, the Asian pariah dog) can bark but rarely do so – and the same is true of wolves. The authors listened to a livestock-guarding dog bark continuously for seven hours on a cold Minnesota night. Since there was nobody around, the authors ask what possible function such barking could have. Their suggestion is that barking is a juvenile trait, since young dogs bark more than adult dogs.[4] If that is the case, it suggests to me a call for attention, for someone, anyone, to fulfil a need. As an attempt to communicate, it is often remarkably successful.

As everybody who lives with dogs knows, the bark can express quite definitive desires: to ward off a supposed threat, to leave the house, to come into the house, to go for a walk – there seems to be an endless series of short commands that the dog attempts to express with different tones, rhythm and volume of barking. If barking is indeed a complex language we don't altogether understand, we rarely fail to get the general drift of our own dogs' barks, even if we are less understanding of others. If scientists were to pay as much attention to barking as they do to bird-song, using all the sophisticated acoustical tools developed for this purpose, we might well discover an entirely unsuspected linguistic world lying close at hand.

This view is strengthened by an experiment conducted by John Paul Scott. The yelps, howls, whimpers and barks of small puppies were recorded and played back to the mothers. 'If the puppies had been removed from the home pen, the mothers responded very strongly, attempting to escape and move toward the source of the sound. On the other hand, if the tapes were played to the mothers while their puppies were with them, they merely gave one glance at the puppies and paid no further attention.'[5] Clearly, then, the function of the puppies' noises was simply to get the mother to pay attention.

The fact that we really do not understand such simple matters as the barking of a dog, or the 'homing' ability that allows the dog to find its way back from places never previously visited, suggests that we must remain humble about the inner life of our canine companions. There is so much we do not know. It may well be that dogs possess senses and abilities which we completely ignore. Michel de Montaigne, in the sixteenth century, wrote: 'I see some animals that live so entire and perfect a life, some without sight, others without hearing: who knows whether to us also one, two, or three, or many other senses, may not be wanting.'[6]

I discussed the homing instinct in dogs with Dr Robert Kirk, the beloved teacher of many vets who graduate from the Cornell Veterinary Medical Teaching Hospital. He was sceptical about stories that involve vast distances, but he was sure that dogs did find their way back home. I asked him how he thought they did it. 'I haven't a clue. Perhaps they use a sense we do not yet know about.' Dogs are still mysterious creatures in spite of more than ten thousand years of companionship with humans.

Dogs are such social creatures, meant to be with others of their kind and with humans, that they feel deprived when these conditions are not met. Above all the dog is a communicating animal. That is what we have bred the dog to be, and we have been successful. Coppinger and Feinstein tell the story of the Institute of Cytology and Genetics in Siberia, where in only twenty generations (two decades) Russian geneticists, by breeding the most docile and the tamest wild silver foxes, succeeded in creating an animal that behaved very much like a dog.[7] They approached humans and greeted them with tail-wagging, face-sniffing, and licking; the foxes developed floppy rather than prick ears and went into heat twice a year, a characteristic of domestic dogs. The foxes even sounded like dogs. These foxes needed people, wanted people, sought people out, exactly the way young puppies do. Dogs need to speak and be spoken to, touch and be touched, love and be loved. This may be true of all humans, and all sentient animals, but nowhere in the animal kingdom is the lesson so strongly evident as in the dog. That is why we need the dog so badly and why we love the dog so much.

When Leila and I take separate routes at the Marina while out walking the dogs, I will tell the dogs as we get close to Leila: 'There she is, there is *Leila!*' The dogs will start looking in every possible direction. If they do not see her immediately, they will look at me, and the look on their faces is so clearly the canine equivalent of 'Where?' that I can read it as easily as I can hear a friend ask me 'Where?' It is an unmistakable direct translation. When I point, the all dogs look in that direction. As soon as they locate Leila with their eyes, they go bounding off in that direction.

Many writers have felt the urge to translate what the dog is thinking into human words. Tolstoy did it in *Anna Karenina*, when he wrote:

> 'Fetch it, fetch it!' shouted Levin, giving Lask a shove from behind. But I can't go, thought Lask: Where can I go to? From here I can smell them, but if I move forward I won't know where or what they are. But there he was nudging her with his knee and muttering to her in an excited whisper: 'Fetch it, Laska darling, fetch it!' Well, if that's what he wants I'll do it, but I no longer accept any responsibility for it now, she thought, and hurled herself forward between the hummocks. She was no longer on the scent, but simply used her eyes and ears without understanding anything.[8]

A version of this desire to give words to dogs is our desire to talk to dogs. We chatter at them. Why? What do we think they get out of it? Dogs certainly pick up the emotional tone of our speech. They know when we are pleased with them and are telling them so, and they delight in our praise. It is not the words, as everybody recognises, but the sound of our voices which lets them know that we are happy.

Brian Vesey-Fitzgerald points out that 'the dog has an absolutely uncanny knack of knowing what we are thinking, even of what we are feeling . . . but I do not really understand my dogs. Many and many a time I have been aware that they have been trying to tell me something. But I am unable to cross the frontier into the dog's mind. They, it seems to me, can cross the frontier into mine whenever they wish. The fact is that the dog can live, happily and at ease, in two worlds: his and our own. We can live only in our own. The dog is cleverer than we are.'[9]

Just how tuned in an animal can be to our moods and emotions is made clear from the story of Clever Hans, the horse who apparently could do mathematics. In the early 1900s a retired German mathematics professor discovered that his beloved horse, Hans, was a prodigy. Hans would tap his foot in answer to the questions of Herr von Osten. Oskar Pfungst, an experimental psychologist, conducted an intensive study of Clever Hans, as he was by then known. He determined that the horse could only respond if the questioner or the observers knew the answers. It turned out that the horse was taking his cues from unconscious, almost imperceptible shifts of head and body posture in his owner or members of the audience. When the horse reached the correct value, the human would involuntarily relax his tension. Herr von Osten was not a fraud; the horse was! He was so intimately in touch with his owner that he perceived, *even when the owner did not*, what the owner wanted, what he was trying to communicate. Clever Hans's gift was one of extraordinary empathy, one more mysterious and infinitely more interesting than the ability to count or do simple mathematics.[10]

Thomas Mann recorded what he supposed his dog was feeling at having been left at the vet's for two weeks: 'He seemed to be oppressed by a feeling of dark hopelessness – and contempt. "Since you have been capable," his attitude seemed to declare, "of having me put into this cage, I expect nothing more from you." And was it not in truth enough to make him despair of all reason and justice? What had he done that this should happen to him? How came it that I not only permitted it, but even took the initial steps?'[11]

Obviously, there is no way in which to verify the accuracy of such a translation project. However, the more knowledge about dogs we acquire, the more accurate our translations are likely to be. Some writers, of course, merely use the dog to underscore some aspect of human behaviour. This was certainly the case in Cervantes' *El Coloquio de los Perros*, written in 1599,[12] and Kafka's 'Investigations of a Dog'.[13] Other literature on the behaviour of dogs is based on information that is inaccurate, and often biased.

Some writers have had the courage to admit that we can be perplexed by the seemingly simple behaviour of the dog. The smelling ritual of dogs is particularly puzzling, especially when it extends beyond the gathering of information. It seems that Thomas Mann felt the same intellectual impotence. In *A Man and his Dog* he writes: '[the] usually transparent behaviour became inscrutable to me – I found it impossible to effect a sympathetic penetration in the feelings, laws, and tribal customs which form the basis of this behaviour. In reality the meeting in the open of two dogs strange to each other belongs to the most poignant, arresting, and pathetic of conceivable happenings . . . I mention these things in order to indicate how strange and alien so close a friend may appear under certain circumstances – times when his entire nature reveals itself as something eerie and obscure.'[14]

To understand how a dog faces the world it is important to know something of its sensory equipment. This is not to say that dogs are confined to their sensory experiences any more than we are. Humans may be primarily visual, but the blind lead lives as complex as those of the sighted. I have often wondered why it is that Rani will stop to taste and then eat almost any edible object she encounters on her walks. I think it is because taste is not important to a dog. In fact, they have one taste bud for every six of ours. Humans enjoy a highly differentiated sense of taste, which is why we have so many restaurants that cater to different likes. Dogs either like the way something tastes or they don't, with the possible exception of being merely indifferent.

The sharp command 'leave it' is the one I use most often on walks with the dogs. Especially in the hills, they love to take into their mouths objects that are disgusting, at least to me – coyote faeces, horse manure, even human excrement.

It is this lack of nuance, I imagine, that allows dogs to eat the same food every day and remain seemingly content. They do have favourite foods, however, and I always run the danger of becoming a cook for my dogs. It was only my vet's strict admonition that saved me from becoming a kitchen slave and them from becoming overweight. Eating does not seem to provide dogs with the same aesthetic pleasure that it gives us. On the other hand, when they are gnawing a fresh bone, they seem to be in a state of ecstasy, so much so that, although a vegetarian, I cannot refrain from offering them this delicacy at least once a week. I think it is some old memory from their days as wolves.

A dog's vision is comparable to that of a human, although it is not as good. Dogs lack the yellow spot in the retina, the light-sensitive membrane at the back of the eye which enables us to see objects very clearly when we focus that portion of the eye upon them.[15] Often I leave Sima, Sasha and Rani tied to a post while I go into a library or a store. Upon coming out, I notice that they look at every person emerging with equal intensity. It is only when I am fairly close to them (within about thirty feet) that they recognise me. On the other hand, if I take them walking in the park at night, they are able to go racing about the hills where I can see only a few feet in front of me. This is because they are more sensitive to light than I am. While we have greater binocular vision, which allows us to focus on details, dogs have sixty degrees more peripheral vision than we do, which is useful in hunting.

A dog's eyes are also more sensitive to movement. I see my three dogs freeze and suddenly go racing forward in pursuit of something I have not seen. What they chase in such cases is never imaginary: they notice squirrels and other smaller rodents at great distances. What they see is the characteristic movement. They can perceive direction, speed, and trajectory. At dusk my dogs, like horses, are easily spooked: they will become terrified of a post, a paper bag, a statue, and only when they have sniffed it thoroughly are they convinced of its harmlessness. Since they see much better than I do in the dark, I am not sure why this should be so. The other day we passed a bronze bear in full daylight, and all three dogs backed off. They could see that it had all the contours of a wild animal, but it was not moving. Although at first they did not know what to make of it, they learnt fast: on the way back, the same statue was of no concern to them. Do wolves see better than dogs? Apparently so. L. David Mech, the foremost expert on wolf behaviour, reports how he watched a two-year-old wild male wolf stare across an Arctic valley at some speck far away, then dash out and suddenly seize a young grey Arctic hare: 'That observation told me a wolf can see a camouflaged hare 400 yards away.'[16] It may, however, have been the movement that the wolf saw.

Until very recently, it was claimed that dogs are colour blind.[17] Apparently, this is not true.[18] Dogs can be trained to discriminate colours.[19] They have just enough cones (centre of vision receptors) and rods (for peripheral vision) for us to say that they may not see colours as well as we do (and we see them less well than certain birds), but dogs almost certainly have some sense of colour. It is hard to test this. How do we know that another human sees the same 'yellow' we see? Dogs do not need to discriminate colours for survival, and I have no anecdotal evidence that a dog will prefer some object because of the way it is coloured, though this does not mean they are completely unaware of its colour. Perhaps they can avoid a bright red poisonous frog for the same reason that other animals learn to stay away: its colour is a warning; what is called aposematic colouring – that is, red and black, or yellow and black, which keeps many little creatures from being eaten. Some dogs, such as retrievers and the so-called sight or gaze hounds, see much better than other breeds, and it is likely that there are individual differences within breeds as well.

None the less, sight does not play the crucial role in the life of a dog that some of the other senses do. Dogs hear much better than we do, for example. A dog can hear sounds from four times farther away than a human. Dogs are constantly freezing, one paw up so as to make less noise, indicating that they have heard something outside of our range. One ear scans for the sounds, while the other funnels the sound waves. A dog can locate a source of sound in six-hundredths of a second.[20] This is why we often see our dogs stop, listen, and then immediately go racing off in a specific direction. They are also able to detect higher-pitched sounds than we can, which may explain why they always find chipmunks, squirrels, and other ground rodents which emit high frequency warning signals outside the range of the human ear. Some hunters claim that dogs can hear sounds much too low in volume for human ears to detect, such as waterfowl touching down on water over half a mile away.[21] When floppy-eared dogs hear something they lift up their ears, much as we cup our hands behind our ears to hear something better. Sasha, with her large German shepherd ears, always bends one of them forward, the better to hear. Dogs can move their ears independently and so can get a better directional fix than humans. As with us, hearing is selective in dogs. Sasha may be sound asleep until she hears my car pull up in the driveway, when instantly she is awake. A fire engine wailing in front of our house last week failed to rouse any of the sleeping dogs. My friend Michael Parenti tells me that his dog can hear a coming storm before he could. The dog will show fear, salivate and hide under the bed. Michael says he is puzzled until five minutes later when a thunderstorm breaks. Evidently dogs can smell the electricity in the air.

A dog's sense of touch is exquisite: the entire body, even the paws, is covered with tactile nerve endings. They sense airflow through touch-sensitive hairs called vibrissae that are located above the eye, on the muzzle, and below the jaw. This explains in part why dogs raise their heads to the sea breezes. Raising the head also enhances their ability to smell.

Footsteps can be detected by dogs through ground vibrations. So when we see our dogs stop and stare, and we notice nothing, they could easily be sensing something far away beginning to move in their direction. Wolves were able to do this with the herds of bison they hunted.

When it comes to touch, dogs seem to surpass us in their ability to express themselves. It is a rare dog who does not like to be stroked, patted, scratched and lovingly touched. Dogs touch one another constantly, though not as much as wolves do. Rani is constantly soliciting touch by putting her paw on my arm to remind me of her due. Sasha wants it too, but only for a moment. She cannot pass anybody in the street without asking for a quick touch, but the token is enough for her. Her need is satisfied in seconds, and she will break contact if it lasts longer. This could be part of the aloofness of the German shepherd breed, or peculiar to Sasha. Sima loves to kiss – must kiss – and when she is stroked she closes her eyes in ecstasy. The importance of touching for dogs could be analogous to the importance of touching for humans, which is related to the mother-infant bond. Generally, a puppy gets plenty of cuddling from its mother, and evidently never forgets it. Infants may be cuddled by their mothers, but cuddling seems to be a source of embarrassment for many adults. Perhaps we would do well to take our cues from the unabashed dog.

To understand the dog's world, we must appreciate that smell is central to a dog's experience of reality. Dogs (like cats and cows) are specially equipped for specific scent-capturing with the vomero-nasal organ (also called Jacobson's organ), consisting of a pouch lined with receptor cells, much like those used for olfaction, situated in the roof of the mouth. Its function is little known, but it allows the dog literally to taste the air. As Roger Caras has remarked, 'A dog's nose is something for us to wonder at. It is perfectly remarkable and reminds us that there is a world out there that we can never know – at least, not as human beings.'[22] As noted in Chapter Five, dogs have more than forty times the number of olfactory cells as humans have, each cell containing several small hair-like structures called cilia. A human being has 6 to 8 cilia per olfactory cell, while the dog has 100 to 150 cilia per cell. The information that a dog receives from a scent is carried directly to an emotional centre in the brain. This immediate connection means that, when a dog smells something, it has an intense emotional response.[23] In theory, this intensity is true for humans as well, but most people are able to suppress emotional reactions to smells, as this ability is seen as a carry-over from our more primitive lives and is not now highly esteemed. A smell to which we humans have absolutely no access can excite, intoxicate, and enchant a dog. A whole world thus remains closed to us. Roger Caras has remarked that we don't know how many senses dogs have, which means that we don't really know how they relate to their surroundings.[24]

In her book, *Perfume*, Susan Irvine speaks of a man who, perhaps through taking a certain drug, became hyperosmic: that is, he was able to smell as vividly as a dog. He would recognise people with one sniff before he saw them and could find his way around New York by smell alone. Unlike a dog, however, the man was miserable because of his gift, only wishing to be a scent-poor human once again.[25]

It is the intimate relationship between emotions and sensory experience that allows the dog to be in constant touch with an emotional core and is why we see the dog live through such a range of emotions in any one day. Dogs *are* pure emotion, because a dog's sensory world is in constant intercourse with its emotional world. James Thurber observed this many years ago:

> The effect upon the dog of his life with Man is discernible in his eyes, which frequently are capable of a greater range of expression than Man's. The eyes of the sensitive French poodle, for example, can shine with such an unalloyed glee and darken with so profound a gravity as to disconcert the masters of the earth, who have lost the key to so many of the simpler magics. Man has practiced for such a long time to mask his feelings and to regiment his emotions that some basic quality of naturalness has gone out of both his gaiety and his solemnity. The dog is aware of this, I think. You can see it in his eyes sometimes when he lies and looks at you with a long, rueful gaze.[26]

Looking back upon my training and later experience as a psychoanalyst,[27] I find only a few ideas of lasting significance. One is Freud's notion that a person could be in love with somebody without knowing it because access to his own emotions remain so blocked that he might not learn about it until years later, usually when it is too late to do anything about it. Freud's earliest theory about the origin of human unhappiness has also had a profound effect on me. He believed that the causes of human misery lay in the real traumas we experience in our childhood, ones that were imposed upon us from the outside world. This suggested that society could be altered, that the world could be made different, so that children grew up in a happier, safer, more compassionate environment.

When I think about these discoveries and try to apply them to dogs, I run up against certain difficulties. Dogs, it should be apparent by now, do not require psychoanalysis or any kind of analysis before they can recognise their own feelings; indeed they have the ability, so rare in humans, to be always and continuously feeling their own internal emotions. This is so apparent that it must play no small role in our love for dogs. At the same time, if a dog grows up in a loving home, it will not experience unhappiness and will not develop into an unhappy animal, one prone to sadness or what we think of as a neurosis. Even if the dog has had its share of misery – and here is the great lesson we can take from dogs – it somehow manages, without the benefit of analysis, to overcome the past, to emerge from a time of sorrow with a strange kind of optimism: it wishes to love again. It must love again. We are drawn to this capacity in a dog; it corresponds to something in us which has been lost somewhere in our evolutionary past, and which we long to recover.

Perhaps it harks back to a time when humans were more like dogs, more spontaneous, more capable of expressing joy, able to experience intense emotions and enjoy the world outside our skins more immediately, in the same way as we see our dogs doing. Children, I believe, retain this dog-like capacity for spontaneous joy until they unlearn it from their elders. This might explain the intense bond that has always existed between children and dogs. Both know something we adults seem to have lost and must now try to recover. Fortunately we have both children and dogs to help us in our quest for happiness.

In Search of the Soul of the Dog

IN *The Unbearable Lightness of Being*, the Czech writer Milan Kundera ends his novel by reminding us that:

> The very beginning of Genesis tells us that God created man in order to give him dominion over fish and fowl and all creatures. Of course, Genesis was written by a man, not a horse. There is no certainty that God actually did grant man dominion over other creatures. What seems more likely, in fact, is that man invented God to sanctify the dominion that he had usurped for himself over the cow and the horse. Yes, the right to kill a deer or a cow is the only thing all of mankind can agree upon, even during the bloodiest of wars.[1]

He goes on to say that 'true human goodness, in all its purity and freedom, can come to the fore only when its recipient has no power. Mankind's true moral test, its fundamental test (which lies deeply buried from view), consists of its attitude towards those

186

who are at its mercy: animals. And in this respect mankind has suffered a fundamental debacle, a debacle so fundamental that all others stem from it.' More and more people are coming to similar conclusions, me among them. It is no accident that Kundera uses this comment towards the end of the book, for the ending is intimately tied to the love of Tereza for Karenin, her dog. She is visited with the sacrilegious thought that her love for Karenin was greater than her love for Tomas, that in fact love for a dog is greater than any love between a man and a woman, for it is a completely voluntary and selfless love.

Slowly, very slowly, our world is beginning to understand, perhaps for the first time in history, that humans are not the apex, the very pinnacle of creation, but only part of a larger world. This means that we must share our planet with many other creatures, sentient and not, who have as much right to its bounty and purity as we. Most children seem to have an easier time with this seeming blow to our narcissism than adult humans. I would guess that the children who do understand this essential truth, have had an early relation with that most domesticated of all domesticated animals, the dog.

Love for a dog during childhood is one of the deepest and purest emotions we are ever likely to have, and it remains with us for the rest of our lives. For some people, their first experience of love is with a dog. The fact that the dog returns the love so fiercely, so openly, so unambivalently, is for many children a unique and lasting experience. Mary Midgley argues that even children who have not had any experience with an animal, actively seek it. 'Animals,' she says, 'like song and dance, are an innate taste.' Morris Berman, in *Coming to our Senses*, points out that for the child, the 'Other is a source of awe or excitement, not of fear; and it makes a deep sense of confidence in the body possible – an ontological confidence, one that is not going to develop into a need to "purify" the world by destroying it.'[3]

I have written about a dog's compassion for humans; I think it is appropriate to end on a note of our love and compassion for dogs. The enormous (over 100,000 verses) Indian epic known as the *Mahabharata* (written some time between 500 B.C. and A.D. 500) ends with a wonderful story about a dog.[4] The great emperor Yudhishthira, at the end of his reign, has set off on a final trek north, towards the Himalaya. He is accompanied by his four

187

brothers, the Pandavas as they are known, and their common-wife, Draupadi. A small pariah dog attaches himself to the retinue as well. Slowly, every member of this royal troupe dies along the way. The four brothers and the wife all succumb. Yudhishthira and the dog continue on their way alone. Eventually, they reach the end of their journey. At the gates of heaven. Indra, the King of the Gods, comes to greet the emperor in a golden chariot. He invites him to climb into the chariot and accompany him in regal and godly splendour into heaven. Yudhishthira replies:

'This dog, O Lord of the Past and the Present, has been a constant and faithful companion to me. He should go with me. My heart is full of compassion for him.'

The King of the Gods says to him:

'Immortality equal to mine, O king, prosperity extending over all the earth, renown and all the joys of heaven have you won today. Leave the dog. There is nothing cruel in this.'

Yudhishthira says: 'O god of a thousand eyes, O you of righteous behaviour, I have always behaved righteously, it is hard now to perpetrate an act that is unrighteous. I do not wish for wealth for whose sake I must abandon one that is devoted to me.'

Indra says: 'There is no place in Heaven for persons with dogs. Besides, the deities called the Krodhavasas take away all the merits of such persons. Think about this, O King of the righteous. Abandon the dog. It is not cruelty.'

Yudhishthira tells the King of the Gods:

'I will in no circumstances abandon this dog now to achieve happiness for myself.'

The King of the Gods tries to convince him one last time:

'If you give up the dog, you will acquire the world of heaven. You have already given up your brothers and wife. You have obtained heaven through your very own deeds. You have already abandoned everything. How can you be so confused as not to give up a mere dog?'

Yudhishthira still refuses, saying he abandoned his wife and brothers because they were already dead, but he will not abandon this living dog.

At that point, the dog reveals himself to be none other than the God of Righteousness himself.[5] How appropriate that in India, a country not noted for kindness to dogs nowadays, this animal should be linked, perhaps five hundred years before Christ, so explicitly with loyalty, devotion, and especially love.

Here is a modern parallel. Over the Internet, the Board of Governors of the Dalmatian Club of America in Memphis, Tennessee, sent out a notice on 8 June 1996: 'If you are the owner of a deaf Dalmatian and are having problems with the dog, don't feel guilty about it. Consider starting over with a healthy, hearing pup. And *do* have the deaf dog put down.' They argue that deaf pups should never be sold, placed, or given away, as they are hard to raise, difficult to control, and often become snappish or overly aggressive. 'It is important that deaf pups be dealt with in a responsible and *humane* fashion' – in other words, killed. Well, Steven Doleac, an emergency medical technician for the Model Secondary School for the Deaf and a pre-college athletic trainer, was not having any of it. He had already adopted a deaf Dalmatian, Kendall (after Kendall Green, part of Gallaudet University). Her sign name is the sign letter 'K', shaking the hand left-to-right, like her wagging tail. Steve taught his dog American Sign Language and he has devoted his time and energies to taking other deaf dogs who would otherwise be killed and placing them with deaf people who can teach them sign language and communicate as completely with them as anyone can with a hearing dog.[6] They are every bit as intelligent, as devoted, as kind-hearted as any other dog. Steve is showing compassion to these dogs, returning a little bit of the immense debt of compassion dogs have shown to us over the last 10,000 years. I wish him and all his dogs saved from death success and long life.

People often dismiss dogs as being entirely creatures of their senses, slavishly dependent on the external world to provide them excitement and interest. Such people note in particular the dog's evident delight in its sense of smell, but what a dog smells has a complex effect on its emotional life. Why not compare the effect of scent on the inner life of the dog to the effect of taste on a person's inner life? Marcel Proust gives a poignant description of this effect in *Swann's Way*. His protagonist bites into a 'petite madeleine' cookie soaked in tea and is suddenly overtaken with a feeling of exquisite pleasure. This pleasurable feeling, stimulated by the taste of the madeleine, is linked to a childhood memory. He suddenly remembers that, when he was a little boy, his aunt

Léonie would give him such a madeleine, having dipped it first into her own cup of tisane, but 'when from a long-distant past nothing subsists, after the people are dead, after the things are broken and scattered, taste and smell alone, more fragile but more enduring, more insubstantial, more persistent, more faithful, remain poised a long time, like souls, remembering, waiting, hoping amid the ruins of all the rest; and bear unflinchingly, in the tiny and almost impalpable drop of their essence, the vast structure of recollection . . . in that moment all the flowers in our garden and in M. Swann's park, and the water-lilies on the Vivonne and the good folk of the village and their little dwellings and the parish church and the whole of Combray and its surroundings, taking shape and solidity, sprang into being, town and gardens alike, from my cup of tea.'[7]

Perhaps smells evoke a similar magical response in dogs. It seems as if every smell reminds them of other smells, and dogs are able to have an almost mystical experience of intense pleasure not unlike the one so memorably described by Proust. Perhaps dogs experience nostalgia for lost friends, dogs and humans, for places they have lived in and walks they have taken, every bit as intensely as we do. Anyone who has seen the face of a dog when it fears it has been abandoned knows that the emotions it is experiencing are of the deepest kind.

When asked if a dog had a soul, the Italian dog expert, Piero Scanziani – who gave the National League for the Defence of the Dog, which he founded, this motto: 'Let us demonstrate that man knows how to defend a friend' – answered that we may as well ask if a dog has a body. It is just as evident that a dog has a psychic existence as that it has a corporeal one. The soul of a dog is immensely rich, he tells us, because of the many deeply felt emotions dogs experience.[8]

There is a marvellous account in an old book, written in 1789, about ancient Hawaii, that shows the deep feelings a person can have for a dog:

A remarkable circumstance . . . shows the great regard the natives have for their dogs; in making a considerable way along the shore, he [Mr Goulding] met with an Indian and his wife; she had two puppies, one at each breast; the oddity of the circumstances induced him to endeavour to purchase one of them, which the woman could not, by all his persuasions or temptations, be induced to part with; but some of the nails [her husband was offered in exchange for the dog] had such powerful attractions upon the husband, that he insisted upon her parting with one of them; at last, with every sign of real sorrow she did, giving it at the same time an affectionate embrace. Although he was at this time a considerable way from the ship, the woman would not part with him till they arrived where the boat was lying to take him on board, and just upon his quitting the shore she very earnestly entreated to have it once more before they parted; upon his complying with which, she immediately placed it at the breast, and after some time returned it to him again.[9]

It could well be that, years later, this compassionate Hawaiian woman would dream with intense longing about these dogs. And who is to say whether the dogs themselves might not, smelling something that reminded them of Hawaii, be visited with the same nostalgia for those happy days long gone?

It has been often said that humans are on an arrogant mission when they seek out life on other planets before they have adequately understood the alien lives on our own planet. I think this is particularly true when it comes to dogs, for here is another life-form that is both immediately understandable and familiar, while at the same time there is some unyielding mystery at the heart of a dog. Just when we think we know them completely, we look into the eyes of a family dog and something about their radiance, their depth, gives us pause. 'Who are you, really?' we are inclined to ask at that moment. The dog might smile, a familiar smile, but will not answer. They keep their deepest mysteries to themselves.

I am not a religious man, and I pause before using the word soul, but my experiences with the dogs in my life, and now with Sasha, Sima, and Rani, convince me that there is some profound essence, something about being a dog, which corresponds to our notion of an inner soul, the core of our being that makes us most human. In human animals, this core, I am convinced, has to do with our ability to reach out and help a member of another species, to devote our energy to the welfare of that species, even when we do not stand to benefit from the other; in short, to love

191

the other for its own sake. If any species on earth shares this miraculous ability with us (and perhaps there are many more we do not yet know about), it is the dog, for the dog truly loves us, sometimes beyond expectation, beyond measure, beyond what we deserve, more indeed than we love ourselves.

Because the soul of the dog is love, the dog can love other animals, itself, and us, with a completeness, a purity and an intensity, that we can admire, and perhaps even learn to emulate. Dogs as gurus? As purveyors of wisdom, the wisdom of love? We have done worse. And, after all, no dog will ever lie to us above love.

NOTES AND REFERENCES

Preface *In Search of Feelings in Dogs*

1. The passage is to be found on page 175 of the first edition of Darwin's *On the Origin of Species by Means of Natural Selection*, 1859.
2. Louis Robinson, *Wild Traits in Tame Animals*, p. 45.
3. German authors distinguish between 'hard' dogs, who will not rest until they master a skill, and 'soft' dogs who would rather play and enjoy themselves.
4. J. E. R. Staddon, 'Animal psychology: the tyranny of anthropocentrism'. In *Perspectives in Ethology*, vol. 8: *Whither Ethology?* edited by P. P. G. Bateson and Peter H. Klopfer.

Chapter 1 *Recognising the Emotions of a Dog*

1. George J. Romanes, *Animal Intelligence*, p. 438.
2. Scott and Fuller, *Genetics and the Social Behavior of the Dog*, p. 131.
3. Quoted in Marjorie Garber's *Dog Love*, p. 74.
4. Dogs have other kinds of ambivalence, however. When I run and Leila walks, the dogs appear confused. They want to be with both of us and the look on their faces is unmistakably one of pure ambivalence. They could not understand why we were parting. The only person who takes marital separation harder than a dog is a child – another trait that children have in common with dogs.
5. P. Leyhausen, *Cat Behavior*.
6. Michael Fleischer, *Hund und Mensch*, pp. 70–71.
7. Jared Diamond, 'Zebras and the Anna Karenina Principle'. *Natural History*, 9, 1994.
8. Juliet Clutton-Brock, 'The Unnatural World', in *Animals and Human Society* (edited by A. Manning and J. A. Serpell), pp. 23–35.
9. Michael Fox, 'The influence of domestication', in *Abnormal Behavior in Animals,* edited by M. W. Fox, p. 71.
10. H. Hediger, *Studies of the Psychology and Behaviour of Captive Animals in Zoos and Circuses*.

11. Eberhard Trumler, *Mit dem Hund auf Du*, p. 169.
12. Voltaire, *Dictionnaire philosophique*.
13. Quoted in Keith Thomas, *Man and the Natural World*, p. 107.
14. Cited in Helen and George Papashvily, *Dogs and People*.
15. Ambrose Bierce, *The Devil's Dictionary*, p. 19.
16. I have taken these from the chapter 'Perfect Dogs' in Constance Perin's *Belonging in America*, p. 118.
17. See *The Macmillan Book of Proverbs*.
18. Joel S. Savishinsky, 'Pet Ideas', in *New Perspectives on Our Lives with Companion Animals*, edited by Aaron Katcher and Alan Beck, p. 126.
19. James Thurber, *Thurber's Dogs,* pp. 205-206.
20. Frances and Richard Lockridge, *Cats and People*. Cited in *Animals and Man in Historical Perspective*, edited by Joseph and Barrie Klaits, p. 114.
21. Elizabeth Marshall Thomas notes that her husband's dog ritually shows his belly first thing in the morning, like a morning devotion. She compares the human humbly kneeling to pray and a dog showing its belly – demonstrating submission – to a person. See *The Hidden Life of Dogs*, XVII-XVIII.
22. Donald Griffin, *Animal Thinking*. See also his *The Question of Animal Awareness* and *Animal Minds*.
23. Roger Caras, *A Dog is Listening*, p. 147.
24. Hastings, *The Encyclopedia of Religion and Ethics* (1908), Ch. 2.
25. R. J. Zwi Werblowsky, 'On Anthropomorphism', in *The Encyclopedia of Religion* (edited by Mircea Eliade), pp. 316-20.
26. I have dealt with the question of anthropomorphism in greater detail in *When Elephants Weep*, pp. 30-38. See, too, Kennedy, *The New Anthropomorphism*; Fisher, 'Disambiguating Anthropomorphism', and Eddy, 'Attribution of Cognitive States to Animals'.
27. Quoted by Elizabeth Lawrence in 'The Sacred Bee, the Filthy Pig, and the Bat Out of Hell: Animal Symbolism as Cognitive Biophilia'. In *The Biophilia Hypothesis*, edited by Stephen R. Kellert and Edward O. Wilson, p. 321.
28. Quoted by Yi-Fu Tuan in *Landscapes of Fear*, pp. 14-15. For a totally different viewpoint about these fascinating animals, see Stebbins and Cohen, *A Natural History of Amphibians*. They report that at the first World Congress of Herpetology held at Canterbury, England, in 1989, participants noted that amphibians, particularly frogs and toads, were declining from widely separated parts of the world, and many species were already extinct. Our world may be far more intimately connected to salamanders, frogs and toads and others of the more than 4,500 known living species of amphibians than Linnaeus ever suspected.
29. Mary Midgely, 'Why knowledge matters', in *Animals in Research*, edited by D. Sperlinger.

Chapter 2 *Why We Cherish Dogs*

1. Roger Caras, in his introduction to *Beautiful Joe* by Marshall Saunders, points out that racing greyhound breeders still kill fifty thousand perfectly

healthy dogs every year because they can no longer perform at the track.

2. *Animal Biography*, London: G. Virtue, 1840, p. 79. The book is anonymous.
3. Cited in Jon Winokur's *Mondo Canine*, p. 248.
4. Anatole France, 'The Coming of Riquet', in *Best Dog Stories*, p. 86.
5. Roger Caras, *A Dog is Listening*, p. 52.
6. G. H. Brückner, 'Ueber einen zweibeinigen Hund', *Zeitschrift für Hundeforschung*, 1938, pp. 1–16.
7. I have taken this quote from the fascinating early article by W. Fowler Bucke: 'Cyno-psychoses. Children's thoughts, reactions, and feelings toward pet dogs'. In *The Pedagogical Seminary*, 10, pp. 509, 1903.
8. J. K. Wise and J. J. Yang, 'Dog and cat ownership, 1991–1998'. In *Journal of the American Veterinary Association*, 204 (1994), pp. 1166–67.
9. This is also the theme of a poem quoted by E. V. Lucas, 'The More I see of Men' (which I have taken from Vesey-Fitzgerald's *Animal Anthology*, p. 86), which begins with the lines:

> A heart to love you till you die –
> That's the thing that money can buy.

and ends with these lines:

> Wherever dogs are offered for sale,
> These are things that money can buy.

10. The exceptions have been described by Vicki Hearne in a series of her books, especially *Bandit* and *Adam's Task*.
11. Quoted in Brian Vesey-Fitzgerald's *Animal Anthology*, p. 86.
12. Marjorie Garber, *Dog Love*, pp. 82–88.

Chapter 3 *Love: The Master Emotion of Dogs*

1. A. J. Brodbeck, 'An exploratory study on the acquisition of dependency behavior in puppies'. In *Bulletin of the Ecological Society of America*, 35 (1954), p. 73.
2. People have asked me how, then, is one to explain the fact that some dogs kill people. There are approximately 18 deaths per year caused by dogs in the United States. Some of these deaths are of sleeping infants, although far more infants are killed every year by their fathers than by dogs. I think an explanation can be found in every case, which does not make the death more bearable, but a detailed study would contribute to the psychology of the dog. I have yet to hear of a single normal relationship between a dog and a person that ends in this kind of tragedy. For references on fatal dog bites, see below, p. 206.
3. Roger Caras, *A Dog is Listening*, p. 136.
4. Michael Fox, *The Dog: Its Domestication and Behavior*, p. 259.
5. E. Dechambre, 'La théorie de foetalisation'. In *Mammalia* 13 (1949), pp. 129–237.
6. Since so much praise has been heaped upon Konrad Lorenz (1903–89), who won the Nobel Prize for Medicine in 1973, it seems only fair to let the reader know that, from 1938, he had a shameful association with the

Nazi party, and became a member of the party's Office of Race Policy. In his papers written in the 1940s, he classified people into those of 'full value' (*vollwertig*) and those of 'inferior value' (*minderwertig*); he spoke of 'socially inferior human material' (*sozial minderwertigen Menschenmaterials*) and even of the 'elimination of the ethically inferior' (*Ausmerzung ethisch Minderwertiger*). See by Ute Deichmann, *Biologists Under Hitler*, p. 189.

7. From Konrad Lorenz's *King Solomon's Ring: New Light on Animal Ways*.
8. Erich Klinghammer and Patricia Ann Goodmann, 'Socialization and management of wolves in captivity', in *Man and Wolf: Advances, Issues, and Problems in Captive Wolf Research* (edited by H. Frank), p. 45.
9. Stephen Jay Gould, 'Mickey Mouse Meets Konrad Lorenz'. In *Natural History*, vol. 88 (5), pp. 30-36.
10. Konrad Lorenz, 'Der Kumpan in Der Umwelt des Vogels'. John Paul Scott comments in *Genetics and the Social Behavior of the Dog*, p. 142, that Lorenz's word for imprinting is *Prägung*, which means impress, and this might have been a better translation. Young birds seem to be deeply 'impressed' or 'imprinted' by experiences early in life.
11. The time lapse can be extremely important. Scott and Fuller, in *Genetics and the Social Behavior of the Dog*, p. 129, point out that if a lamb is taken from its mother at birth and returned at any time within four hours, she will accept it and allow it to nurse. After this time she rejects it, along with any other strange lambs.

Chapter 4 *On Loyalty and Heroism*

1. Senator George Graham Vest, 1830–1904, Eulogy on the Dog, Johnson County Circuit Court, Warrensburg, Missouri. See Gustav Kobbé, *A Tribute to the Dog: Including the Famous Tribute by Senator Vest*, 1910.
2. R. H. Smythe, *Animal Psychology*, pp. 232-33. It has been suggested that this tremendous loyalty derives from the great maternal love that some dogs display: 'I have a record of one retriever bitch which travelled two miles across a town, retrieved her puppy from a large saucepan in which it had been "drowned", carried it home, and resuscitated it.' Op.cit., p. 229.
3. Quoted by Scott and Fuller in *Genetics*, p. 47.
4. The French psychiatrist A. Brion, in an article entitled 'Suicide et automutilations chez les animaux', writes of 'observations d'animaux domestiques, chiens le plus souvent, qui cessent de manger, dépérissent et meurent lorsqu'ils ont perdu leur maître. Ce fait est indéniable'. – (observations made on domestic animals, generally dogs, who cease eating, waste away, and die when they lose their masters. This fact is undeniable).
5. Edward Jesse, *Anecdotes of Dogs*, p. 465.
6. Cervantes, *A Dialogue between Scipio and Berganza, Two Dogs belonging to the city of Toledo*. p. 135.
7. Rhoda Lerman, *In the Company of Newfies*, p. 158. While mentioning Newfoundlands, I cannot refrain from telling the story, repeated in

Carson Ritchie's *The British Dog*, p. 150, about a Newfoundland dog in the audience where a performance of *Jesse Vere* was being given at the theatre in Woolwich. During the play, a man beats a young girl. The dog was so incensed by seeing this that he jumped the footlights and 'was only pulled away from the actor impersonating the villain with the greatest difficulty'.

8. Gregory Zompolis, *Operation Pet Rescue*, pp. 28-29.
9. Barbara Cohen and Louise Taylor, *Dogs and Their Women*, p. 94.
10. R. H. Smythe, *The Mind of the Dog*.
11. Göran Bergman, *Why Does Your Dog Do That?*, p. 124. In this book, Bergman discusses the question of homing in general. He summarises his conclusions about a dog's orientation as follows: 'It can be said that a dog very quickly learns to know areas it regularly inhabits, and that within this area, it learns to use roundabout routes, short cuts, and easy connecting routes such as paths and roads....There is no real evidence that dogs possess the ability to find their way home over a longer distance.'
12. Michael Fox, *Superdog*.
13. A minor exception is the book by L. Huyghebaert, *Le Chien: Psychologie – Olfaction – Mécanisme de l'Odorat*. He is convinced that the dog finds its way home exclusively through scent and is completely opposed to seeking 'un sens supplémentaire'. (p. 54). Michael Fox in 'The Extra Sense of Man and Beast' (in *Between Animal and Man*, p. 29-32) suggests that dogs and cats find their way home by geomagnetic influences from the earth. 'It seems there is a sense of place and, possibly related to this, what we often refer to as a "spirit of place".'
14. The article by Bastian Schmid is entitled 'Vorläufiges Versuchsergebnis über das hundliche Orienterungsproblem'. (Preliminary results on the problem of canine homing ability). It was published in the *Zeitschrift für Hundeforschung*, vol. 2, (1932), pp. 133-56. (This remarkable journal for the scientific study of the dog was published between 1931 and 1951.) There is an English summary of this article called 'How does the dog find his way home?' in his book *Interviewing Animals*, pp. 182-202.
15. Schmid, in *Von de Aufgaben der Tierpsychologie*, p. 178, says that dogs in these circumstances, 'are plagued by a kind of homesickness' (dass er von einer Art Heimweh geplagt).
16. Op. cit. p. 138.
17. 'When one analyses the evidence, one finds that the number of cats removed from their homes which do *not return* is very large compared with those that come back . . . the same conclusion applies to the return home of dogs. Huge numbers of dogs change hands, many escape and get lost, either temporarily or entirely, but very few find their way home, and the extraordinary cases that are reported in print now and again are almost certainly not examples of the supposed homing instinct, but of luck, of sheer flukes, that have enabled the wanderer to get back.' So Frances Pitt wrote in *Animal Mind*, pp. 159-62.

18. Reported in *The Times*, 5 September 1996, and in the *Daily Mail* the same day.

19. *The Boston Herald*, 18 March 1996, first edition.

20. The story is told in many books and articles, but I have been unable to find a more elaborate account in English.

21. Personal communication from Jean E. Kundert, 10 May 1996.

22. *Dayton Daily News*, 30 March 1996.

Chapter 5 *Dogs Smell What We Cannot See*

1. Quoted in Jon Winokur's *Mondo Canine*, p. 255.

2. See the chapter 'Odour Preferences of Animals' in R.W. Moncrieff's, *Odour Preferences*. He notes that 'Sophisticated flower smells are liked much better by the over 25's than by young adults' (p. 316).

3. Fernand Mery, *The Life, History and Magic of the Dog*, p. 144.

4. Walter Neuhaus, 'Ueber die Riechschärfe des Hundes'. The article contains a complete bibliography on the topic. More recently, see Becker, Markee and King, 'Studies on olfactory acuity in dogs', and Moulton, Ashton and Eayrs, 'Studies in olfactory acuity'. Some researchers think this figure is too high. See Desmond Morris's *Dogwatching*, p. 58, and the literature cited in Syrotuch's *Scent and the Scenting Dog*. One can find many other figures cited as well. Michael Fox, one of America's foremost dog experts, says in *Superdog* that 'dogs love to roll in obnoxious organic material because they have a highly evolved sense of smell, probably a million times better than ours, and I believe they have an aesthetic sense in this modality: they like to wear odors much as we, a more visually oriented species, like to wear bright clothes or something different for a while'. While there is no doubt that a dog's sense of smell is far superior to our own, it is probably impossible to put an exact figure on it. It is a little like attempting to measure intelligence, which is never a good idea.

5. Roger Caras, *A Dog is Listening*, p. 59.

6. Eberhard Trumler, *Mit dem Hund auf Du*, p. 122.

7. I have taken this quote from the article by W. F. Bucke, 'Cyno-Psychoses', p. 475.

8. Elizabeth Marshall Thomas, *Certain Poor Shepherds*, p. 34.

9. Eberhard Trumler, in his book *Mit dem Hund auf Du* (pp. 242 ff.), maintains that dogs can tell from smelling faeces whether the dog who left the faeces is male or female, its physical and sexual condition, at what time the pile was left and whether the dog is known to them or not. They seem also to be able to put together the smell of the faeces with that of the sweat on the footprints. For wolves in the wild, this kind of information can be life-saving.

10. Sigmund Freud, *Civilization and its Discontents* (1929), p. 100, note. Actually what Strachey translates as 'an animal whose dominant sense is that of smell' is a single word in Freud's original German, *Geruchstier*, literally 'a smelling-animal'.

Chapter 6 *Submission, Dominance and Gratitude*

1. Rudolf Schenkel, 'Submission: its features and functions in the wolf and dog'. *American Zoologist*, 7 (1967), pp. 319-30.

2. Sometimes the nomenclature can be confusing. Mammals include a subgroup known as carnivores. There are two superfamilies: Canidea and Felidae (cats, civets and hyenas). Canidae include the dog, bear, sea lion, weasel, seal and racoon families. One subgenus is Canis (the canids), which includes dogs, wolves, coyotes and jackals.

3. Desmond Morris, *Dogwatching*, pp. 60-62.

4. Michael Fox, *Behavior of Wolves, Dogs and Related Canids*, p. 189. Another interesting explanation is found in *The Mind of the Dog* (p. 75), where R. H. Smythe sees the origin among dog scavengers rather than hunters, living on the kills or leavings of the larger carnivora. 'This particular instinct resembled that of bees which, when they found rich honey-bearing flowers, would return home and by their special dance advise all the other members of the hive of their discovery. The other bees would realize instinctively from this behavior that they must follow the dancing bee and so were led to the nectar. Similarly, other dogs, charmed by the smell of the highly scented animal, followed it around until they, too, were able to locate the feast and share in the banquet.'

5. 'Rather than fighting directly for the goods they desire, animals are likely to try out their strengths in a way that does not seriously damage anyone. They do not usually use their most dangerous weapons against their rivals, and losers accept their lot. They may even (in disaster areas) let themselves starve to death while the dominant few eat relatively well. This last phenomenon need not be interpreted as a conscious suicide for the good of the tribe. It is more likely to be a byproduct of the usually "successful" strategy of "wait and see": better to wait for the dominant's leavings and hope for a return match later on than risk a real fight now. Conversely, it is often better for the dominants (those successful in the contests that define the eating and mating orders) to allow their subordinates lives of their own, sometimes even to assist them, and not to press home their attacks lest their victim turn upon them with the courage of despair.' Stephen Clark, 'Good dogs and other animals', in *In Defense of Animals* edited by Peter Singer, pp. 48-49.

6. R. Lockwood, 'Dominance in wolves: useful construct or bad habit?' In *The Behavior and Ecology of Wolves*, edited by E. Klinghammer, pp. 225-44.

7. Elizabeth von Arnim, *All the Dogs of My Life*, p. 116. Elizabeth von Arnim (1866–1941), the cousin of Katherine Mansfield, (E. M. Forster tutored her children), wrote this autobiography, a charming account of her dogs, while living on the French Riviera in 1936.

8. The definitive article on subordination concludes: 'It is argued on conceptual grounds – not for the first time – but also demonstrated on empirical grounds that dominance should be treated as a phenomenon at the level of social relationships and not as an individual or motivational attribute.' Jan van Hoof and Josep Wensing, 'Dominance and its

behavioral measures in a captive wolf pack'. In *Man and Wolf: Advances, Issues, and Problems in Captive Wolf Research*, edited by H. Frank, p. 250.

9. George Romanes, *Animal Intelligence*, p. 444.

Chapter 7 *The Great Dog Fear: Loneliness and Abandonment*

1. D. L. Allen, *The Wolves of Minong*, p. 291. Cf. Lois Crisler, *Arctic Wild*, p. 283.
2. David Mech, *The Wolf*, p. 288.
3. J. P. Scott, 'Editor's comments'. In *Critical Periods*, p. 17.
4. Some of the best are: *Dog Problems* by Carol Lea Benjamin; *Behavior Problems in Dogs* by William Campbell; *People, Pooches & Problems* by Michael Job Evans (who also wrote, with the monks of New Skete, the excellent *How to Be Your Dog's Best Friend*); *Canine and Feline Behavioral Therapy* by Benjamin and Lynette Hart; and *When Good Dogs Do Bad Things* by Mordecai Siegal and Matthew Margolis.
5. Carol Lea Benjamin, *Mother Knows Best*.
6. Desmond Morris, *Dogwatching*, p. 89.
7. Houpt and Wolski: *Domestic Animal Behavior*, pp. 298–99.
8. Mordecai Siegal, *UC Davis School of Veterinary Medicine Book of Dogs*, p. 80.
9. Charles Darwin, *The Variation of Animals and Plants under Domestication*, p. 27: 'The habit of barking, however, which is almost universal with domesticated dogs, forms an exception, as it does not characterize a single natural species of the family, though I am assured that the *Canis latrans* of North America utters a noise which closely approaches a bark.' The quote in the text above follows this passage. Desmond Morris in *Dogwatching*, p. 15, reports that wolves kept near to domestic dogs learn to give the amplified dog-bark after a while. I am sceptical.
10. I do not know who first suggested this. I have seen it mentioned in a nineteenth-century text by P. Hachet-Souplet, *Examen psychologique des animaux*, quoted in L. Huyghebaert, op. cit., p. 79: 'Le Chien dans l'état sauvage n'aboie pas plus que le loup. L'un et l'autre, il est vrai, apprennent très vite à aboyer dans l'état domestique. Il semble que leur aboiment est un essai d'imitation très grossière du parler humain.' (In the wild the dog does not bark any more than the wolf. Both, it is true, quickly learn to bark when they are domesticated. It seems that their barking is a very awkward attempt to imitate human speech.) According to W. Fowler Bucke, in *Cyno-psychoses*, Darwin had already suggested this idea in *The Descent of Man*. Richard Katz, in 'Talks with Dogs' (*Solitary Life*, p. 233), writes that 'the barking of a dog to whom no human being talks is less expressive than the sound made by a dog whose master is in the habit of talking to him'.

Chapter 8 *Compassion: The Essence of a Dog's Inner Life*

1. See, for example, C. R. Badcock, *The Problem of Altruism*; Alfie Kohn, *The Brighter Side of Human Nature*; Samuel and Pearl Oliner, *The Altruistic Personality*.

2. Diane Ackerman, *A Natural History of Love*, p. 289.
3. Frans de Waal, *Good Natured*, p. 52. The book contains many other examples of compassion among the great apes.
4. *Los Angeles Times*, December 1995.
5. Morgan's cannon (named after Lloyd Morgan, the nineteenth-century English scientist) warns that we should never assume a higher level of explanation than is absolutely necessary and should always interpret animal behaviour as the outcome of the more simple mental faculties. Sometimes this is a useful caution but it is one that to my mind is over employed.
6. Dennis L. Krebs, 'Altruism – An examination of the Concept and a Review of the Literature'. In *Psychological Bulletin*, 73 (1970), pp. 258-302.
7. Irenäus Eibl-Eibesfeldt, *Love and Hate*, p. 89.
8. Rick McIntyre, 'The East Fork Pack', in *Out Among the Wolves*, edited by John A. Murray, p. 190.
9. Moobli, a German shepherd, features also in 'Tomkies' other books about Scottish Highland wildlife, notably *A Last Wild Place* and *Out of the Wild*.
10. See the story as reported in the *St. Louis Post-Dispatch*, vol. 118, no. 72 (Tuesday, 12 March 1996).
11. Barry Lopez, *Of Wolves and Men*, p. 69.
12. See Hank Whittemore and Caroline Hebard, *So That Others May Live*.
13. Philip Gonzalez and Leonore Fleischer, *The Dog Who Rescues Cats: The True Story of Ginny*.
14. Roger Caras, *A Dog is Listening*, pp. 103-08.

Chapter 9 *Dignity, Humiliation and Disappointment*

1. Ludwig Wittgenstein, *Zettel*. Translated by G. E. M. Anscombe, p. 91.
2. R. H. Smythe, *The Mind of the Dog*, p. 63.
3. George Romanes, *Animal Intelligence*, p. 444.
4. Henri Bergson, *Le Rire: essai sur la signification du comique*.
5. Barbara Woodhouse, *Talking to Animals*, p. 212.
6. Ludwig Wittgenstein, *Philosophical Investigations*, p. 174.
7. In Chapter 21 of 'Le Petit Prince' by Antoine de Saint Exupéry, the fox asks the little prince to tame him by coming every day at the same time, so that he can anticipate the happiness he will feel at the time, and ends by saying: 'Il faut des rites' (Everybody needs rituals).
8. Anne Lamott, *Operating Instructions*, p. 182.

Chapter 10 *Dog Dreams*

1. J. Allan Hobson, *The Chemistry of Conscious States*.
2. See H. Hediger, 'Vom Traum Der Tiere'. See too S. S. Campbell and I. Tobler, 'Animal sleep: A review of sleep duration across phylogeny'. The cat is the most studied of animals in terms of dreams. For a complete bibliography, see *Experimental Studies of Dreaming*, edited by Herman A. Witkin and Helen B. Lewis. An elaborate account by one of the pioneers of research on sleep, especially animal sleep, is given in an article by M.

Jouvet and D. Jouvet, 'Le sommeil et les rêves chez l'animal', in *Psychiatrie animale*, edited by A. Brion and Henri Ey, pp. 149-67.

3. Peretz Lavie, 'Do Fish Dream?' in *The Enchanted World of Sleep*, p. 102.
4. See Y. Shimazono, et al., 'The correlation of the rhythmic waves of the hippocampus with the behavior of dogs'.
5. Edgar A. Lucas et al., 'Baseline Sleep-Wake Patterns in the Pointer Dog', *Physiology & Behavior*, vol. 19, pp. 285-91. Jouvet and Jouvet, in the article cited above ('Le sommeil et les rêves chez l'animal', p. 164), claim that dogs and cats dream about the same amount of time, namely 20 per cent, but they cite no authority and do not claim to have undertaken any research themselves on the subject.
6. Frederick Snyder, 'In Quest of Dreaming', in *Experimental Studies of Dreaming*, edited by Herman A. Witkin and Helen B. Lewis, p. 55. Also Howard P. Roffwarg, Joseph Muzio and William Dement: 'Ontogenetic development of the human sleep-dream cycle', *Science* 152 (1966), pp. 604-19. The authors of this study observe that dream activity is associated with a segment of the brainstem that develops early. A fascinating study would be to compare REM behaviour in neo-nates and in dogs.
7. James L. Gould and Carol Grant Gould, *The Animal Mind*, p. 169.
8. Merrill M. Mitler, William C. Dement et al., 'Narcolepsy-Cataplexy in a Female Dog', *Experimental Neurology*, 45 (1974), pp. 332-240.
9. Virginia Woolf, *Flush: A Biography*, 1933. Quoted in *The Oxford Book of Creatures*, edited by Fleur Adcock and Jacqueline Simms, p. 137.
10. Bruce Max Feldman, a Berkeley veterinarian, suggests that I have someone else, without me present, take Sima towards a person whom she has met before. He thinks it would be interesting and possibly illuminating to do so. I welcome these kinds of benign experiments.
11. R. H. Smythe, *The Mind of the Dog*, p. 104.

Chapter 11 *Nature versus Nurture: Dogs at Work and Play*

1. William Koehler, *The Koehler Method of Dog Training*. Koehler trained the dogs for the Disney film, *The Incredible Journey*.
2. The cover picture on the December 1994 issue of *National Geographic* (vol. 186, no. 6, 'Animals at Play'), shows a polar bear playing with a husky dog. Everyone who saw the photograph was amazed and delighted. Something about this kind of play (where one expects murder) is particularly affecting.
3. Jeffrey Masson, *Lost Prince*.
4. Robert Fagen: *Animal Play Behavior*, p. 492.
5. Ibid.
6. Michael Fox, *The Wolf*, p. 224.
7. Robert Fagen, *Animal Play Behavior*, p. 487.
8. See the book edited by Alistair Lawrence and Jeffrey Rushen: *Stereotypic Animal Behaviour*. Such stereotypical movements are never seen in the wild, only in captive and domestic animals. In zoos one sees it in wolves, bears, hyenas and elephants, but also in horses and many captive bird

species. (An excellent account of these movements in zoo animals can be found in Vickie Croke's *The Modern Ark*). Monique Meyer-Holzapfel, who has studied these movements at the Bern zoo, thinks they are the results of emotional misery. See her: 'Mouvements stéréotypés chez les animaux: expression de malaises psychiques', in Brion and Ey, pp. 295-98. Many people who own hamsters derive pleasure from watching them run for hours in their wheels. But this, too, is the result of deprivation. See H. Petzsch: 'Ueber Bewegungsstereotypien bei kleinen Nagetieren in Gefangenschaft – Hamster (*Cricetus L.*) und Eich-hörnchen (*Sciurus vulgaris L.*). *Mitteilungen für Naturkunde und Vorgeschichte*, 1950, vol. 2, pp. 113-128 (Museum Magdeburg).

9. Scott and Fuller, *Genetics and the Social Behavior of the Dog*, p. 137.
10. R. D. Lawrence, *In Praise of Wolves*, p. 3.
11. Thomas Mann, *A Man and His Dog*, p. 97.
12. Roger Caras, *A Dog is Listening*, pp. 130-32.
13. See the many articles by Marc Bekoff, in particular: 'Social play and play-soliciting by infant canids', *American Zoologist* 14 (1974), pp. 323-40; 'Social communication in canids: Evidence for the evolution of a stereotyped mammalian display', *Science* 197 (1977), pp. 1907-99.
14. S. A. Altmann, 'Social behavior of anthropoid primates', in *Roots of Behavior*, edited by E. L. Bliss, pp. 277-85.
15. Dr Robert Kirk informs me that he believes this is not a sign of aggression but of dominance, and comes from the fact that a mother dog or wolf grasps the puppy by the scruff of the neck. This makes the puppy feel secure but dominated.
16. Roger Caras, *A Dog is Listening*, pp. 138-39.
17. Brian Vesey-Fitzgerald, *Animal Anthology*, p. 83.
18. Michael Fox speaks of 'the canid analogue of the human greeting grin'. This is distinct from the submissive grin and open-mouth play face of dogs. This facial expression is mimicked by the dog and has only been observed in man-dog interactions and not between dog and dog.
19. Erasmus Darwin: *Zoonomia* (1794-6), as quoted by Keith Thomas in *Man and the Natural World: A History of the Modern Sensibility*, p. 121.

Chapter 12. Cats and Dogs

1. Charles Darwin, *Journal of Researches into the Geology and Natural History of the Various Countries Visited by HMS 'Beagle'*, p. 142.
2. Billy Arjan Singh, *Eelie and the Big Cats*. See too his *Tiger! Tiger!* and *Prince of Cats*.
3. In the chapter 'The Mind of the Cat' in Frances and Richard Lockridge's *Cats and People*.
4. Jane Vessels, 'Koko's Kitten'. In *National Geographic*, January 1985, 167 (1), pp. 110-13.
5. People who have cats and dogs recognise that they often become extremely close friends. To test this scientifically, Michael Fox raised cats and dogs together in a series of experiments which clearly show the degree to which they can come to think of one another as a brother or

sister. I am not entirely certain whether they see themselves as a member of the other species. See his *Integrative Development of Brain and Behavior in the Dog*, as well as his article, 'Behavioral effects of rearing dogs with cats during the critical period of socialization', *Behavior*, 35 (1969), pp. 273–80.

6. Carl van Vechten, *The Tiger in the House*. 'Dieu a fait le chat pour donner à l'homme le plaisir de caresser le tigre.' Méry.

7. See R. Tabor, *The Wildlife of the Domestic Cat*. Also Juliet Clutton-Brock, *Cats Ancient and Modern*.

8. Maurice Maeterlinck, quoted in, *The Double Garden*, pp. 11-46.

9. Carl van Vechten, *The Tiger in the House*, p. 1.

Chapter 13 *Dogs and Wolves*

1. L. David Mech in *Wolf!*, p. 9.

2. 'It would appear that domestication of the dog took place in south-west Asia on the eve or the inception of the Mesolithic as early as 10,000 B.C.' H. Epstein, *The Origin of the Domestic Animals of Africa*, p. 145.

3. Juliet Clutton-Brock and Kim Dennis-Bryan, *Dogs of the Last Hundred Years at the British Museum (Natural History)*, 1988.

4. J. P. Scott, 'The social behavior of dogs and wolves', *Annals New York Academy of Sciences*, 51 (1950), p. 1012.

5. Peter Steinhart, *In the Company of Wolves*.

6. This was noted by L. David Mech in *The Way of the Wolf*, p. 26.

7. See Christine Gentry, *When Dogs Run Wild*. Also Alan Beck, *The Ecology of Stray Dogs: A Study of Free-Ranging Urban Animals*.

8. Erik Zimen, *The Wolf: His Place in the Natural World*, p. 33. See also his *Wölfe und Königspudel: Vergleichende Verhaltensbeobachtungen*, where he speaks in great detail of the crosses he bred between wolves and poodles.

9. John C. Fentress, 'Observations on the behavioral development of a hand-reared male timber wolf'. In *American Zoologist*, 7 (1967), pp. 339-51, especially p. 344.

10. John Paul Scott and John L. Fuller, *Genetics and the Social Behavior of the Dog*, p. 137. Desmond Morris states otherwise on pp. 19-20 of *Dogwatching*, where he maintains that puppies do not fully develop tail-wagging until six or seven weeks of age, and in adult dogs it signals an ambivalent frame of mind in which the dog is torn between staying and fleeing. No evidence is given, but Dr Morris says it can be observed. My observations, and those of several other dog and wolf experts, tell me a different story.

11. Michael Fox, in the chapter entitled 'Love, Dependence and Perpetual Infants' in *Between Animal and Man*, p. 58.

12. This point is well summed up by Louis Robinson in his 1897 book *Wild Traits in Tame Animals*, (p. 66) as follows: 'Finally, the instinct of association has, in the case of the domestic dog, become more exactly fitted to the new conditions of environment. He makes himself thoroughly at home with us because he feels that he is with his own

proper pack, and not among strangers or those of an alien race. The wild animal, on the contrary, still has the perception that those who would palm themselves off as his comrades are creatures of an alien nature. He sturdily refuses to become a party to the fraud, and remains suspicious of their intentions; and, whatever they may do to propitiate him, he keeps on the *qui vive* as against a possible enemy.'

13. Rudolf Schenkel, 'Ausdruckstudien an Wölfen', *Behavior* 1 (1947).

14. Peter Steinhart, *In the Company of Wolves*, pp. 345.

15. 'Packs of domestic dogs which have become feral lack the stability and complex interrelationships observed in the truly wild canine species.' Leo K. Bustad, 'Man and Beast Interface', in *Man and Beast Revisited*, edited by Michael H. Robinson and Lionel Tiger. The phenomenon of wild and stray dogs is the subject of an excellent article by the Italian wolf expert, Luigi Boitani, in the Italian nature magazine *Airone*, November 1996.

16. Vicki Hearne, *Adam's Task*, pp. 22-23.

17. Konrad Lorenz, *Man Meets Dog*, p. 24.

18. J. P. Scott, 'The evolution of social behavior in dogs and wolves', p. 377. Wolves, dogs, and probably jackals have the same number of chromosomes: 78. Moreover, as Epstein notes, 'the fact that the jackal has a smaller brain than a dog of its size excludes it . . . from the ancestry of the domestic dogs'. *The Origin of the Domestic Animals of Africa*, p. 139. Jackals and dogs do mate, and the offspring are fertile, however, as Christine Gentry (*When Dogs Run Wild*) notes.

19. Ian Dunbar, *Dog Behavior*, p. 178.

20. Fred H. Harrington and L. David Mech, 'Wolf-vocalizations', edited by Roberta L. Hall and Henry S. Sharp, in *Wolf & Man: Evolution in Parallel*, p. 130.

21. Desmond Morris, *Dogwatching*, p. 17.

22. Scott and Fuller, *Genetics and the Social Behavior of the Dog*, p. 28. The full quote reads: 'What kind of an animal is a dog? In evaluating the answers we would find that a dog is not a four-legged and childish human being dressed up in a fur coat. Our dogs could therefore give us answers to other questions only as dogs, closely related to human beings through social contacts but basically carnivores in their heredity.'

23. Deborah M. Warrick, 'Dogs and wolves'. In *Animals' Agenda*, vol. IX, no. 11, Dec. 1989.

24. Erkki Pulliainen, 'Ecology of the Wolf in the Settled Areas of Finland', in *The Behavior & Ecology of Wolves*, edited by Erich Klinghammer, p. 90.

25. Richard H. Polsky, 'Wolf hybrids'. In *Veterinary Medicine*, December 1995, pp. 1122-24.

26. The list of problems in owning a wolf-hybrid are numerous: they can be very destructive; they are difficult if not impossible to housebreak; if they bite somebody they can (by United States law) be destroyed and then tested for rabies; there is no approved rabies vaccine available for the wolf dog, and so on. See 'Wolf dogs: pets who aren't quite pets', in *Best Friend Magazine*, June 1996, p. 6. For a somewhat different

view, see also Dorothy Prendergast, *The Wolf Hybrid*.

27.   Peter Steinhart, *In The Company of Wolves*, p. 306.

28.   Ibid., p. 344.

Chapter 14 *Canine Aggression: Real or Feigned?*

1.   It is striking how the so-called negative emotions are thoroughly researched in animals, whereas the more positively toned ones are not. For example, 'The ontogeny of fear in animals' (in *Fear in Animals and Man*, edited by W. Sluckin, pp. 125-164) by Eric Salzen of the Department of Psychology at Aberdeen University, is a scholarly compilation listing hundreds of articles written on fear. There is no parallel article in the scientific literature about compassion, or gratitude, or even love in animals.

2.   Scott and Fuller, *Genetics and the Social Behavior of the Dog*, p. 117.

3.   Ibid., p. 112.

4.   John Paul Scott, 'Investigating Behavior: Toward a Science of Sociality', in *Studying Animal Behavior: Autobiographies of the Founders*, edited by Donald A. Dewsbury, p. 412.

5.   John Paul Scott, *Animal Behavior*.

6.   The very fact that wolf cubs can be raised almost exactly like a dog shows how closely related the two species are. See the important work by F. E. Zeuner, *A History of Domesticated Animals*.

7.   Niko Tinbergen, 'On War and Peace in Animals and Man', in *Man and Animal: Studies in Behavior*, edited by Heinz Friedrich, p. 135.

8.   The origin of this term comes, I believe, from Konrad Lorenz's *Man Meets Dog*: 'Should the tactlessly importunate human being persist in his attentions [to a shy dog trying to avoid human touch] and actually touch the dog, the terrified animal may lose control of itself and snap like lightning and with punishing severity at the offending hand. A considerable number of dog bites are attributable to this kind of biting from fear.'

9.   See Jeffrey J. Sacks, 'Fatal Dog Attacks', *Pediatrics*, vol. 97, no. 6, June 1996, pp. 891-95.

10. Wolves evidently also release an odour of submission: 'He [a subordinate wolf] showed all the appropriate visual displays of passive submission. At the same time, while lying on the ground, he yelped with each muzzle poke of Chippewa's and urinated, liberating a chemical substance in his urine with a powerful musky odor which was immediately detectable from several meters away ... expression of extreme submission and fear...' Ronald Schassburger, *Vocal Communication in the Timber Wolf, Canis lupus, Linnaeus*, p. 46.

11. When human emotions are compared to animal emotions, these tend to be the negative ones. Thus Walton Cannon's book *Bodily Changes in Pain, Hunger, Fear and Rage*, opens with these lines: 'Fear, rage, and pain and the pangs of hunger are all primitive experiences which human beings share with the lower animals.' It would never have occurred to Cannon to include love, compassion and gratitude.

12. This work has been carried on by his student and successor, I. Eibl-Eibesfeldt. See his *Love and Hate*. The term 'ritualised fighting' was first used by Schenkel in a paper entitled 'Submission: its features and function in the wolf and dog'. (*American Zoologist*, 7 (1967), pp. 319-29), published many years after his pioneering work in the field, the 1947 study, 'Ausdrucks-Studien an Wölfen'.

13. This is true not only of dogs. In his article 'On War and Peace in Animals and Man' (p. 122), Niko Tinbergen writes: 'In animals, intraspecific fighting is usually of distinctive advantage. In addition, all species manage as a rule to settle their disputes without killing one another; in fact, even bloodshed is rare. Man is the only species that is a mass murderer, the only misfit in his own society.' We know from the more recent field studies of Jane Goodall that chimpanzees will kill baboons and even other chimps. They go to war. Still, they do so only very rarely, and the carnage bears no resemblance to human destructiveness. It appears that only man can pose a threat to the very existence of other species.

14. Charles Darwin, *The Expression of the Emotions in Man and Animals*, p. 119.

15. See under Aggression in *The Oxford Companion to Animal Behaviour*, edited by David McFarland.

16. Tim Jones, *Dog Heroes*, p. 58. The best book about the use of dogs in war that I have seen is Michael G. Lemish's *War Dogs*. Lemish, who is the official historian of the Vietnam Dog Handler Association and a member of the National Association for Search and Rescue, gives a more elaborate account of the story of Chips.

17. Quoted in Michael Lemish's *War Dogs*, p. 4.

18. From Isaiah Spiegel's 'A Ghetto Dog', in *A Treasury of Yiddish Stories*, edited by Irving Howe and Eliezer Greenberg, 1954.

19. We are often told that to have done so would have been tantamount to signing one's own death certificate, but this was not so. In fact there were a number of occasions when concentration camp guards did ask to be re-assigned and were not punished. I think it is much more likely that the guards came to enjoy their work – they became sadists, a term that cannot be applied, in my opinion, to dogs, since dogs do not enjoy the suffering of others. See the book by Daniel Goldhagen, *Hitler's Willing Executioners*.

20. E. S. Humphrey and L. Warner reported in 1934 that teaching the German shepherd to bite a man was the most difficult part of the police course. Even the most courageous fighters showed unwillingness to bite, and with a substantial number of dogs it was found to be impossible to 'overcome their prejudice against violating the person of man'. They quote various authors (e.g., S. Dangerfield) to the effect that biting has been the unforgivable sin for such countless generations that to refrain from biting has become almost second nature in dogs. *Genetics of the Dog: The Basis for Successful Breeding*, Marca Burns and Margaret N. Fraser, p. 143.

21. Vicki Hearne, *Adam's Task*, p. 208.

Chapter 15 *Being Alone: The Sadness of Dogs*

1. I am not alone: 'At one moment she reclined on the front porch, staring somnolently into space. The next moment she was gone – vanished – evaporated. . . . At one moment the front porch was empty – deserted. The next moment she was there, staring somnolently at nothing and smelling richly of ripe fish or rotted seaweed.' 'Dogs in a Big Way' by Kenneth and Anna Roberts, in *Best Dog Stories*, edited by Lesley O'Mara, p. 158.
2. American Psychiatric Association, *Diagnostic and Statistical Manual of Mental Disorders*, p. 219.
3. Ibid., p. 220.
4. Vol. 8, no. 4 (1996), p. 18. The caption under the vivid photo reads: 'A group of dogs – all of whom are about to die – watch while another is fatally injected on the killing table.'
5. Michael Fox, *Returning to Eden*, p. 3. See too Eleanor Atkinson, *Greyfriars Bobby*, and Sarah Bolton, *Our Devoted Friend the Dog*, p. 28, for other accounts.
6. Roger A. Caras, *A Dog is Listening*, p. 123.
7. *Heroic Dogs in the News*, p. 215.
8. Personal communication from Vasos Panagiotopoulos, New York, April 1996.
9. Quoted in *Mondo Canine*, edited by Jon Winokur, p. 234.
10. Personal communication from Al Graber, 20 May 1996.
11. Personal communication from Veronique Richard on 27 May 1996.
12. Personal communication from Marjorie Riddle, April 1996.
13. Yi-Fu Tuan, *Dominance and Affection: The Making of Pets*.
14. In 1963, Fuller showed a film called 'Canine Kaspar Hausers' to the American Society of Zoologists in Cleveland. Kaspar Hauser was a so-called feral or wild child who appeared in Nuremberg in 1828, unable to speak or walk. Later it was learned that he was kept for most of his life, at least 12 years, in an unlighted dungeon where he heard no sounds, saw no living creatures, spoke to nobody and ate nothing but bread and water. He was murdered five years later by an unknown assailant. It is widely believed now that he was the legitimate heir to the throne of Baden. The psychiatric condition known as the Kaspar Hauser syndrome refers to children who have been raised in complete isolation. So a canine Kaspar Hauser would be a dog raised in total isolation. See Jeffrey Masson, *Lost Prince*.
15. John L. Fuller, *Readings in Animal Behaviour*, pp. 197-210.
16. John Paul Scott, 'Separation in Infant Dogs', in *Separation and Distress*, edited by E. Senoy, p. 14.
17. Scott, 'The Evolution of Social Behavior in Dogs and Wolves', *American Zoologist*, 7, p. 375.
18. Michael Fox, *The Dog: Its Domestication and Behavior*, p. 156.
19. Martin Seligman, 'Chronic Fear Produced by Unpredictable Shock', in

the *Journal of Comparative and Physiological Psychology*, 66 (1968), pp. 402–11. Also his 1973 article in *Psychology Today*, 'Fall into helplessness'. See too E. C. Senay's 'Toward an animal model of depression', *Journal of Psychiatric Residency*, 4 (1966), pp. 65–71.

20. C. P. Richter. 'On the phenomenon of sudden death in animals and man'. *Psychosomatic Medicine*, 19 (1957), pp. 191–98.

21. Martin Seligman, *Helplessness: On Depression, Development and Death*, pp. 58–59.

22. Andrée Collard and Joyce Contrucci, in their book *Rape of the Wild*, describe the experiment of Ronald Melzack and T. H. Scott on Scottish terriers deprived of sensory and social experiences. The experimenters then used strong electric shock and burning to test the dogs' reactions: 'To the astonishment of the observers, seven of the ten restricted dogs made no attempt to get away from E [the experimenter] during stimulation . . . and E was able to touch [the noses of four dogs] with the flame as often as he wished.' The authors comment: 'Melzack and Scott have shown through animal torture what torturers throughout history have known all along: it is possible to traumatize the sense out of living creatures and bring them to the point at which they submit to any atrocity without a whimper while becoming hopelessly dependent upon their torturers.' The article they refer to is called 'The effects of early experience on the response to pain'. *Journal of Comparative and Physiological Psychology*, 50 (1957), p. 158.

23. D. Pratt: *Alternatives to Pain in Experimentation on Animals*, p. 68.

24. The Humane Society of the United States says these dogs are 'forced to spend their entire lives in cramped cages, with not enough food and water or shelter from adverse weather. The females are bred every time they come in season – for these animals the puppy mills are truly living hells.' *The True Nature Newsletter*, vol. II, no. 2, p. 1.

25. How ironic that we should use the most friendly of dogs, the beagle, to do the most horrendous of experiments. In one report, entitled 'Comparison of Tracheal Damage from Laser-Ignited Endotracheal Tube Fires', a blowtorch-type airway fire was produced in the anaesthetised dog's throat, producing acute inflammation and ulceration. The tests were performed by Northwestern University Medical School, Chicago and the Medical College of Wisconsin, Milwaukee, in the 1980s. The test was reported by R. H. Ossoff et al. in *Annals of Otology, Rhinology & Laryngology*, vol. 92 (1983), pp. 333–36. I have taken this information from the useful article by Dr Robert Sharpe (who wrote *The Cruel Deception* about the uses of animals in laboratories) – 'Man's Best Friend', published in *The Antivivisectionist*, February 1994, pp. 4–7. See 'Pet Theft in America, A Report to Congress', compiled by *Last Chance for Animals*, (an animal protection group in Los Angeles), p. 14. As far back as 1966 (4 February issue), *Life Magazine* reported that 'Laboratories now need almost 2 million dogs a year'. In 1996 Harvard Medical School dropped all dog labs from its curriculum. No medical school in the United States now forces students to participate in mandatory animal labs.

26. Gerald Carson, *Men, Beasts, and Gods: A History of Cruelty and Kindness to Animals*, pp. 197-98.

27. Quoted from *Rape of the Wild: Man's Violence against Animals and the Earth* by Andrée Collard and Joyce Contrucci, p. 62.

28. I. T. Kourtsine, 'La conception Pavlovienne des névroses expérimentales base de la psychopathologie des animaux', in A. Brion and H. Ey, *Psychiatrie animale*, pp. 204-10. The sentence cited comes from p. 207.

29. V. K. Fedorov, 'A propos de certaines anomalies du comportement chez les animaux'. In Brion and Ey, *Psychiatrie animale* pp. 211-15.

30. Andrée Collard and Joyce Contrucci, *Rape of the Wild*, p. 61.

31. *The Dayton Daily News*, 27 March 1996.

Chapter 16 *Thinking Like a Dog*

1. See M. J. Wells, 'What the Octopus makes of it: Our world from another point of view'. In *American Scientist*, 49 (1961), pp. 215-27.

2. Stanley Coren, *The Intelligence of Dogs*, p. 105.

3. Jean Craighead George, *How to Talk to Your Animals*.

4. R. P. Coppinger and M. Feinstein, 'Why dogs bark', *Smithsonian Magazine*, January 1991, pp. 119-29.

5. J. P. Scott, 'Observation', in *Animal Communication,* edited by T. A. Sebeok, pp. 17-30.

6. Quoted in Marjorie Spiegel's *The Dreaded Comparison*, p. 23.

7. Another account of the Soviet biologist, D. K. Belyaev, who conducted the experiment can be found in Stephen Budiansky, *The Covenant of the Wild*, pp. 95-97.

8. Leo Tolstoy, *Anna Karenina*.

9. Brian Vesey-Fitzgerald, *Animal Anthology*.

10. See Oskar Pfungst, *Clever Hans*. Gould and Gould, who retell the story, note that 'Clever Hans was marvellously perceptive – but not in the way most observers had hoped.' *The Animal Mind*, pp. 1-3.

11. Thomas Mann, *A Man and His Dog*, p. 202.

12. Cervantes, *A Dialogue Between Scipio and Bergansa: Two Dogs belonging to the City of Toledo*.

13. In *Kafka: The Complete Stories and Parables*, edited by Nahum N. Glatzer, foreword by Joyce Carol Oates. Introduction, p. XI. The story was not published during Kafka's lifetime. Einstein is said to have remarked to Thomas Mann, regarding Kafka's short prose pieces, that 'this is too much for the human mind to grasp'.

14. Thomas Mann, *A Man and His Dog*, p. 81.

15. R. H. Smythe, *The Mind of the Dog*, p. 66.

16. L. David Mech, 'Joining a Wolf Pack', *Audubon*, 98, no. 6 (December 1996), p. 82.

17. See John Horgan, 'See Spot See Blue', *Scientific American* 262 (January 1990), p. 20. Even such an authority as R. H. Smythe, who was the examiner for the Diploma of Membership of the Royal College of Veterinary Surgeons in London, could write that 'Dogs, of course, have no colour vision.' *The Mind of the Dog*, p. 69.

18. See R. F. Ewer, *The Carnivores,* and the literature he cites. He points out that 'for many years it was believed that, apart from man and the higher primates, all mammals were colour blind. This, however, is not the case.' (p. 130).

19. See *The Waltham Book of Dog and Cat Behaviour*, in which the author cites A. Rosengren, 'Experiments in colour discrimination in dogs', *Acta Zoological Fennica*, 12 (1969), pp. 1-19.

20. Bruce Fogle, *The Encyclopedia of the Dog*, p. 41.

21. See the excellent chapter on dog hearing in Roger Caras's *A Dog is Listening: The Way Some of Our Closest Friends View Us,* p. 41. I cannot recommend this book too highly for many of the topics in this chapter.

22. Caras, *A Dog is Listening*, p. 69.

23. 'This scenting apparatus transmits information directly to the limbic system, the part of the brain most intimately involved in emotional behavior.' Bruce Fogle, *The Dog's Mind*, p. 41.

24. Caras, *A Dog is Listening*, p. 113.

25. Susan Irvine, *Perfume*, p. 151.

26. James Thurber, p. xiii of his Introduction to *The Fireside Book of Dog Stories*, edited by Jack Goodman.

27. My views on this subject are given in an earlier book, *Final Analysis: The Making and Unmaking of a Psychoanalyst*.

Conclusion *In Search of the Soul of the Dog*

1. Milan Kundera, *The Unbearable Lightness of Being*.

2. Mary Midgley, *Animals and Why They Matter*, p. 118.

3. Morris Berman, 'The Wild and the Tame', in *Coming to our Senses*, p. 103.

4. Liz Rosenberg, in a poem called 'Elegy for a Beagle Mutt', mentions a Buddhist saint 'who waited at the gates of heaven ten thousand years with his faithful dog, till both were permitted in'. Quoted in *Dog Music: Poetry about Dogs*, p. 193.

5. This is my translation from the original Sanskrit. I have taken the text from volume four of the *Critical Text of the Mahabharata*, edited at the Bhandarkar Oriental Research Institute, 17.3.7ff. The text can also be found in volume twelve of the P. C. Roy translation of the *Mahabharata*, published by the Oriental Publishing Co., Calcutta.

6. Susan McCarthy, my co-author on *When Elephants Weep*, is writing a book about what people should know before they buy a purebred dog (*The Honest Dog Book*), and she tells me that there has been a move to teach bilaterally deaf dogs and their owners to communicate with hand signs. Caroline Crosby runs a School for Deaf Dalmatians in Santa Fe, which advises on training and placement of (neutered) deaf dogs. Many of the dogs go to families where some or all members are deaf. 'I've had really good success with families that have a deaf child. The children can identify with the dog,' Ms Crosby told Susan. These dogs learn between ten and forty signals. Crosby's dog, Miss Dotties, is a watchdog who barks whenever Crosby signs 'door'.

7. Marcel Proust, *Remembrance of Things Past*, Swann's Way, Overture.
8. Piero Scanziani, *Enciclopedia del Cane*, p. 193: 'Il cane ha memoria, volontà, intelligenza et tutta una gamma di sentimenti, fra cui amore, dedizione, fedeltà, gioia, rimpianto, paura, dolore, disperazione, collera, gelosia, vergogna, orgoglio, fantasia, curiosità, perplessità e via via. Non solo il cane ha un'anima, ma ha un'anima assai ricca.' (The dog has memory, will, intelligence, and experiences the entire gamut of emotions, among them love, dedication, faithfulness, joy, regret, fear, sorrow, desperation, anger, jealousy, shame, pride, imagination, curiosity, perplexity, and on and on. Not only does the dog have a soul, but it has a very rich soul.)
9. Margaret Titcomb, *Dog and Man in the Ancient Pacific with Special Attention to Hawaii*, p. 9.

BIBLIOGRAPHY

Items marked with an asterisk (*) were of particular value in writing this book. I have omitted classics referred to in the text that are still readily available in many editions.

Abrantes, R. A. B., 'The expression of emotions in man and canid', In: Canine Development throughout Life, Waltham Symposium No. 8, edited by A. T. B. Edney. *Journal of Small Animal Practice* (USA), 28, (1987): pp. 1030-36.

Ackerley, J. R., *My Dog Tulip*. London: Bodley Head, 1956.

Ackerman, Diane, *A Natural History of Love*. New York: Random House, 1994.

Adams, G. J., and K. G. Johnson, 'Sleep-wake cycles and other night-time behaviours of the domestic dog, *Canis familiaris*'. *Applied Animal Behavior Science* (USA), 36, (1993): pp. 233-48.

Adcock, Fleur, and Jacqueline Simms (eds.), *Oxford Book of Creatures*. Oxford University Press, 1995.

Adell-Bath, M. et. al., *Do We Need Dogs: A Study of Dogs' Social Significance to Man*. Gothenburg; University of Gothenburg Press, 1979.

Agrawal, H. C., 'Neurochemical and behavioral effects of isolation rearing in the dog'. *Life Sciences* (USA), 6, (1967): pp. 71-8.

Allen, D. L., *The Wolves of Minong*. University of Michigan Press, 1993.

Allen, G. M., 'Dogs of the American aborigines'. *Bulletin of the Museum of Comparative Zoology*, Harvard Collection, vol. 63, (1920): pp. 431-617.

Altmann, S. A., 'Social behavior of anthropoid primates: analysis of recent concepts'. In *Roots of Behavior*, edited by E. L. Bliss. New York: Harper & Row, 1962.

Anderson, A. C. (ed.), *The Beagle as an Experimental Dog*. Ames: Iowa State University Press, 1970.

Anderson, R. S. (ed.), *Pet Animals in Society*. New York: Macmillan, 1975.

Arluke, A., 'Understanding Nazi animal protection and the Holocaust', *Anthrozoös*, (USA) 5, (1992): pp. 6-32.

*Arnim, Elizabeth von, *All the Dogs of My Life*. London: Virago Press, 1995.

213

Bibliography

Atkinson, Eleanor, *Greyfriars Bobby*. New York: A. L. Burt, 1912.

Badcock, C. R., *The Problem of Altruism*. Oxford: Basil Blackwell, 1986.

Baillie, J., 'The behavioural requirements necessary for guide dogs for the blind in the United Kindgom'. *British Veterinary Journal*, 128, 1972.

Barloy, J. J., *Man and Animals: One Hundred Centuries of Friendship*. Translated by H. Fox. New York: Gordon and Cremonesi, 1974.

Barrette, C., 'The "inheritance of dominance", or an aptitude to dominate'. *Animal Behavior* (USA), 46, (1993): pp. 591-93.

Beck, A. M., *The Ecology of Stray Dogs: A Study of Free-Ranging Urban Animals*. Baltimore: York Press, 1973.

Becker, F., J. E. Markee and J. E. King, 'Studies on olfactory acuity in dogs. 1. Discriminatory behavior in problem box situations'. *Animal Behavior* (USA), 5, (1957): pp. 94-103.

Bedichek, Roy, *The Sense of Smell*. London: Michael Joseph, 1960.

Bekoff, Marc, 'Social play and play-soliciting by infant canids'. *American Zoologist*, 14, (1974): pp. 323-40.

Bekoff, Marc, 'Social communication in canids: Evidence for the evolution of a stereotyped mammalian display'. *Science* (USA) 197, (1977): pp. 1907-99.

Bekoff, Marc, 'Social play: Structure, function, and the evolution of a cooperative social behavior'. In *The Development of Behavior: Comparative and Evolutionary Aspects*, edited by G. Burdhardt and M. Bekoff. New York: Garland, 1978.

Bekoff, Marc, and J. Diamond, 'Life-history patterns and sociality in canids: body size, reproduction and behavior'. *Oecologia* (USA), 50, (1981): pp. 386-90.

*Bekoff, M., 'Play signals as punctuation: the structure of social play in canids'. *Behaviour*, 132, (1995): pp. 419-29.

Benjamin, Carol Lea, *Dog Problems*. New York: Howell Book House, 1981.

*Benjamin, Carol Lea, *Mother Knows Best: The Natural Way to Train your Dog*. New York: Howell Book House, 1985.

Bergin, Bonnie, *Bonnie Bergin's Guide to Bringing Out the Best in Your Dog*. Boston: Little, Brown, 1995.

Bergler, R., *Man and Dog: The Psychology of a Relationship*. Oxford: Blackwell Scientific Publications, 1988.

Bergman, Göran, *Why Does Your Dog Do That?* New York: Howell Book House, 1971. (Translated from the Finnish; original publication 1967.)

Bergson, Henri, *Le Rire: essai sur la signification du comique*. Paris: Presses Universitaires de France, 1900.

Berman, Morris, 'The Wild and the Tame'. In *Coming to our Senses: Body and Spirit in the Hidden History of the West*. New York: Simon & Schuster, 1989.

Bierce, Ambrose, *The Devil's Dictionary: A Selection of the Bitter Definitions of Ambrose Bierce*. Mt. Vernon, N.Y.: Peter Pauper Press, 1958.

Boitani, Luigi, 'Randagi: Una vita da cani'. *Airone*, 187, (November, 1996), pp. 43-53.

Bolton, Sarah Knowles, *Our Devoted Friend the Dog*. Boston: Page & Co., 1902.

Bowlby, John A., 'Critical phases in the development of social responses in man and other animals'. *New Biology*, No. 14 (1953): pp. 25-37.

214

Brion, A., and Henri Ey (eds.), *Psychiatrie animale*. Paris: Bibliothèque neuro-psychiatrique de langue française. Paris: Desclée de Brouwer, 1976.

Brodbeck, A. J., 'An exploratory study on the acquisition of dependency behavior in puppies'. *Bulletin of the Ecological Society of America*, 35, 1954.

Bromfield, Louis, 'Dogs of Malabar Farm'. Excerpts from *Pleasant Valley*. New York: Harper & Row, 1943.

Brown, L. T., 'Affection for people as a function of affection for dogs'. *Psychological Reports* (USA), 31, (1972): pp. 957-58.

Brückner, G. H., 'Ueber ein zweibeinigen Hund'. *Zeitschrift für Hundeforschung*. Neue Folge, vol. 13, (1938): pp. 1-16.

Bucke, W. Fowler, 'Cyno-psychoses. Children's thoughts, reactions, and feelings toward pet dogs'. *The Pedagogical Seminary*, 10, (1903): pp. 459-513.

Budiansky, Stephen, *The Covenant of the Wild: Why Animals Chose Domestication*. New York: William Morrow Co., 1992.

Bueler, Lois E., *Wild Dogs of the World*. New York: Stein & Day, 1973.

*Burns, Marcia, and Margaret N. Fraser, *Genetics of the Dog: The Basis for Successful Breeding*, second edition. Edinburgh: Oliver and Boyd, 1966.

Burroughs, John, *My Dog Friends*. Edited by Clara Barrus. Boston: Houghton Mifflin, 1928.

Burt, M. R., 'The animal as Alter Ego; cruelty, altruism, and the work of art'. In *Animals and People Sharing the World*, edited by Andrew N. Rowan, Hanover, N.H.: University Press of New England, 1988.

Bustad, Leo K., 'Man and Beast Interface'; In *Man and Beast Revisited*, edited by Michael H. Robinson and Lionel Tiger. Washington D.C.: Smithsonian Institution Press, 1991.

Buytendijk, Frederik, *The Mind of the Dog*, translated by Lilian A. Clare. Boston: Houghton Mifflin, 1936.

Cairns, R., 'Behavior development in the dog. an interspecific analysis'. *Science*, N.Y., 158, (1967): pp. 1070-72.

Campbell, S. S., and I. Tobler, 'Animal sleep: A review of sleep duration across phylogeny'. *Neuroscience and Bio-behavioral Reviews* (USA), 8: (1984): pp. 269-300.

Campbell, William E., *Behavior Problems in Dogs*. Santa Barbara, California: American Veterinary Publications, 1975.

Cannon, Walter B, *Bodily Changes in Pain, Hunger, Fear and Rage: An Account of Recent Researches into the Frontiers of Emotional Excitement*. New York: D. Appleton & Co., second edition, 1929. (First edition 1915.)

Caras, Roger A., *A Celebration of Dogs*. New York: Times Books, 1982.

*Caras, Roger A., *A Dog is Listening: The Way Some of Our Closest Friends View Us*. New York: Summit Books, 1992.

Carson, Gerald, *Men, Beasts, and Gods: A History of Cruelty and Kindness to Animals*. New York: Scribner's, 1972.

Case, D. B., 'Dog ownership; a complex web'. *Psychological Reports* (USA), 60,: pp. 247-59.

Cattell, R. B., 'The isolation of temperament dimensions in dogs'. *Behavioral Biology* (USA), 9, (1973): pp. 15-30.

Clarke, R. S., W. Heron, M. L. Fetherstonhaugh, D. G. Forgays and D. O.

Hebb, 'Individual differences in dogs: preliminary report on the effects of early experience'. *Canadian Journal of Psychology*, 5, (1951): pp. 150-6.

Clark, Stephen R. L., 'Good dogs and other animals'. In *In Defense of Animals*, edited by Peter Singer. New York: Basil Blackwell, 1985, pp. 41-51.

Clutton-Brock, Juliet, (ed.), *The Walking Larder: Patterns of Domestication, Pastoralism, and Predation*. London: Unwin Hyman, 1980.

Clutton-Brock, Juliet, 'The domestication of the dog with special reference to social attitudes of the wolf'. *Carnivores* (USA), 3, (1980): pp. 27-33.

*Clutton-Brock, Juliet, *Domesticated Animals from Early Times*. Austin: University of Texas, 1983.

Clutton-Brock, Juliet and Kim Dennis-Bryan, *Dogs of the Last Hundred Years at the British Museum (Natural History)*. London: British Museum, 1988.

Clutton-Brock, Juliet, *Cats Ancient and Modern*. Harvard University Press, 1993.

Clutton-Brock, Juliet, 'The Unnatural World: behavioural aspects of humans and animals in the process of domestication'. In *Animals and Human Society: Changing Perspectives*, edited by A. Manning and J. A. Serpell, London: Routledge, 1994.

Cohen, Barbara, and Louise Taylor, *Dogs and Their Women*. Boston: Little, Brown, 1989.

*Collard, Andrée, and Joyce Contrucci, *Rape of the Wild: Man's Violence against Animals and the Earth*. London: Women's Press, 1988.

Collier, V. W. F., *Dogs of China and Japan in Nature and Art*. London: William Heinemann, 1921.

Coppinger, R. P., and Lorna Coppinger, 'Dogs in sheep's clothing guard flocks'. *Smithsonian Magazine*, April 1982.

*Coppinger, R. P., and M. Feinstein, 'Why dogs bark'. *Smithsonian Magazine*, January 1991.

Coren, Stanley, *The Intelligence of Dogs: Canine Consciousness and Capabilities*. New York: Free Press, 1994.

*Crisler, Lois, *Arctic Wild*. New York: Harper, 1958.

Crisler, Lois, *Captive Wild*. New York: Harper & Row, 1968.

Croke, Vickie, *The Modern Ark: The History of Zoos: Past, Present and Future*. New York: Scribner's, 1997.

Dale-Green, P., *Lore of the Dog*. Boston: Houghton Mifflin, 1967.

Dangerfield, S., 'The R.A.F. Police Dogs'. *Animal Health* (UK) 2, (1964): pp. 1-5.

Darwin, Charles, *Journal of Researches into the Geology and Natural History of the Various Countries Visited by H.M.S. Beagle*. London: H. Colburn, 1839; new edition, Cambridge University Press, 1956.

Darwin, Charles, *On the Origin of Species by Means of Natural Selection*, London: John Murray, 1859; new edition with an introduction by J. W. Burrow, Penguin Books, 1982.

Darwin, Charles, *The Descent of Man and Selection in Relation to Sex*. London: John Murray, 1871.

*Darwin, Charles, *The Expression of the Emotions in Man and Animals*. London: John Murray, 1872. New editions: University of Chicago Press, 1965; Friedman, 1978; UK, Greenwood Press, 1994.

Bibliography

Darwin, Charles, *The Variation of Animals and Plants under Domestication*, London: John Murray, second edition, 1875. (First edition, 2 vols., 1865.)

Davidar, E. R. C., 'Wild dogs (*Cuon alpinus*) and village dogs'. *Journal of the Bombay Natural History Society*, 62, (1965): pp. 146-48.

Davis, Hank, and Dianne Balfour (eds.), *The Inevitable Bond: Examining Scientist-Animal Interactions*. Cambridge University Press, 1992.

Dechambre, E., 'La théorie de foetalisation et la formation des races de chiens et de porc'. *Mammalia* (France), 13, (1949): pp. 129-237.

Deichmann, Ute, *Biologists Under Hitler*, translated by Thomas Dunlop. Harvard University Press, 1966.

Diamond, Jared, 'Zebras and the Anna Karenina Principle'. *Natural History* (USA), 9, 1994.

Dodman, Nicholas, *The Dog Who Loved Too Much: Tales, Treatments and the Psychology of Dogs*. New York: Bantam, 1996.

Downs, James, 'Domestication: An examination of the changing relationships between man and animals'. *Kroeber Anthropological Society Papers*, 22, 1960.

*Duemer, Joseph, and Jim Simmerman (eds.), *Dog Music: Poetry About Dogs*. New York: St Martin's Press, 1966.

Dunbar, Ian, and Michael Berman, 'The Social Behavior of Free Ranging Suburban Dogs'. *Applied Animal Ethology* (USA), 10, (1983): pp. 5-17.

Dunbar, Ian, *Dog Behavior*, Neptune, New Jersey: T. H. F. Publications, 1979.

Eddy, Timothy, Gordon Gallup Jr., and Daniel Povinelli, 'Attribution of Cognitive States to Animals: Anthropomorphism in Comparative Perspective'. *Journal of Social Issues* (USA), 49, (1953): pp. 87-101.

Eibl-Eibesfeldt, Irenäus, 'Dominance, submission, and love: Sexual pathologies from the perspective of ethology'. In *Pediophilia*, edited by J. R. Feierman. New York: Springer, 1990, pp. 150-175.

Eibl-Eibesfeldt, Irenäus, *Love and Hate: The Natural History of Behavior Patterns*. New York: Shocken, 1974.

Eisenberg, J. F., and W. S. Dillon (eds.), *Man and Beast: Comparative Social Behavior*, preface by S. Dillon Ripley. Washington, D.C.: Smithsonian Institution Press, 1971.

Ensminger, M. E., *The Complete Book of Dogs*. New York: A. S. Barnes, 1977.

Epstein, H., *The Origin of the Domestic Animals of Africa*. Revised with I. L. Mason (Vol. 1): New York: Africana Publishing Corp. 1971.

Evans, Michael Job, *People, Pooches and Problems*. New York: Howell Book House, 1991.

Ewer, R. F., *The Carnivores*. Cornell University Press, 1973.

*Fagen, Robert, *Animal Play Behavior*. New York: Oxford University Press, 1981.

Feddersen-Petersen, Dorit, 'Observations on social play in some species of Canidae'. *Zool. Anz.* 217 (1/2): 1986.

Feddersen-Petersen, Dorit, *Hunde und ihre Menschen*. Stuttgart: Franckh-Kosmos, 1992.

Feddersen-Petersen, Dorit, *Hundepsychologie: Wesen und Sozialverhalten*. Preface by Konrad Lorenz. Stuttgart: Kosmos: Gesellschaft der Naturfreunde Franckh'sche Verlagshandlung, 1986.

217

Bibliography

*Feddersen-Petersen, Dorit, *Ausdruchsverhalten beim Hund*. Jena: Gustav Fischer, 1995.

Feddersen-Petersen, Dorit, *Fortplanzungsverhalten beim Hund*. Jena: Gustav Fischer, 1994.

Fentress, John C., 'Observations on the behavioral development of a hand-reared male timber wolf'. *American Zoologist*, 7, (1967): pp. 339-51.

*Fiennes, R., and A. Fiennes, *The Natural History of Dogs*. Garden City, N.Y.: The Natural History Press, 1970.

Fischel, Werner, *Tierpsychologie und Hundeforschung*. Leipzig: Verlag Dr. Paul Schöps, 1941.

*Fischel, Werner, *Die Seele des Hundes*. Berlin-Hamburg: Paul Parey, 1961.

Fisher, John, *Why Does My Dog...?* New York: Howell Book House, 1991.

*Fisher, John Andrew, 'Disambiguating Anthropomorphism: An Interdisciplinary Review'. *Perspectives in Ethology* (USA), 9, 1991.

Fleischer, Michael, *Hund and Mensch: Eine semiotische Analyse ihrer Kommunikation*. Tübingen: Stauffenburg Verlag, 1987.

Fogle, Bruce, *The Dog's Mind: Understanding Your Dog's Behavior*. New York: Howell Book House, 1990.

Fogle, Bruce, *The Encyclopedia of the Dog*. New York and London: Dorling Kindersley, 1995.

Fox, Michael W. (ed.), *Abnormal Behavior in Animals*. Philadelphia: W. B. Saunders, 1968.

Fox, Michael W., 'The influence of domestication upon behavior of animals'. In *Abnormal Behavior in Animals*, edited by M. W. Fox. Philadelphia: W. B. Saunders, 1968.

Fox, Michael W., 'The anatomy of aggression and its ritualization in Canidae: a developmental and comparative study'. *Behavior* (USA), 35, (1969): pp. 242-58.

*Fox, Michael W., *Behavior of Wolves, Dogs and Related Canids*. New York: Harper & Row, 1971.

Fox, Michael W., *Integrative Development of Brain and Behavior in the Dog*. University of Chicago Press, 1971.

Fox, Michael W., *The Wolf*. New York: Coward, McCann and Geoghegan, 1973.

Fox, Michael W. et al., 'Behavior and ecology of a small group of urban dogs (Canis familiaris)'. *Applied Animal Ethology* (USA) 1, (1975): pp. 119-37.

*Fox, Michael W. and Marc Bekoff. 'The behaviour of dogs'. In *The Behaviour of Domesticated Animals*, edited by E. S. E. Hafez. London: Balliere Tindall, third edition, 1975, pp. 370-409.

Fox, Michael W., 'Evolution of Social Behavior in Canids'. In *The Wild Canids*, edited by M. W. Fox. New York: Van Nostrand Reinhold, 1975, pp. 429-59.

Fox, Michael W., *Between Animal and Man*. New York: Coward, McCann & Geoghegan, 1976.

*Fox, Michael W., *The Dog: Its Domestication and Behavior*. (First published 1978.) Malabar, Florida: Robert E. Krieger Publishing Co., 1987.

Fox, Michael W., *The Soul of the Wolf*, Boston: Little, Brown, 1980.

Bibliography

Fox, Michael W., *The Whistling Hunters: Field Studies of the Asiatic Wild Dog* . Albany: State University of New York Press, 1984.

Fox, Michael W., *Superdog: Raising the Perfect Canine Companion*. New York: Howell House Books, 1990.

France, Anatole, 'The Coming of Riquet'. In *Best Dog Stories,* with an introduction by Gerald Durrell, edited by Lesley O'Mara. London: Brockhampton Press, 1990.

Frank, Harry (ed.), *Man and Wolf: Advances,. Issues and Problems in Captive Wolf Research*. Dordrecht: Kluwert Academic Publishers, 1987.

Frank, Harry, and M. G. Frank, 'On the effects of domestication on canine social development and behavior'. *Applied Animal Ethology* (USA), 8, (1982): pp. 507-25.

Freedman, D. G., 'Constitutional and environmental interactions in rearing of four breeds of dogs'. *Science* (USA) 127, (1955): pp. 585-86.

Freedman, D. G., J. A. King and O. Elliot, 'Critical periods in the social development of dogs'. *Science* (USA), 133, (1961): pp. 1016-17.

Freud, Sigmund, *Civilization and its Discontents* (1929). Included in *The Standard Edition of the Complete Psychological Works of Sigmund Freud*, translated and edited by James Strachey, Volume xxi. London: The Hogarth Press, 1961.

Fuller, John L., 'Experimental deprivation and later behavior'. In *Readings in Animal Behavior*, edited by Thomas E. McGill. New York: Holt, Reinhart & Winstone, 1973.

*Garber, Marjorie, *Dog Love*. New York: Simon & Schuster, 1996.

Genoways, Hugh, and Marion Burgwin (eds.), *Natural History of the Dog*. Pittsburgh: Carnegie Museum of Natural History, 1984.

Gentry, Christine, *When Dogs Run Wild: The Sociology of Feral Dogs and Wildlife*. Jefferson, N. C.: McFarland & Co., 1983.

George, Jean Craighead, *How to Talk to Your Animals*. New York: Harcourt Brace Jovanovich, 1985.

Gilbert, E. M., and Thelma R. Brown, *K-9 Structure and Terminology*. New York: Howell Book House, 1995.

Ginsburg, Benson E., and Laurie Hiestand, 'Humanity's "best-friend": the origins of our inevitable bond with dogs'. In *The Inevitable Bond: Examining Scientist-animal Interactions,* edited by Hank Davis and Dianne Balfour. Cambridge University Press, 1992.

Goldhagen, Daniel, *Hitler's Willing Executioners*. London: Little, Brown, 1996.

*Gonzalez, Philip, and Leonore Fleischer, *The Dog Who Rescues Cats: The True Story of Ginny*, with an introduction by Cleveland Amory. New York: HarperCollins, 1995.

Goodman, Jack (ed.), *The Fireside Book of Dog Stories*. New York: Simon & Schuster, 1943.

Gottlieb, A., 'Dog: ally or traitor?' *American Ethnologist*, 13, (1986): pp. 477-88.

Gould, James L., and Carol Grant Gould, *The Animal Mind*. New York: Scientific American Library, 1994.

Gould, Stephen Jay, 'Mickey Mouse Meets Konrad Lorenz'. *Natural History* (USA), vol. 88 (5), (1979) pp. 30-36.

Graven, Jacques, *Non-human Thought: The Mysteries of the Animal Psyche*, translated from the French by Harold J. Salemson. New York: Stein & Day, 1967.

*Griffin, Donald, *The Question of Animal Awareness: Evolutionary Continuity of Mental Experience*. New York: Rockefeller University Press, 1976 (new edition, 1981).

*Griffin, Donald, *Animal Thinking*. Harvard University Press, 1984.

*Griffin, Donald, *Animal Minds*. University of Chicago Press, 1992.

Grossman, Loyd, *The Dog's Tale: A History of Man's Best Friend*. London: BBC Books, 1993.

Hafez, E. S. E. (ed.), *The Behaviour of Domestic Animals*. London: Bailliere, Tindall and Cox, 1962.

Hall, C. S., 'Temperament: a survey of animal studies'. *Psychological Bulletin* (USA), 38, (1941): pp. 305-43.

Hall, Roberta L., and Henry S. Sharp (eds.), *Wolf and Man: Evolution in Parallel*. New York: Academic Press, 1978.

Halliburton, Judith, *Raising Rover*. New York: St Martin's Press, 1996.

Haltenorth, T., *Rassehunde – Wildhunde*. Heidelberg, Winter, 1958.

Harrington, Fred H., and L. David Mech, 'Wolf-vocalizations'. In *Wolf and Man: Evolution in Parallel*, edited by Roberta L. Hall & Henry S. Sharp. New York: Academic Press, 1978.

Hart, B. L., and L. A. Hart, 'Selecting pet dogs on the basis of cluster analysis of breed behavioral profiles and gender'. *Journal of the American Veterinary Medical Association*, 186, (1985): pp. 1181-85.

Hart, B. L., and L. A. Hart, *Canine and Feline Behavioral Therapy*. Philadelphia: Lea & Febiger, 1985.

Hart, B. L., and M. F. Miller, 'Behavioral profiles of dog breeds', *Journal of the American Veterinary Medical Association*, 186, (1985): pp. 1175-80.

*Hearne, Vicki, *Adam's Task: Calling Animals by Name*. New York: Knopf, 1987.

Hearne, Vicki, *The White German Shepherd*. New York: The Atlantic Monthly Press, 1988.

Hearne, Vicki, *Bandit: Dossier of a Dangerous Dog*. New York: HarperCollins, 1991.

Hearne, Vicki, *Animal Happiness*. New York: HarperCollins, 1994.

Heidger, H., 'Vom Traum der Tiere', *Ciba-Z.*, 9: 1945.

Heidger, H., *Studies of the Psychology and Behavior of Captive Animals in Zoos and Circuses*, translated by Geoffrey Sircom. New York: Criterion Books, 1955.

Henshaw, R. E. and R. O. Stephenson, 'Homing in the Gray Wolf'. *Journal of Mammalogy* (USA) 55 (1), (1974): pp. 234-37.

Heroic Dogs in the News. New York: The Paebar Co., 1946.

Herre, Wolf, and Manfred Röhrs. *Haustiere – zoologisch gesehen*. Stuttgart: Gustav Fischer Verlag, second edition 1990.

Hetts, S., 'Psychologic well-being: behavioral measures and implications for the dog'. *Advances in Companion Animal Behavior* (USA), 21, (1991): pp. 369-87.

Hobson, J. Allan, *The Chemistry of Conscious States*. Boston: Little, Brown, 1994.

Bibliography

Honig, Werner K., and P. H. R. James (eds.), *Animal Memory*. New York: Academic Press, 1971.

Hopkins, S. G., T. A. Schuber and B. L. Hart, 'Castration of adult male dogs: Effects on roaming, aggression, urine marking and mounting'. *Journal of the American Veterinary Medical Association*, 186, (1985), pp. 1175-80.

Horgan, John, 'See Spot See Blue: Curb That Dogma! Canines Are Not Color-blind'. *Scientific American* 262 (January 1990): p. 20.

Houpt, Katherine A., and Thomas R. Wolski, *Domestic Animal Behavior for Veterinarians and Animal Scientists*. Ames: Iowa State University Press, 1982.

Hume, C.W., 'In praise of anthropomorphism'. In *Man and Beast*. Potters Bar, Herts: UFAW, 1962.

*Humphrey, E. S., and L. Warner, *Working dogs: an attempt to produce a strain of German Shepherds which combines working ability and beauty of conformation*. Baltimore: Johns Hopkins Press, 1934.

Hunt, Morton, *The Compassionate Beast: What Science is Discovering about the Humane Side of Humankind*. New York: William Morrow, 1990.

Huyghebaert, L, *Le Chien: Psychologie – Olfaction – Mécanisme de l'Odorat*. Paris: Les éditions de l'éleveur. n.d. (approx. 1914).

Indiana, Gary, *Living with the Animals*. London: Faber & Faber, 1994.

Irvine, Susan, *Perfume: The Creation and Allure of Classic Fragrances*. New York: Crescent Books, 1995.

Jesse, Edward, *Anecdotes of Dogs*. London: George Bell & Sons, 1897.

Johns, Bud (ed.), *Old Dogs Remembered*. New York: Carroll & Graf, 1993.

Jones, E. Gwynne, *A Bibliography of the Dog*. London: The Library Association, 1971. (Based on a thesis for the Library Association Fellowships, 1970.)

Jones, Tim, *Dog Heroes: True Stories about Extraordinary Animals Around the World*. Researched by Christine Ummel. Fairbanks/Seattle: Epicenter Press, 1996

Jouvet, M., and D. Jouvet, 'Le sommeil et les rêves chez l'animal'. In: A. Brion and Henri Ey, eds. *Psychiatrie animale*. Paris: Bibliothèque neuro-psychiatrique de langue française. Paris: Desclée de Brouwer, 1976, pp. 149-67.

Jouvet, M., and J. P. Sastre, 'Le comportement ironique du chat'. *Physiology and Behavior*, 22, (1979): pp. 979-89.

Kalmus, H., 'The discrimination by the nose of the dog of individual human odors and in particular of the odors of twins'. *Animal Behavior* (USA), 3, 1955.

Katz, Richard, 'Talks with Dogs', in *Solitary Life*, translated from the German by Hetty Kohn. New York: Reynal & Co., 1958.

Keehn, J. D., *Origins of Madness: Psychopathology in Animal Life*. Oxford, Pergamon Press, 1979.

Keehn, J. D., *Animal Models for Psychiatry*. Boston: Routledge & Kegan Paul, 1986.

Kennedy, John S., *The New Anthropomorphism*. Cambridge University Press, 1992.

King, J. A., 'Closed social groups among domestic dogs'. *Proceedings of the American Philosophical Society*, 98, (1954): pp. 327-36.

Klaits, Joseph, and Barrie Klaits (eds.), *Animals and Man in Historical Perspective*. New York: Harper and Row, 1974.

Kleiman, D. G., and J. F. Eisenberg, 'Comparisons of canid and felid social systems from an evolutionary perspective'. *Animal Behavior* (USA), 21, (1973): pp. 637-59.

Kobbé, Gustav, *A Tribute to the Dog: Including the Famous Tribute by Senator Vest*. New York: Frederick A. Stokes, 1910.

Koehler, William, *The Koehler Method of Dog Training*. New York: Howell Book House (Macmillan), 1962.

Kohn, Alfie, *The Brighter Side of Human Nature: Altruism & Empathy in Everyday Life*. New York: Basic Books, 1990.

Krebs, Dennis, L., 'Altruism – An Examination of the Concept and a Review of the Literature'. *Psychological Bulletin* (USA), 73, (1970): pp. 258-302.

Krushinksii, L. V., *Animal Behavior: Its Normal and Abnormal Development*. New York: Consultant's Bureau, 1962.

Kundera, Milan, *The Unbearable Lightness of Being*. New York: Harper & Row, 1984.

Lamott, Ann, *Operating Instructions: A Journal of My Son's First Year*. New York: Pantheon Books, 1993.

Lansbury, Coral, *The Old Brown Dog: Women, Workers, and Vivisection in Edwardian England*. University of Wisconsin Press, 1985.

Lavie, Peretz, *The Enchanted World of Sleep*, translated by Anthony Berris, with a foreword by Michel Jouvet. Yale University Press, 1996.

Lawrence, Alistair B., and Jeffrey Rushen, (eds.), *Stereotypic Animal Behaviour: Fundamentals and Applications to Welfare*. Wallingford (Oxon): Cab International, 1993.

Lawrence, Elizabeth Atwood, 'The Sacred Bee, the Filthy Pig, and the Bat Out of Hell: Animal Symbolism as Cognitive Biophilia', in *The Biophilia Hypothesis,* edited by Stephen R. Kellert and Edward O. Wilson. Washington: Island Press, 1993.

Lawrence. R. D., *In Praise of Wolves*. New York: Henry Holt, 1986.

*Leach, Maria, *God Had a Dog: Folklore of the Dog*. New Brunswick: Rutgers University Press, 1961.

*Lemish, Michael G., *War Dogs: Canines in Combat*. Washington: Brassey's, 1996.

*Lerman, Rhoda, *In The Company of Newfies: A Shared Life*. New York: Henry Holt, 1996.

Lessac, M., 'Effects of early isolation on the later adaptive behavior of Beagles'. *Developmental Psychology* (USA) 1, (1969): pp. 14-25.

Lewis, Michael, and Jeannette M. Haviland, *Handbook of Emotions*. New York: Guilford Press, 1993.

Leyhausen, P., *Cat Behavior: The Predatory and Social Behavior of Domestic and Wild Cats*, translated by B. A. Tonkin. New York: Garland STPM Press, 1979.

Lipman, E. A., 'Comparative auditory sensitivity of man and dog', *American Journal of Psychology*, 55, (1942): pp. 84-89.

Lockridge, Frances, and Richard, *Cats and People*. New York: Lippincott, 1950

222

Bibliography

Lockwood, R., 'Dominance in wolves: useful construct or bad habit?' In *The Behavior and Ecology of Wolves*, edited by E. Klinghammer (pp. 225-44). New York: Garland STPM Press, 1979.

*Lopez, Barry, *Of Wolves and Men*. New York: Scribner's, 1987.

Lorenz, Konrad, 'Der Kumpan in der Umwelt des Vogels'. *Journal of Ornithology*, 83, (1935): pp. 137-213, 289-413.

*Lorenz, Konrad, *So kam der Mensch auf den Hund*. Munich: DTV, 1950.

Lorenz, Konrad, *King Solomon's Ring, New Light on Animal Ways*. London: Methuen, 1952.

Lorenz, Konrad, *On Aggression*. New York: Harcourt Brace, 1966.

Lorenz, Konrad, 'Companions as factors in the bird's environment'. In *Studies in Animal and Human Behaviour*, Vol. 1, translated by Robert Martin. Harvard University Press, 1970.

*Lorenz, Konrad, *Man Meets Dog*, with a new introduction by Donald McCaig, translated by Marjorie Kerr Wilson. New York: Kodansha America, 1994.

Lubbock, J., *On the Senses, Instincts, and Intelligence of Animals*. New York: Appleton, 1888.

Lucas, Edgar A. et al., 'Baseline Sleep-Wake Patterns in the Pointer Dog'. *Physiology & Behavior* (USA), Vol. 19, (1977): pp. 285-91.

MacCaskill, Bridget, *The Blood is Wild* (with photographs by Don MacCaskill). London: Jonathan Cape, 1995.

Macgregor, Forbes, *Greyfriars Bobby: The Real Story at Last*. London: Gordon Wright, 1990.

The Macmillan Book of Proverbs, Maxims, and Famous Phrases, selected and arranged by Burton Stevenson. New York: Macmillan, 1948.

Maeterlinck, Maurice, *The Double Garden*, translated by Alexander Teixera de Mattos. New York: Dodd, Mead, 1905.

Mahut, H., 'Breed differences in the dog's emotional behaviour'. *Canadian Journal of Psychology*, 12, (1958): pp. 35-44.

Malcolm, J. R., 'African wild dogs play every game by their own rules'. *Smithsonian* 11 (8), (1980): pp. 62-72.

*Mann, Thomas, *A Man and His Dog*. New York: Knopf, 1930. (Originally published as *Herr und Hund*, S. Fischer, 1918.)

Manning, A., and J. A. Serpell (eds.), *Animals and Human Society: Changing Perspectives*. London: Routledge, 1994.

Mason, I. L., *Evolution of Domesticated Animals*. London: Longman, 1984.

Mason, Marcus, W. *Bibliography of the Dog*. Iowa State University Press, 1959.

Masson, Jeffrey Moussaieff, *Final Analysis: The Making and Unmaking of a Psychoanalyst*. New York: Addison Wesley, 1991; London: HarperCollins, 1991.

Masson, Jeffrey Moussaieff, and Susan McCarthy, *When Elephants Weep: The Emotional Lives of Animals*. London: Jonathan Cape, 1994; New York: Delacorte Press, 1995.

Masson, Jeffrey Moussaieff, *Lost Prince: The Unsolved Mystery of Kaspar Hauser*. New York: The Free Press, 1996.

*McCaig, Donald. *Nop's Trials*. New York: Crown Publishers, 1984.

McCaig, Donald, *Eminent Dogs Dangerous Men: Searching Through Scotland for a Border Collie*. New York: HarperCollins, 1991.

McElroy, Susan Chernak, *Animals as Teachers and Healers: True Stories and Reflections*, with a foreword by Michael W. Fox. Troutdale, Origon: New Sage Press, 1996.

McFarland, David (ed.), *The Oxford Companion to Animal Behaviour*, Oxford University Press, 1987.

McGill, Thomas E. (ed.), *Readings in Animal Behavior*, edited by Thomas E. McGill. New York: Holt, Rinehart & Winston, second edition, 1973.

McIntyre, Rick, 'The East Fork Pack', from: John A. Murray (ed.), *Out Among the Wolves: Contemporary Writings on the Wolf*. Anchorage: Alaska Northwest Books, 1993.

McLoughlin, John C., *The Canine Clan: A New Look at Man's Best Friend*. New York: Viking, 1983.

Mech, L. David, *The Wolves of Isle Royale*. Fauna of the National Parks of the United States, Fauna Series, No. 7. Washington D.C.: Government Printing Office, 1966.

*Mech, L. David, *The Wolf: The Ecology and Behavior of an Endangered Species*. New York: Natural History Press, 1970.

Mech, L. David, *Wolf!* Wolves in American Culture Committee. Ashland, Wisconsin: Northworld, 1986.

Mech, L. David, *The Way of the Wolf*. Stillwater MN, USA: Voyageur Press, 1991.

Mech, L. David, 'Joining a Wolf Pack'. *Audubon*, 98, no. 6, December 1996.

Melzack, R., 'Irrational fears in the dog'. *Canadian Journal of Psychology*, 6, (1952): pp. 141-47.

Melzack, R., 'The genesis of emotional behavior: an experimental study of the dog'. *Journal of Comparative and Physiological Psychology.*(USA), 50, (1954): pp. 155-61

Melzack, R., 'Effects of early experience on social behavior'. *Canadian Journal of Psychology*, 10, (1956): pp. 82-90.

Melzack, R., 'The effects of early experience on the response to pain'. *Journal of Comparative Physiological Psychology* (USA), 50, (1957): pp. 155-61.

Merritt, Clifton, 'Heroic Dogs'. In *Animal People* (USA), Vol. V, no. 4, May 1996.

Méry, Fernand. *The Life, History and Magic of the Dog*. New York: Grosset & Dunlap, 1970 (original French edition published in 1968 by Robert Laffont, Paris).

Midgley, Mary, *Animals and Why They Matter*. University of Georgia Press, 1983: London: Penguin Books, 1983.

Midgley, Mary, 'Why knowledge matters', in D. Sperlinger (ed.), *Animals in Research*. New York: John Wiley, 1981.

Milani, Myrna M., *The Body Language and Emotion of Dogs: A Practical Guide to the Physical and Behavioral Displays Owners and Dogs Exchange and How to Use Them to Create a Lasting Bond*. New York: William Morrow, 1986.

Mitler, Merrill, M. William, C. Dement et al., 'Narcolepsy-Cataplexy in a Female Dog'. *Experimental Neurology* (USA), 45, 1974.

Bibliography

Moncrieff, R. W., *Odour Preferences*. London: Leonard Hill, 1966.

*The Monks of New Skete, *How to Be Your Dog's Best Friend: A Training Manual for Dog Owners*. Boston: Little, Brown, 1978.

*Morris, Desmond, *Dogwatching*. London: Jonathan Cape, 1986; New York: Crown Publishers, 1986.

Morris, Willie, *My Dog Skip*. New York: Random House, 1995.

Moulton, D. G., E. H. Ashton, and J. T. Eayrs, 'Studies in olfactory acuity. 4. Relative detectability of n-aliphatic acids by the dog'. *Animal Behavior* (USA), 8, (1960): pp. 117-28.

Mowat, Farley. *The Dog Who Wouldn't Be*. Boston: Little, Brown, 1957.

Mugford, R. A., 'Attachment versus dominance: an alternative view of the man-dog relationship'. In *The Human-Pet Relationship*, pp. 157-65. Vienna: IEMT, 1985.

Neuhaus, Walter, 'Ueber die Riechschärfe des Hundes Fer Fettsäuren', *Zeitschrift zur Vergleichende Physiologie*, 35, 1953.

Neville, Peter, *Do Dogs Need Shrinks?* New York: Carol Publishing Group, 1992.

Oatley, K., 'The importance of being emotional'. *New Scientist* (London), 19, August 1989.

O'Farrell, V., *Manual of Canine Behavior*. Cheltenham, Glos.: BSAVA Publications, 1986.

Ogden, Paul, *Chelsea: The Story of a Signal Dog*. Boston: Little, Brown, 1992.

Oliner, Samuel P., and Pearl M. Oliner, *The Altruistic Personality*. New York: The Free Press, 1988.

Olsen, Stanley J., *Origins of the Domestic Dog, the Fossil Record*. Tucson: University of Arizona Press, 1985.

O'Mara, Lesley (ed.), *Best Dog Stories*, introduction by Gerald Durrell. London: Brockhampton Press, 1990.

Papashvily, Helen, and George Papashvily, *Dogs and People*. Philadelphia: Lippincott, 1954.

Parker, S. T., R. W. Mitchell, and M. L. Boccia (eds.), *Self-Awareness in Animals and Humans: Developmental Perspectives*. Cambridge University Press, 1994.

Paulsen, Gary, *Winterdance: The Fine Madness of Running the Iditarod*. New York: Harcourt Brace, 1994.

Pavlov, I. P., *Conditioned Reflexes: An Investigation of the Physiological Activity of the Cerebral Cortex*. Oxford University Press, 1927.

Perin, Constance, 'Perfect Dogs'. In *Belonging in America – Reading Between the Lines*. Madison: University of Wisconsin Press, 1988.

Pfaffenberger, C. J., 'The relationship between delayed socialization and trainability in guide dogs. *Journal of Genetic Psychology* (USA), 95, (1959): pp. 145-55.

*Pfaffenberger, C. J., *The New Knowledge of Dog Behavior*. New York: Howell Books, 1963.

Pfaffenberger, C. J. (ed.), *Guide Dogs for the Blind: Their Selection, Development and Training*. Amsterdam: Elsevier, 1976.

Pfungst, Oskar. *Clever Hans: (The Horse of Mr. von Osten): A Contribution to Experimental, Animal and Human Psychology*, translated from the German by

Carl L. Rahn, with an introduction by C. Stumpf, and preface by James R. Angell. New York: Henry Holt, 1911 (reprinted 1965).

Phelps, Gilbert, and John Phelps (compilers), *Between Man and Beast*. New York: Bonanza Books, 1979.

Pitt, Frances, *Animal Mind*. New York: Frederick A. Stokes, 1926.

Porter, V., *Faithful Companions: The Alliance of Man and Dog*. London: Methuen, 1989.

Powers, W. K., and M. N. Powers, 'Putting on the dog'. *Natural History* (UK), vol. 95, no. 2, (February 1986): pp. 6-16.

Pratt, D., *Alternatives to Pain in Experimentation on Animals*. New York: Argus Archives, 1980.

Prendergast, Dorothy, *The Wolf Hybrid*. Gallup, New Mexico: Rudelhaus Enterprises, 1989.

Pulliainen, Erkki, 'Ecology of the Wolf in the Settled Areas of Finland'. In: *The Behavior & Ecology of Wolves*, edited by Erich Klinghammer. New York: Garland STPM Press, 1979.

Ratner, Stanley C., and Robert Boice, 'Effects of Domestication on Behaviour'. In *The Behaviour of Domestic Animals*, edited by E. S. E. Hafez, London; Balliere Tindall, third edition, 1975.

Reitman, Judith, *Stolen for Profit: The True Story Behind the Disappearance of Millions of America's Beloved Pets*. New York: Kensington Books, 1992.

Rheingold, H., 'Maternal behavior in the dog'. In *Maternal Behavior in Mammals*. New York: John Wiley, 1963.

Rhine, J. B., and Sara R. Feather, 'The Study of Cases of "Psi-Trailing" in Animals'. *Journal of Parapsychology* (USA), 26, 1962.

Ricciuti, E. R., 'Dogs of war'. *International Wildife*, 8 (5), (1978): pp. 36-40.

Richardson, E. H., *Forty Years with Dogs*. London: Hutchinson, 1929.

Richter, C. P., 'On the phenomenon of sudden death in animals and man'. *Psychosomatic Medicine* (USA), 19, (1957): pp. 191-98.

Ritchie, C. I. A., *The British Dog: Its History from Earliest Times*. London: Robert Hale, 1981.

Robinson, Louis, *Wild Traits in Tame Animals (being some Familiar Studies in Evolution)*. Edinburgh & London: William Blackwood, 1897.

Robinson, Michael H., and Lionel Tiger (eds.), *Man and Beast Revisited*. Washington D.C.: Smithsonian Institution Press, 1991.

Roeder, Kenneth D., 'A dog's world view'. *Natural History*, vol. 82, no. 7, (August 1973): pp. 12-18 and 84-85.

Rohan, Jack, *Rags: The Story of a Dog Who Went to War*. New York: Harper & Brothers, 1930.

★Romanes, George J., *Animal Intelligence,* London: Kegan Paul, 2nd edition, 1882.

★Rosen, Michael J. (ed.), *The Company of Dogs: 21 Stories by Contemporary Masters*. New York: Doubleday, 1990.

★Rosen, Michael J. (ed.), *Dog People: Writers and Artists on Canine Companionship*. New York: Artisan, 1995.

Rosengren, A., 'Experiments in colour discrimination in dogs'. *Acta Zoologica Fennica*, 12: 1969.

226

Bibliography

Ruchebusch, V., 'Sommeil et rêves chez les animaux'. In *Psychiatrie animale*, edited by A. Brion & H. Ey. Paris: Desclée de Brouwer, 1964, pp. 139-48.

Salzen, Erid A., 'The Ontegony of fear in animals'. In *Fear in Animals and Man*, edited by W-Sluckin. New York: Van Nostrand Reinhold Co., 1979.

Saunders, Marshall, *Beautiful Joe: An Autobiography*. With a new introduction by Roger A. Caras. Bedford, Mass.: Applewood Books, 1994 (first published 1894).

Savishinsky, Joel S., 'Pet ideas: the domestication of animals, human behavior, and human emotions'. In *New Perspectives on Our Lives with Companion Animals*, edited by Aaron Honori Katcher and Alan M. Beck. Philadelphia: University of Pennsylvania Press, 1983.

Scanziani, Piero, *Enciclopedia del Cane*. Novara: Istituto Geografico de Agostini, 1981.

Schachter, S., *The Psychology of Affiliation*. London: Tavistock, 1959.

Schassburger, Ronald M., *Vocal Communication in the Timber Wolf, Canis lupus, Linnaeus: Structure, Motivation, and Ontogeny*. Berlin: Paul Parey Scientific Publishers, 1993.

Schenkel, Rudolf, 'Ausdruckstudien an Wölfen'. *Behavior* 1, (1947): pp. 81-129.

*Schenkel, Rudolf, 'Submission: its features and functions in the wolf and dog'. *American Zoologist*, 7, (1967): pp. 319-30.

Schmid, Bastian, *Von den Aufgaben der Tierpsychologie*. Berlin: Gebrüder Borntraeger, 1921.

*Schmid, Bastian, 'Vorläufiges Versuchseregebnis über das hundliche Orientierungsproblem'. In *Zeitschrift für Hundeforschung*, Vol 2, (1932): pp. 133-56.

Schmid, Bastian, *Interviewing Animals*. London: George Allen & Unwin, 1936. (German original. *Begegnung mit Tieren*, Munich, 1935.)

Schmidt-Nielson, K., *How Animals Work*. Cambridge University Press, 1972.

Scholtmeijer, Marian, *Animal Victims in Modern Fiction. From Sanctity to Sacrifice*. University of Toronto Press, 1993.

Scott, J. P., 'The social behavior of dogs and wolves: an illustration of sociobiological systematics'. *Annals New York Academy of Sciences*, 51, (1950): pp. 1009-21.

Scott, J. P., *Animal Behavior*. University of Chicago Press, 1958.

*Scott, J. P., and J. L. Fuller, *Genetics and the Social Behavior of the Dog*. University of Chicago Press, 1965.

Scott, J. P., 'The Evolution of social behavior in dogs and wolves'. *American Zoologist*, 7, (1967): pp. 373-81.

Scott, J. P., 'Separation in infant dogs. Emotional and motivational aspects'. In *Separation and Distress*, edited by E. Senoy, AAAS Symposium, 1969.

Scott, J. P., 'Attachment and separation in dog and man: Theoretical propositions'. In: *The Origins of Human Social Relations*. edited by H. R. Schaffer. London: Academic Press, 1972.

Scott, J. P.; John M. Stewart, Victor J. DeGhett, 'Separation in Infant Dogs: Emotional Response and Motivational Consequences'. In *Separation and Depression: Clinical and Research Aspects*, edited by John Paul Scott and Edward C. Senay. Washington: American Association for the Advancement of Science, 1973.

Scott, J. P., 'Editor's comments'. In *Critical Periods*. Benchmark Papers in Animal Behavior, 12. Bowling Green State University: Dowden, Hutchinson & Ross, 1978.

Scott, J. P., 'Investigating Behavior: Toward a Science of Sociality'. In *Studying Animal Behavior: Autobiographies of the Founders*, edited by Donald A. Dewsbury. University of Chicago Press, 1985.

Sebeok, T. A. (ed.), *Animal Communication*. Bloomington: Indiana University Press, 1968.

Seligman, Martin E. P., 'Chronic Fear Produced by Unpredictable Shock', *Journal of Comparative and Physiological Psychology*, 66, (1968): pp. 402-11.

Seligman, Martin E. P., 'Fall into helplessness'. *Psychology Today*, Vol. 7, (1973): pp. 43-48.

Seligman, Martin E. P., *Helplessness: On Depression, Development and Death*. San Francisco: W. H. Freeman & Co., 1975.

Senay, E. C., 'Toward an animal model of depression: A study of separation behavior in dogs. *Journal of Psychiatric Residency* (USA), 4, (1966): pp. 65-71.

Sebeok, Thomas A., *Animal Communication*. Indiana University Press, 1968.

★Serpell, J. A., *In The Company of Animals*. Oxford: Basil Blackwell, 1986.

Serpell, J. A., 'The influence of inheritance and environment on canine behavior: myth and fact'. *Journal of Small Animal Practice*, 28, (1987): pp. 949-56.

★Serpell, J. A. (ed.), *The Domestic Dog: Its Evolution, Behaviour and Interactions with People*. Cambridge University Press, 1995.

★Sheldon, Jennifer W., *Wild Dogs: The Natural History of the Nondomestic Canidae*. San Diego: Academic Press (Harcourt Brace Jovanovich), 1992.

Sheldrake, Rupert, *Seven Experiments that Could Change the World: A Do-It-Yourself Guide to Revolutionary Science*. New York: Riverhead Books, 1995.

Shell, Mark, 'The family pet'. In *Representations*, 15, (1986): pp. 121-53.

Shimazono, Y. et al., 'The correlation of the rhythmic waves of the hippocampus with the behavior of dogs'. *Neurologica Medico-Chirurgìca*, 2, (1960): pp. 82-88.

Shojai, Amy, *A Dog's Life: The History, Culture, and Everyday Life of the Dog*. New York: Friedman/Fairfax, 1994.

Siegal, Mordecai, and Matthew Margolis, *When Good Dogs Do Bad Things*. Boston: Little, Brown, 1986.

Siegal, Mordecai (ed.), *UC Davis School of Veterinary Medicine Book of Dogs: A Complete Medical Reference Guide for Dogs and Puppies*. By the Faculty and Staff, School of Veterinary Medicine, University of California. New York: HarperCollins, 1995.

Singh, Arjan, *Prince of Cats*. London: Jonathan Cape, 1982.

Singh, Arjan, *Tiger! Tiger!*. London: Jonathan Cape, 1984.

Singh, Billy Arjan, *Eelie and the Big Cats*. London: Jonathan Cape, 1987.

Sluckin, W. (ed.), *Fear in Animals and Man*. New York: Van Nostran Reinhold, 1979.

Smythe, R. H., *Animal Psychology*. Springfield, Illinois: Charles C. Thomas, 1958.

Bibliography

*Smythe, R. H., *The Mind of the Dog*. Springfield, Illinois: Charles C. Thomas, 1961.

*Spiegel, Isaiah, 'A Ghetto Dog'. From *A Treasury of Yiddish Stories*, edited by Irving Howe and Eliezer Greenberg. New York: Viking, 1954.

*Spiegel, Marjorie, *The Dreaded Comparison: Human and Animal Slavery*, with a Foreword by Alice Walker (second edition). Princeton: Mirror Books, 1996.

*Staddon, J. E. R., 'Animal psychology: the tyranny of anthropocentrism'. In *Perspectives in Ethology*. Vol. 8: *Whither Ethology?* edited. by P. P. G. Bateson and Peter H. Klopfer. New York: Plenum Press, 1989.

Stebbins, Robert C., and Nathan W. Cohen, *A Natural History of Amphibians*. Princeton University Press, 1995.

*Steinhart, Peter, *In the Company of Wolves*. New York: Knopf, 1995.

Syrotuch, William G., *Scent and the Scenting Dog*. Westmoreland, New York: Arner Publications, 1972.

Tabor, R., *The Wildlife of the Domestic Cat*. London: Arrow Books, 1983.

Tarrant, Bill, *The Magic of Dogs*. New York: Lyons & Burford, 1995.

*Thomas, Elizabeth Marshall, *The Hidden Life of Dogs*. Boston: Houghton Mifflin, 1993; London: Weidenfeld & Nicolson, 1994.

Thomas, Elizabeth Marshall, *The Tribe of Tiger*. Boston: Houghton Mifflin, 1995.

Thomas, Elizabeth Marshall, *Certain Poor Shepherds: A Christmas Tale*. New York: Simon & Schuster, 1996.

Thomas, Keith, *Man and the Natural World: A History of the Modern Sensibility*. New York: Pantheon, 1983.

Thompson, Laura, *The Dogs. A Personal History of Greyhound Racing*. London: Vintage, 1994.

Thompson, W. R., 'Exploratory behavior in normal and restricted dogs'. *Journal of Comparative Physiological Psychology* (USA), 47, (1954): pp. 77–82.

Thorne, Y. C. (ed.), *Waltham Book of Dog and Cat Behavior*. New York: Pergamon Press. 1992.

Thurber, James, *Thurber's Dogs*. New York. Simon & Schuster, 1955.

Tinbergen, Niko, 'On War and Peace in Animals and Man'. In *Man and Animal: Studies in Behavior*, edited by Heinz Friedrich. New York: St Martin's Press, 1968.

Titcomb, Margaret, with the collaboration of Mary Kawena Pukui, *Dog and Man in the Ancient Pacific with Special Attention to Hawaii*. Hawaii: Bishop Museum, 1969.

Tomkies, Mike, *A Last Wild Place*, London: Jonathan Cape, 1983.

Tomkies, Mike, *Moobli*. London: Jonathan Cape, 1988.

*Trumler, Eberhard, *Mit dem Hund auf du: Zum Verständnis seines Wesens und Verhaltens*, with a preface by Konrad Lorenz. Munich: Piper, 1971.

*Trumler, Eberhard, *Your Dog and You*. New York: Seabury, 1973.

*Trumler, Eberhard, *Understanding your Dog*. Translated from the German by Richard Barry. London: Faber & Faber, 1973.

*Trumler, Eberhard, *Hunde ernst genommen: Zum Wesen und Verständniss ihres Verhaltens*. Munich: Piper, 1974.

Tuan, Yi-Fu, *The Landscape of Fear*. New York: Pantheon Books, 1979.

Tuan, Yi-Fu, *Dominance and Affection: The Making of Pets*. Yale University Press, 1984.

Tucker, Michael, *The Eyes that Lead: The Story of Guide Dogs for the Blind*. London: Robert Hale, 1984.

*Turner, Dennis C., and Patrick Bateson (eds.), *The Domestic Cat: The Biology of its Behaviour*. Cambridge University Press, 1988.

Ucko, P. J., and G. W. Dimbleby (eds.), *The Domestication and Exploitation of Animals*. London: Duckworth, 1969.

Van der Post, Laurens, *A Story Like the Wind*. London: Chatto and Windus, 1972.

Van Lawick-Goodall, J., and H. van Lawick-Goodall, *Innocent Killers*. Boston: Houghton Mifflin, 1971.

*Vechten, Carl van, *The Tiger in the House*. New York: Knopf, 1952 (originally published 1920).

*Vesey-Fitzgerald, Brian (ed.), *The Book of the Dog*. Toronto: Borden Publishing, 1948.

Vesey-Fitzgerald, Brian (ed.), *Animal Anthology*. London: Newnes, 1965.

Vessels, Jane, 'Koko's Kitten'. *National Geographic* 167 (1), January 1985.

Vines, G., 'Wolves in dog's clothing'. *New Scientist* (London), 91, 1981.

Vollmer, P. J., 'Do mischievous dogs reveal their "guilt"'? *Veterinary Medicine Small Animal Clinician* (USA). 72: (1977): pp. 1002-05.

Voronoff, Serge, *Love and Thought in Animals and Man*. London: Methuen, 1937.

Waal, Frans de, *Good Natured: The Origins of Right and Wrong in Humans and Other Animals*. Harvard University Press, 1996.

Walther, Fritz R., *Communication and Expression in Hoofed Mammals*. Bloomington: Indiana University Press, 1984.

Warrick, Deborah M., 'Dogs and wolves: canine cousins: a look at wild and domestic canids'. *Animals' Agenda* (USA?), vol. IX, no. 11, December 1989.

Werblowsky, R. J. Zwi, 'On Anthropomorphism'. In: *The Encyclopedia of Religion,* edited by Mircea Eliade, Volume 1. New York: Macmillan, 1987.

White, D. G., *Myths of the Dog-Man*. University of Chicago Press, 1991.

White, Joseph J., *Ebony and White: The Story of the K-9 Corps*. Wilsonville, Oregon: Doral Publishing Co., 1996.

Whittemore, Hank and Caroline Hebard, *So That Others May Live: Caroline Hebard and Her Search-And-Rescue Dogs*. New York: Bantam, 1995.

Wilkin, Herman A., and Helen B. Lewis, *Experimental Studies of Dreaming*. New York: Random House, 1967.

Willis, R. G. (ed.), *Signifying Animals: Human Meaning in the Natural World*. London: Unwin Hyman, 1990.

Willis, Roy, *Man and Beast*. New York: Basic Books, 1974.

*Winokur, John (ed.), *Mondo Canine*. New York: Dutton, 1991.

Wise, J. K., and J. J. Yang, 'Dog and cat ownership, 1991-1998'. *Journal of the American Veterinary Association*, 204, (1994): pp. 1166-67.

Wispé, L., *The Psychology of Sympathy*. New York: Plenum, 1991.

Witkin, Herman A., and Helen B. Lewis (eds.), *Experimental Studies of Dreaming*. New York: Random House, 1967.

Bibliography

Wittgenstein, Ludwig, *Philosophical Investigations* translated by G. E. M. Anscombe. New York: Macmillan, third edition, 1968.

Wittgenstein, Ludwig, *Zettel*, translated by G. E. M. Anscombe and edited by G. E. M. Anscombe and G. H. von Wright. Berkeley: University of California Press, 1970.

Wolfensohn, S., 'The things we do to dogs'. *New Scientist* (London), 14 May 1981.

Woloy, Eleanora M., *The Symbol of the Dog in the Human Psyche*. Wilmette, Illinois: Chiron Publications, 1990.

Woodhouse, Barbara, *Talking to Animals*. London: Penguin Books, 1981 (first published 1954).

Woolf, Virginia. *Flush: A Biography*, London: Chatto & Windus 1933. (Quoted in *The Oxford Book of Creatures,* edited by Fleur Adcock and Jacqueline Simms. Oxford University Press, 1995.)

Woolpy, J. H., 'Wolf socialization: A study of temperament in a wild social species'. *American Zoologist*, 7, (1967): pp. 357-64.

Wright, J. C., 'The development of social structure during the primary socialization period in German Shepherds'. *Developmental Psychobiology*, 13, (1980): pp. 17-24.

*Zeuner, F. E., *A History of Domesticated Animals*. New York: Harper & Row, 1963.

Zimen, Erik, *Wölfe und Königspudel*. Munich: Piper Verlag, 1974.

*Zimen, Erik, *The Wolf: His Place in the Natural World*, translated from the German by Eric Mosbacher. London: Souvenir Press, 1981 (first published 1978).

*Zimen, Erik, *Der Hund: Abstammung-Verhalten – Mensch und Hund*. Munich: Bertelsmann, 1988.

Zompolis, Gregory N., *Operation Pet Rescue: Animal Survivors of the Oakland, California, Firestorm*. Exeter, New Hampshire: Townsend Publishing, 1994.

Zweig, A., 'Ueber die psychischen Leistungen eines Hundes und deren mögliche Beziehungen zur Humanpsychologie'. *Schweizerische Zeitschrift für Psychologie*, Vol. 16, 1957.

INDEX